Contemporary Theories of Career Development

CW00819614

In response to the complexities of social change that have become evident in the 21st century, there is a need for innovation in career theory that takes into account new perspectives and the fluctuating contexts of people's lives. *Contemporary Theories of Career Development: International Perspectives* brings together the contributions of theorists from around the globe whose work represents current, cutting-edge international approaches to career development theory. Emphasizing the new perspectives that are needed for this field to be relevant in a contemporary era, this book considers the cultural applications of theory in a diverse range of populations.

Structured in three parts with chapters written by internationally renowned leaders in the field, this collection features a critical examination of the current history of the field; thirteen theory chapters, each enhanced by a case study; and a final chapter that draws the previous chapters together through key themes, broadening the reader's knowledge of theoretical perspectives and their inter-relations. Each theory chapter author comments on and critiques his or her own theory, inviting readers to engage with these theories at both a practical and theoretical level through the case studies.

Detailed, with reader-friendly descriptions and supplemented by international research, case examples, and discussion questions, *Contemporary Theories of Career Development: International Perspectives* is the ideal reference work for students studying the topic as well as a stimulus for researchers and practitioners looking to implement the theories in their work.

Nancy Arthur is a Professor in the Werklund School of Education, University of Calgary, Canada.

Mary McMahon is an Honorary Senior Lecturer in the School of Education, The University of Queensland, Australia.

Contemporary Theories of Career Development

International Perspectives

Edited by
Nancy Arthur and Mary McMahon

Routledge
Taylor & Francis Group

LONDON AND NEW YORK

First published 2019
by Routledge
2 Park Square, Milton Park, Abingdon, Oxon OX14 4RN

and by Routledge
711 Third Avenue, New York, NY 10017

Routledge is an imprint of the Taylor & Francis Group, an informa business

British Library Cataloguing in Publication Data
A catalogue record for this book is available from the British Library

Library of Congress Cataloging-in-Publication Data
Names: Arthur, Nancy, 1957- editor. | McMahon, Mary, 1955- editor.
Title: Contemporary theories of career development : international
perspectives / edited by Nancy Arthur and Mary McMahon.
Description: Abingdon, Oxon ; New York, NY : Routledge, 2019. |
Includes bibliographical references.
Identifiers: LCCN 2018029801| ISBN 9781138279971 (hardback) |
ISBN 9781138279988 (pbk.) | ISBN 9781315276175 (ebook)
Subjects: LCSH: Career development. |
Cross-cultural counseling. | Counseling.
Classification: LCC HF5381 .C68718 2019 | DDC 650.101--dc23
LC record available at https://lccn.loc.gov/2018029801

ISBN: 978-1-138-27997-1 (hbk)
ISBN: 978-1-138-27998-8 (pbk)
ISBN: 978-1-315-27617-5 (ebk)

Typeset in Sabon
by Taylor & Francis Books

Printed and bound in Great Britain by
TJ International Ltd, Padstow, Cornwall

Contents

Figures

Tables

Contributors

Nancy Arthur is a professor, Educational Studies in Counselling Psychology, Werklund School of Education, University of Calgary, Canada. Nancy is a registered psychologist (Alberta), an elected Fellow of the Canadian Psychological Association of Canada, and an Honorary Lifetime Member of the Alberta Career Development Association. Nancy currently serves as a vice-president of the International Association of Educational and Vocational Guidance and she served for 8 years on the Board of Governors for the Canadian Career Development Foundation. Nancy's research interests focus on professional education for diversity and social justice, and the international career transitions of students and workers.

Gideon Arulmani, Director of The Promise Foundation, India, holds an M.Phil in clinical psychology, a doctoral degree in career psychology and advanced diplomas in counselling, philosophy and theology. Gideon is interested in the interface between culture and counselling and has published more than 75 papers and book chapters and presented his ideas in a number of invited key note addresses. He is an international development consultant and has executed assignments in 36 countries. He is an international Fellow of NICEC U.K. and the Consortium for Multicultural Psychology Research U.S.A.; a visiting senior lecturer at the University of Canterbury Christ Church, U.K.; a visiting professor at the Martin Luther University, India and a trustee of the Indian Association for Career and Livelihood Planning. Gideon is interested in craft and runs a small, online handmade jewellery business.

Jenny Bimrose is a professor at the Institute for Employment Research, the University of Warwick, England. With over 30 years teaching, researching and managing in higher education, ongoing research interests include: the implications for career guidance of women's career development; supporting careers guidance practitioners in their use of labour market information, and ICT in career guidance; and the role of career adaptability for mid-career changers. She has extensive experience of external project management and consultancy, both in the U.K. and Europe. She is a legacy Fellow of the Career Development Institute, a Fellow of the Higher Education Academy and member of the IAEVG. She has published widely and has contributed as a member of various editorial boards.

David L. Blustein is a professor in the department of counseling, developmental, and educational psychology at the Lynch School of Education at Boston College. His expertise includes the psychology of working, unemployment, decent work, precarious work, relationships and work, the future of work, STEM career development for marginalized high school students, and other aspects of the radically changing world of labor. He is the author of *The Psychology of Working: A New Perspective for Career Development, Counseling, and Public Policy* and the forthcoming book entitled *The Impact of Work an Age of Uncertainty*, which will be published by Oxford University Press. David has consulted with state and national governments in the United States and multinational organizations (including most recently the International Labor Organization) on issues pertaining to career development, the school-to-work transition, long-term unemployment, and the psychological experiences of working.

Jim Bright is a professorial Fellow in career education and development at the Australian Catholic University and a visiting professor of career development at the International Centre for Education and Guidance Studies at the University of Derby. He has a Ph.D. in psychology and is a Fellow of the Australian Psychological Society and a Fellow of the Career Development Association of Australia. He is an honorary international board member of the British Columbia Career Development Association. Jim has published extensively on career development, job search skills, occupational stress, and unconscious biases. He has worked in medico-legal assessment, career coaching of elite sports people, and a wide range of other clients, journalism, and management consultancy for many years in addition to his academic work.

Emily Bullock-Yowell received her Ph.D. in combined counseling and school psychology in 2006 from Florida State University, is currently an associate professor at the University of Southern Mississippi, and licensed psychologist in the state of Mississippi. She studies the career development of a variety of groups from the CIP perspective, often focusing on negative thinking, CASVE-style decision-making, and outcomes associated with mental health and well-being. Additionally, she trains and supervises graduate students in counseling and psychology in the provision of career counseling services using the CIP theory.

AJ Diamonti is a doctoral student in counseling psychology at Boston College. He received a master's degree in mental health counseling from Boston College. His research interest focus on identity development through school and work experiences.

José F. Domene is a professor in educational studies in counselling psychology, Werklund School of Education, at the University of Calgary. His program of research has been funded by the Canada Institutes of Health Research and the Social Sciences and Humanities Research Council of Canada, and includes a focus on the relational contexts of career development, developmental transitions in adolescence and emerging adulthood, the implications of technological change for career development and counselling, and professional issues in Canadian counselling and counselling psychology. Dr. Domene has also worked as a licensed psychologist, whose practice has focused on assisting adolescents and emerging adults presenting with a range of complex academic, career, and mental health difficulties.

Casey Dozier earned her Ph.D. at Florida State University, and she is a licensed psychologist (Florida) and national board certified counselor (NBCC). Publications include refereed journal articles, book chapters, and national presentations. Dr. Dozier has provided clinical interventions in a variety of settings, with an emphasis on personal and career counseling.

Ryan D. Duffy is an associate professor of psychology at the University of Florida and has worked there since 2009. He received his B.A. from Boston College and his M.A. and Ph.D. from the University of Maryland.

Donald H. Ford began his search in 1952 for a sound theory for understanding the development and dynamics of a self-constructing, self-directing, self-regulating and self-controlling person. He discovered general systems theory (GST) soon after its creation by von Bertalanffy (1940, 1950) and its early applications by Shannon and Weaver (1949) and Wiener (1948). His book *Humans as Self-Constructing Living Systems* (1987) served as the theoretical foundation for *A Living Systems Theory of Vocational Behavior and Development* (2014) as well as for M. Ford's motivational systems theory (1992) and for developmental systems theory (1992). Ford is a professor and dean emeritus at Pennsylvania State University. He created and directed the university's Division of Counselling and served as the founding dean of the College of Health and Human Development.

Hugh Gunz has Ph.D.s in chemistry and organizational behaviour, and is a professor of organizational behaviour at the University of Toronto. He has published on the careers of managers, professionals and others, the management of professionals of many kinds, and management education, is the author of the book *Careers and Corporate Cultures* (1989), and the co-editor of the *Handbook of Career Studies* (2007). He serves or has served on the editorial boards of a number of journals, including *Journal of Professions and Organization, Academy of Management Journal*, and *Journal of Managerial Psychology, and Emergence*, and is a former chair of the Careers Division of the Academy of Management.

Ellen Gutowski, M.A., is a doctoral student in counseling psychology at Boston College and has her master's in mental health counseling, also from Boston College. Her research interests include understanding how diverse populations experience and overcome social and economic barriers, with a particular focus on women's experiences, the psychology of working, and the shared spaces between the two.

Paul J. Hartung, Ph.D., is interested in how people (a) explore, choose, and adjust to work over the life span; (b) use work to shape their identities and advance their life stories; and (c) navigate and balance work along with roles in nonwork spheres of life. His interest in career construction grew during 30 years of learning, practicing, studying, and teaching about career development and counselling. He is a professor of family and community medicine at Northeast Ohio Medical University and has more than 50 journal articles, 35 book chapters, and three edited books dealing with career psychology and counselling. He is the current editor for *The Career Development Quarterly* (since 2014) and a Fellow of the International Association of Applied Psychology, American Psychological Association, and the National Career Development Association.

Maureen E. Kenny is a professor in the department of counseling, developmental and educational psychology in the Boston College Lynch School, where she also held the positions of dean and associate dean for Faculty and Academics. Dr. Kenny completed her Ph.D. in counseling and school psychology at the University of Pennsylvania and is a Fellow of Division 17, Society of Counseling Psychology, of the American Psychological Association. Dr. Kenny is the author of more than 50 articles in referred journals, seven books, and 25 book chapters. Her research interests focus on prevention and positive youth development, especially as related to student career development, work-based learning, school engagement, and the development of social-emotional competencies. She is the recipient of the Lifetime Achievement Award in Prevention by the APA Division 17 Section on Prevention.

Wolfgang Mayrhofer is a full professor and head of the Interdisciplinary Institute of Management and Organisational Behaviour, WU Vienna, Austria. He previously has held full-time positions at the University of Paderborn, Germany, and at Dresden University of Technology, Germany. He conducts research in comparative international human resource management and leadership, work careers, and systems theory and management, and has received national and international awards for outstanding research and service to the academic community. He authored, co-authored and co-edited 31 books and more than 130 book chapters and 80 peer-reviewed articles. He is a member of the editorial or advisory board of several international journals and research centres. His teaching assignments at the doctoral, graduate and executive level and his role as visiting scholar have led him to many universities around the globe. He regularly consults to both private and public sector organisations and conducts trainings in the area of HRM, leadership, teams, and self-development by outdoor training/sailing.

Mary McMahon is an honorary senior lecturer in the School of Education at The University of Queensland, Brisbane, Australia, where she taught career guidance and counselling. Mary is the developer with Wendy Patton of the systems theory framework (STF) of career development. She has published extensively in national and international journals, has co-authored and co-edited a number of career development and career counselling books, and has authored and co-authored several chapters in international texts. Mary serves on the editorial boards of a number of national and international journals.

Debra S. Osborn received her Ph.D. in combined counseling and school psychology in 1998 from Florida State University, has been in faculty positions since 1997, and currently works an associate professor at Florida State University. She is also a past president and Fellow of the National Career Development Association.

Wendy Patton is an emeritus professor in the Faculty of Education at Queensland University of Technology, Brisbane, Australia. In addition to serving as head of school and executive dean in the Faculty for a combined 15 years, she maintained a significant research role in career development theory and career counselling. She has taught and researched in the field for more than 25 years, co-authoring and co-editing a number of books and publishing widely in book chapters and articles. Key achievements include the development of the systems theory framework (STF) with Mary McMahon in 1995, and her role as founding series editor of the *Career Development Series* with Sense Publishers from 2005 to 2015. She currently serves as editor emerita of this series. She continues to serve on a number of national and international journal editorial boards.

Gary W. Peterson earned his Ph.D. from Duke University in 1970 and he was clinical training director for the academic program Counseling and Psychological Services in Education, College of Education, Florida State University. He is now professor emeritus and senior research associate in the Center for the Study of Technology in Counseling and Career Development, FSU Career Center. With his research interests in cognition and personality assessment, he contributed to theory and assessments in facilitating how individuals could become better career problem solvers and decision makers.

Laura Phrasavath is a doctoral student in the counseling psychology program at the University at Albany, State University of New York, under the advisement of Dr. Hung-Bin Sheu. Her experiences as a first-generation college student and daughter of working-class immigrant parents in the United States cultivated a seemingly perennial interest and stake in understanding and fostering well-being in all domains of the lives of minority/marginalised populations, particularly within the realms of work, health, and education. She subsequently developed an interest in the conceptualisation of social cognitive career theory (SCCT) frameworks within cultural and intersectional contexts with the hope of contributing to the research and development of interventions and policies seeking to empower those who are disadvantaged to thrive.

Robert Pryor has worked in the field of vocational counselling, organisational development, staff selection and psychological assessment extensively for both public and private organisations. He has also held a range of academic positions and currently is an adjunct professor at the School of Education, Australian Catholic University. He has published widely in psychological assessment, professional ethics, vocational counselling and career development theory. He is a Fellow of both the Australian Psychological Society and the Career Development Association of Australia.

Mary Sue Richardson, Ph.D., is a professor in the department of applied psychology at New York University. She is a counseling psychologist whose major scholarly contributions have been in vocational psychology. Her focus has been to develop a perspective for the field of vocational psychology grounded in contemporary social conditions and intellectual trends, referred to as "counseling for work and relationship." Related to this work, she proposed a dual model of working for both men and women inclusive of market work and unpaid care work. At NYU, Dr. Richardson teaches courses in the counseling psychology Ph.D. program and the counseling for mental health and wellness M.A. program. She maintains an independent psychotherapy practice that complements her academic work.

James P. Sampson, Jr. is a professor emeritus in the department of educational psychology and learning systems and a senior research associate at the Center for the Study of Technology in Counseling and Career Development at Florida State University. He writes and speaks on the appropriate use of computer technology in counseling; on the use of cognitive strategies in the design and delivery of career interventions; and on the integration of theory, research, and practice.

Denise E. Saunders received her Ph.D. in combined counseling and school psychology from Florida State University and is a licensed psychologist in North Carolina, where she maintains a private practice offering career, consultation, and counseling services to clients in higher education, for-profit business, non-profit, and government.

Hung-Bin Sheu is an associate professor in the counseling psychology program at the University at Albany, State University of New York. He has taught graduate-level courses on career theory and counselling, vocational psychology, multicultural counselling, counselling practicum, and structural equation modeling. Social cognitive career theory (SCCT) has been one of the theoretical foundations in his research, teaching, and supervision of students' clinical work. He has published empirical articles and book chapters as well as delivered conference presentations in SCCT with the founders of this theory. At a personal level, he has also found the unifying, comprehensive nature of SCCT useful to his own career choice and development as empirically supported SCCT models offer a roadmap to plan, modify, and execute his career goals.

Logan Vess has practiced career construction counselling and conducted research related to life design for nearly 5 years. Logan's dissertation research under the direction of Mark Savickas focuses on the use and utility of the "My Career Story" workbook, a written assessment in the life-design discourse. He has taught courses based in life design and career construction to undergraduate students. He has also taught a life-design-based career advising course to master's and doctoral students. He is an assistant director for academic internships at John Carroll University, an instructor of family and community medicine at Northeast Ohio Medical University, and a doctoral candidate in counsellor education at Kent State University. He has published several articles related to life design and career construction. He holds a master's degree in counselling from East Tennessee State University and is a nationally certified counsellor and licensed professional counsellor in Ohio.

Fred W. Vondracek's extensive conceptual and empirical work has been focused on the topic of vocational behavior and development. His early theoretical work resulted in a book describing a developmental-contextual framework for understanding life-span career development. Ford's seminal work on living systems inspired him to collaborate with him (and with former student Erik Porfeli) to produce A Living Systems Theory of Vocational Behavior and Development (LSVD). Vondracek is a professor emeritus at the Pennsylvania State University. He started his career as a graduate assistant in Penn State's division of counseling in 1965, and in the intervening half-century served as teacher, scholar, department head and dean in Penn State's College of Health and Human Development.

Mark Watson is a distinguished and emeritus professor at the Nelson Mandela University, South Africa, an honorary professor at The University of Queensland, and a research Fellow at the University of Warwick. He teaches, researches and practices in the field of career development, counselling and assessment. Mark has published extensively in international journals, has co-authored several career psychology books, has contributed chapters to international career books, and is a co-developer of an international qualitative career assessment instrument. He is on the editorial board of several international career journals.

Richard A. Young is a professor of counselling psychology at the University of British Columbia. He is a Fellow of both the Canadian Psychological Association and the American Psychological Association and a registered psychologist in British Columbia. His research interests include the application of action theory and the qualitative action-project method to a variety of research topics, including the transition to adulthood, families, career development, counselling, health, and suicide. His most recent co-edited book, addressing the application of action theory to counselling practice, is *Counseling and Action: Toward Life-Enhancing Work, Relationships, and Identity.*

Preface

We want to begin by acknowledging and respecting the many contributions of theorists whose work historically provided a foundation for career development. The legacy of earlier theories provided pillars from which current writers have transformed the field and envisioned new directions. The complex world of the 21st century has called for innovations in career theory that reflect new perspectives, account for the complexities of social change, and consider the contexts of peoples' lives. As the field of career development has grown and transformed in the last century, so too must theories that explain peoples' career-related behavior.

This edited collection was developed with four aims that guided the writing of the chapters. First, we wanted to develop a career theory book to emphasize and update newer perspectives that are relevant for career development practice in a contemporary era. Second, we were eager to include multidisciplinary perspectives on theories of career development that reflect multiple voices and disciplinary contributions. Third, we wanted to consider the cultural applications of theory to diverse populations within countries and the diversity found between countries where career development practices are implemented. Fourth, we were determined to develop a career theory resource that would make stronger linkage between theory and practice through a case-based approach. With those aims in mind, we sought authors whose work represents theoretical innovations in career theory for the 21st century.

This edited collection is unlike any other in the market because of the selection of theories represented in the book and in the attempt to broaden the base of theoretical perspectives offered to readers away from those that are traditionally featured in theory texts. We brought together internationally renowned leaders in the field of career development whose inspiring theoretical perspectives are moving the field forward in response to long-term critique of the extant theory. The contributors to the 17 chapters are authors working in several different countries, which include Australia, Austria, Canada, England, India, South Africa, and the United States. The chapter authors bring expanded international perspectives through their experience of living and/or working in various countries. The authors have offered leading-edge international approaches to career development theory, including perspectives from the fields of psychology, sociology and organizational development.

Another unique feature of the edited collection is the attention paid to the cultural contexts of people's lives and discussion of the cultural applications of each theory as a component described within each theory chapter. In contemporary society, theorists are called on to be transparent about the underpinning theoretical premises of their work, for whom their theory is directed, and how their theory stands in explaining and supporting the lives of people from diverse cultural contexts and cultural identities. Rather than addressing cultural perspectives as a separate or additional chapter, we invited each chapter author to comment on and critique their own theory. This resulted in substantive content about the application of theory to culturally diverse populations within countries. Several chapter authors spontaneously added perspectives about international influences on the world of work and the potential strengths and limitations of career theory across international contexts.

It is important that practitioners have access to resources that depict current theoretical perspectives. It is also important that such perspectives are written in accessible language and that they provide directions for career development practice. Too often, practitioners do not see the connections between career theory and practice, and this is a gap that we are trying to address in both the content and format of the edited collection. We wanted to be responsive to the feedback from both students and seasoned career practitioners who expressed that they needed resources from which to draw stronger linkage between theory and practice. To that end, we offered a challenge to our chapter authors to provide foundational information about their theories and apply their theories to the unique and original case studies they developed. In doing so, chapter authors have offered a wide range of case studies and customized the particularities of the concepts within their theory that they wanted to highlight for practice. The latter component is highly desirable for both student and practitioner audiences through making the content of theory more directly related to their practice contexts, and through highlighting the strong linkages between theory and practice. To this end, each chapter was written according to a structure designed to enhance accessibility to students new to the field, and to practitioners and researchers who may be unfamiliar with the theoretical perspective.

The edited collection is structured in three parts. Part I of the book offers three chapters in which the authors overview and critique the history and current status of the field. The content of these chapters sets an agenda for advancement in career theory and its integral relationship with practice. Part II of the book offers 13 chapters in which the chapter authors detail a contemporary theory and illustrate its application through a case study. In this section of the book, readers will find chapters on well-established theories with updates the authors have presented for the first time, emerging theories that are newer in the field, and theories that have been developed to more intentionally link applications beyond the individual to organizations and broader social systems. Part III of the book offers one chapter that synthesizes the key themes raised in the book and poses questions for future theory development, research, and practice. It is our hope that the detailed, reader-friendly description of theory supplemented by research and case examples will provide a stimulus for researchers and practitioners to implement the theories and further test and refine them. Moreover, we hope that continuing to expand the international authorship will ensure continued growth and vitality in the development of career theory and its relevancy for practice in countries around the world. We also hope that this book will stimulate ongoing conversations about career theory, its challenges and responses, and its cultural and practical applications in an ever-changing world that continue beyond the publication of this book.

– Nancy Arthur and Mary McMahon

Part I

Career theory

History, challenges, and practical applications

Part I sets the stage for this book by presenting three chapters that overview the history of career development as a professional discipline and its foundational theories, consider the importance of theory for informing practice, and critique the status of career development theories.

1 Career development theory

Origins and history

Mary McMahon and Nancy Arthur

Learning objectives

The purpose of this chapter is to:

- introduce the origins of career theory,
- overview historical trends in career theory, and
- consider the relationship between theory and practice.

Introduction to the chapter

The origins of career development, as a helping profession designed to assist individuals with work and learning decisions, has a long history that spans many, primarily Western, countries. Characteristic of the early history of career development in the mid to late 1800s, is its emergence in periods of rapid economic development and social change such as urbanisation, industrialisation, and immigration, and associated rising social inequality. The first documented efforts to provide career guidance were committed to achieving socially just employment outcomes for individuals who may have been disenfranchised as a result of such changes. Assistance was originally provided in the 1800s primarily in the form of placement services (Patton, forthcoming; Pope, 2000). For example, in Australia, an early attempt to assist people to find work is that of Carolyn Chisholm who in the 1840s, assisted young women arriving in the fledgling colony from England to find safe employment (Patton, forthcoming).

Vocational guidance, as the forerunner of career development, emerged toward the end of the 19th century and in the early 20th century in Europe and the USA (Watts, 1996b) and other Western countries such as Australia (Patton, forthcoming), Canada (Van Norman, Shepard, & Mani, 2014), England and Scotland (Killeen & Kidd, 1996; Law, 1996). For example, in Canada, guidance was first introduced in 1851 when the YMCA provided "character education, and vocational and education programming" (Van Norman et al., 2014, p. 13) to young people and assisted people who were unemployed and those in the "emerging middle class to discover their sense of identity" (p. 13). Subsequently in Canada, in the early 20th century, Etta St. John Wileman, a believer in social responsibility and "a true pioneer in career development" (Van Norman et al., 2014, p. 13), advocated for the establishment of government labour employment services, the first of which was established in Hamilton Ontario in 1914. In England, Juvenile Employment Bureaux were established in the early 20th century when the school leaving age was thirteen or fourteen and children could be exempted from school at age eleven or twelve if they had part-time employment (Killeen & Kidd, 1996). Concern was expressed at this time that too many children were drifting into unskilled work with poor long-term prospects. The purpose of the Bureaux was to advise young people and their parents to take a longer-term view and to encourage them to consider skilled employment and taking advantage of educational opportunities (Killeen & Kidd, 1996). In Scotland, the Scottish Education Act (1908) and the Education (Choice of Employment) Act (1910) permitted local authorities to offer services that assisted young people to transition into work (Killeen & Kidd, 1996). Labour Exchanges were established nationally in 1909 and separate Juvenile Employment Offices were created. China witnessed the emergence of career guidance in the early 20th century when, in 1916, career development lectures were organised by Mr. Zhou Yichun to assist students choose majors and overseas universities (Jin, 2017). In Japan, vocational guidance was introduced in 1915 and Dr. Hiraku Sandaya was a pioneer in providing vocational guidance for youth, including youth with disabilities (Mimura, 2016).

The international nature of the emergence of vocational guidance is frequently overlooked, possibly as a result of the influential work of Frank Parsons (1909), a social reformer who in 1908 founded the Vocation Bureau in Boston and wrote one of the earliest theoretical works on vocational guidance, *Choosing a Vocation*. Reflecting its origins in social reform, Brewer (1919) described vocational guidance as a "civic force", a "moral force" and an "agent of culture" (p. viii). In these words, Brewer provided insight into the potential contribution of career development to individuals and to society. These early social reform efforts to assist people to find jobs and make occupational decisions paved the way for the development of numerous theories and models that focus on vocational guidance and career development.

In orienting this chapter to introduce career theory, it is useful to first consider the nature of theory and what purpose it serves. According to Swanson and Fouad (2015), "theories guide us in making sense of complex sets of information about how humans behave to help us understand them and to predict their behaviour in the future" (p. 12). More simply, theory may be regarded as a map, a guide, a hypothesis, a model, or an explanation that helps us to understand a phenomenon such as career development (McMahon, 2014); career theories are "used to understand and describe people's career development and work experiences" (Ali & Brown, 2017, p. 73).

Since the time of Parsons (1909), a myriad of theories has been proposed and offer explanations for the many facets of career development including personal traits, developmental stages over time, the career decision-making process, the career learning process, and contextual influences on career development. Some of these theories that may be regarded as foundational in the field were developed in the early to mid-20th century and naturally reflected the context and time in which they were developed. Moreover, theories reflect the disciplines in which they were developed and theories about career development have been proposed in disciplines such as vocational psychology, sociology, and organisational psychology. As the 21st century approached and the world was again witnessing rapid economic and social change, scholars pondered how well career theories positioned the field for the more complex, diverse, and challenging world that was shaping (e.g., Savickas & Lent, 1994). New theories began to emerge that were more accommodating of the contemporary world and provide the focus for this book. This chapter however, considers the origins and history of career development theory. The aim is to introduce and overview foundational career theories that have influenced career development for more than half a century and continue to do so. It is not possible in the space of this chapter to provide detailed accounts of career theories. Rather, a brief description of highly influential theories is presented. Cultural considerations related to the extant theory are also presented.

Overview of career theory

Career theory may be confusing to those new to the field who find themselves confronted with many theories, each with a different focus. Those new to the field may wonder if they should choose one theory to focus on, and if so, how to choose it, or attempt to gain a broad understanding of as many theories as possible. Career development, however, is a complex and multifaceted phenomena that recognises the inseparability of work and life as reflected in this description proposed almost half a century ago that continues to resonate well with contemporary thinking:

> Career development involves one's whole life, not just occupation. As such, it concerns the whole person. . . . More than that, it concerns him or her in the ever-changing contexts of his or her life. The environmental pressures and constraints, the bonds that tie him or her to significant others, responsibilities to children and aging parents, the total structure of one's circumstances are also factors that must be understood and reckoned with. In these terms, career development and personal development converge. Self and circumstances – evolving, changing, unfolding in mutual interaction – constitute the focus and drama of career development.
>
> (Wolfe & Kolb, 1980, pp. 1–2)

A further cause of confusion to those new to the field of career development is the array of terms that by and large are used synonymously and, in addition to career development, include vocational guidance, vocational psychology, career psychology, and career/s guidance. Within the confines of this chapter, it is not possible to consider in detail the origins of each term, suffice it to say that the terms may reflect disciplinary allegiances and the time and place in history when they were introduced.

The contribution of Frank Parsons

To begin to understand career development, it is necessary to turn to one of the earliest theoretical formulations, that of Frank Parsons (1909). In providing assistance to young people who were poor and disadvantaged, Parsons advocated a tripartite model, which has provided a foundation for career development to the present day, specifically:

1   A clear understanding of yourself, aptitudes, abilities, interests, resources, limitations, and other qualities;
2   A knowledge of the requirements and conditions of success, advantages and disadvantages, compensation, opportunities, and prospects in different lines of work; and
3   True reasoning on the relations of these two groups of facts

(Parsons, 1909, p. 5).

Parsons' tripartite model encouraged a 'matching' of self-knowledge with world of work knowledge to arrive at a career decision. This matching process underpins the trait-and-factor and more recent person–environment fit approaches which have made a lasting impact on career development.

Parsons invited his clients to complete a "personal record and self-analysis" (p. 27) questionnaire comprising over 100 questions. The questionnaire sought information on personal traits such as abilities and interests, as well as contextual influences such as clients' health, resources, financial status, mobility, friends, and relatives, who were also asked to participate in an interview. In essence, Parsons pioneered career assessment and career counselling and emphasised the need to understand the world of work, all of which remain key elements of career development services. Parsons subsequently worked briefly with Hugo Münsterberg, who is widely regarded as the founder of applied psychology and who proposed the first theory of vocation, which was not widely accepted or adopted (Porfeli, 2009). This association represents the beginning of career development's longstanding association with the discipline of psychology.

Parson's (1909) theoretical work also warrants consideration in relation to two philosophical positions (worldviews) that underpin career theory, logical positivism, and constructivism. Logical positivism is reflected in the seemingly simple matching process proffered by Parsons in that it emphasises a rational linear approach based on objective knowledge. Core assumptions which underpin logical positivism include the following: behaviour is measurable, observable, and linear; individuals can be studied separately from their environments; and context is less important than action (Patton & McMahon, 2014).

Constructivism, however, emphasises contexts and posits that individuals are active agents in the construction of their lives across time and that they make meaning of their contextually based experiences and in doing so construct their identity (Patton & McMahon, 2014). Reflecting the tenets of constructivism, Parsons encouraged the individuals with whom he worked to take an active role in self-analysis and to consider a wide range of contextual influences on their career decision-making. That evidence of both worldviews coexist in Parsons' work is significant as they have sometimes been polarised in career development; both worldviews however, have a contribution to make to how career development is understood and practice is enacted.

Career theory evolves

Psychological career theory has, to date, made a significant contribution to understanding career development. Indeed, two strands of psychology have strengthened our understanding of career development, specifically vocational and organisational psychology. Vocational psychology has contributed to our understanding of individual career development including that of children, adolescents, and adults and focuses more on how career decisions and choices are made. Both organisational psychology and the discipline of management have focused primarily on adult career development after career choice has been made (M. B. Arthur, 2009) and contribute to our understanding of the interface between individuals and the organisations in which they work. Psychology is not, however, the only discipline that has contributed to understandings of career development; individuals' participation in work is also highly relevant to management and to many social science disciplines, including anthropology, economics, education, geography, history, political science, and sociology (Gunz, 2009), and reflects Audrey Collin's (2009) claim that career development's "richness, complexity and ambiguity cannot be grasped from one perspective alone" (p. 3). To the present day, however, career theory and research in these disciplines has remained siloed despite calls for multidisciplinarity (e.g., Collin & Patton, 2009).

Subsequent to the work of Parsons (1909), vocational guidance expanded its influence into the field of education in many countries in the form of educational and vocational guidance in schools, colleges, and universities (Law, 1996; Patton, forthcoming; Pope, 2000; Watts, 1996a), stimulated in the United States by federal legislation (Hoyt, 2001). Publicly provided career services for adults have continued to remain less available and tend to be provided primarily in relation to unemployment, rehabilitation, and outplacement. Although there has been a rise in independent or private practice, career development services for adults remain limited in most countries despite a Council of the European Union (2004) resolution for the provision lifelong access to guidance in the EU countries.

The mid-20th century saw considerable advancement in theoretical explanations of career development. In particular, two of the most influential theorists in career development, Donald Super (1957) and John Holland (1959), proposed theories that continue to stimulate research and practice. Also of interest in the 1950s is the work of the sociologist Everett Hughes (1958) who published the significant text *Men and Their Work*. All three theorists had long and distinguished careers. Sociology, unlike career development which focuses on individuals, focuses more broadly on the social and institutional enablers and constraints of career development such as education and labour market policy, gender, socioeconomics, and social class (Johnson & Mortimer, 2002; Roberts, 2012). Hughes and Super broadly agreed on career being viewed as a sequence of occupations over time, yet, it seems, they did no collaborative work (M. B. Arthur, 2009), evidencing the long tradition of the disciplinary siloing of career development.

Categorising career theory

Within the field of vocational psychology, given the proliferation of so many career theories, several attempts have been made to categorise them. For example, Crites (1969) used the categories psychological theories and non-psychological theories, thus reflecting the siloing of disciplines. Other categories have emerged within vocational psychology itself. For example, Osipow and Fitzgerald (1996) proposed the five categories of (1) trait-factor (reflecting the work of Parsons), (2) society and career choice, (3) developmental/self-conceptions, (4) vocational choice and personality, and (5) behavioural. These categories reflect the breadth and focus of career theories.

Another categorisation is that of Patton and McMahon (2014), who proposed the four categories of (1) theories of content, (2) theories of process, (3) theories of content and process, and (4) wider explanations. Theories of content are steeped in the tradition of Parsons (1909) that have been widely referred to as matching approaches, trait-and-factor approaches, and person–environment fit approaches. The best-known theory of content is that of John Holland (1997) which is described in detail in the following sections. The theory of work adjustment (TWA; Dawis, 2005; Dawis & Lofquist, 1984) has also played an influential role as a theory of content and is briefly described. Theories of process recognise that career is a developmental process beginning in childhood and continuing across the life span, passing through a series of stages. The best-known theory of process is that of Donald Super (1990), which we describe in detail in the following sections. Linda Gottfredson's (1981) theory of circumscription and compromise is also briefly described. Theories of content and process recognise the dynamic and contextual nature of career development. One of the best-known theories of content and process is that of John Krumboltz and his colleagues (e.g., Krumboltz, A. M. Mitchell, & Jones, 1976; A. M. Mitchell, Jones & Krumboltz, 1979; L. K. Mitchell & Krumboltz, 1990), who recognised the important role to career development of learning in context beginning in childhood; this theory is described in more detail in the following sections. Career theories categorised as wider explanations by Patton and

McMahon (2014) are those which account for the career development of people in nondominant groups who have largely been ignored by career theory, and include people with a disability; people with nondominant racial and ethnic identities; people who identify as gay, lesbian, bisexual, or transgendered; and people who have been disadvantaged because of social class. The section on cultural considerations provides some background to the need for such a body of theory.

Person–environment fit theory

Following in the matching tradition of Parsons (1909), Holland (1959) published a theory of vocational choice which remains the most influential trait-and-factor/person–environment fit theory specifically, and more generally, one of the most influential career development theories (Nauta, 2013). Holland set out to develop a simple and practical theory (Nauta, 2013) and developed a parallel classification of people and environments according to six types. Holland believed vocational interests were an aspect of personality and he developed a typology comprising six types: realistic, investigative, artistic, social, enterprising, and conventional, commonly referred to as a RIASEC model and represented on the corners of a hexagon. In keeping with the psychological traditions of his theory, Holland (1985) developed one of the world's most widely used career assessment instruments, the Self-Directed Search (SDS). Individuals who complete the SDS obtain a score on each of the six personality types, but Holland ultimately focuses on the highest three scores (e.g., social, investigative, and artistic [SIA]). Holland also used his typology to categorise occupations. Individuals can match their three-letter code to those of occupations. Reflective of a person–environment fit approach, Holland contended that individuals seek out work environments that are congruent with their type; the higher the degree of congruence between an individual and their work environment, the more satisfied and successful they will be. Throughout his distinguished career, Holland continued to refine his theory, culminating in the publication in 1997 of his book *Making Vocational Choices: A Theory of Vocational Personalities and Work Environments*.

Another person–environment fit theory that is also worthy of mention is the theory of work adjustment (TWA; Dawis, 2005; Dawis & Lofquist, 1984) which focuses primarily on the interaction between individuals and their work environments. The relationship between individuals and their work environments is dynamic as continual adjustments are made to achieve satisfactory relationships. Adjustment from an individual perspective may be influenced by variables such as personality and values, both of which are emphasised in theories of content. Both the worker and the work environment have needs, and if these needs cannot be met then dissatisfaction may occur. Adjustment is the process of trying to achieve a good match between the worker and the environment, which, in TWA, is termed correspondence. If correspondence is not achieved, or, in other words, discorrespondence exists, the worker may leave the work environment.

Developmental stage career theory

In the early 1950s, in a move away from trait-and-factor accounts of career development, the process of career development was theorised as a series of stages beginning in childhood. The first such theory was that of Ginzberg, Ginsberg, Axelrad, and Herma (1951), who proposed three developmental stages beginning in childhood and ending in early adulthood. Despite being visionary for its time, its influence was diminished by acceptance of the notion of life-span career development, the first proponent of which was Donald Super.

Super advanced thinking about career development by shifting the focus away from differential psychology perspectives and taking a broader view of career as a developmental process across the lifespan. Subsequent to his first major theoretical statement in 1953, *A Theory of Vocational Development*, Super (1957) also shifted thinking from vocation to careers with the publication of his book *The Psychology of Careers*. Super refined his theory throughout his career and the publication of his life-span, life-space theory in 1990, which remains his best-known theoretical contribution. As reflected in the name of this theory, Super was the first theorist to take account of the contextual location of career development and its relationship with other life roles across time. Super proposed that career development is an implementation of self-concept over time beginning in childhood and he identified a series of five stages through which individuals pass, specifically growth, exploration, establishment, maintenance, and decline (later termed disengagement) which reflect the life-span stages of childhood, adolescence, adulthood, middle adulthood, and old age. During each stage, Super identified tasks that individuals complete. He depicted chronological ages, his stages, the life roles individuals occupy across time (e.g., child, student, worker). Super's life-space concept refers to the context of career development and he acknowledged that work roles may be only one of a number of life-roles that an individual occupies at one time. He depicted the context of career development in his archway of career determinants which centrally featured the self and a range of personal determinants (e.g., values, aptitudes, interests) and situational determinants (e.g., labour market, society, school, family) that influences career development in the two pillars of the arch. Super's legacy to career development is lasting. His recognition of the life-span process of career "led to a redefinition of vocational guidance" and a "career developmental orientation" that became widely accepted (Pope, 2000, p. 204), and remains so to the present day.

Like Super, Linda Gottfredson (1981) proposed a career theory based on a sequence of four stages beginning in childhood. Gottfredson, however, also described how the processes of circumscription and compromise influence career choice. Circumscription is a process of eliminating alternatives from a range of possible careers on the basis of self-concept in a series of four age-related stages. For example, Gottfredson posits that children between the ages of three and five realise that adults work and that between the ages of six and eight, they reject (circumscribe) occupations on the basis of gender. As children become more capable of abstract thought, typically between the ages of nine and thirteen, they circumscribe occupations on the basis of perceived social status. From age fourteen, children begin to weigh up acceptable alternative occupations in terms of their accessibility and personal preferences and begin to implement career decisions. Compromise is the process of relinquishing preferred alternatives for those that are more accessible on the basis of social and environmental circumstances such as geographic location or socioeconomic circumstances. Unlike Super's lifespan theory, Gottfredson's primary focus was on childhood and adolescence.

Career theory, context, and process

Another of the early theorists to recognise the importance of context in the 1950s was Anne Roe. Her theory of personality development and career choice focused on the relationship between occupational behaviour and personality (Roe, 1956; Roe & Lunneborg, 1990). She focused on parent–child relations and career choice. Roe was one of the first to develop an occupational classification system that was a forerunner to Holland's (1959, 1997) RIASEC model described earlier. Roe was one of the first theorists to acknowledge a broad range of variables on career development, including gender, the economy, family background, physical attributes and impairments, and chance.

A further foundational theory is the social learning theory of career decision-making (SLTCDM) developed by John Krumboltz and his colleagues and first published in 1976 (Krumboltz, A. M. Mitchell, & Jones). In adapting Bandura's (1977) social learning theory, A. M. Mitchell, Jones, and Krumboltz (1979) attempted to explain the content and process of career development. Essentially, SLTCDM posits that "individuals learn about themselves, their preferences, and the world of work through direct and indirect experiences" (Patton & McMahon, 2014, p. 96) and subsequently take action based on their learning. This theory identifies four groups of factors that influence career decision-making, specifically genetic endowment and special abilities (e.g., gender, ability), environmental conditions and events (e.g., job and training opportunities, social policy, natural disasters, families), learning experiences (i.e., instrumental and associative learning experiences), and task approach skills (e.g., work habits, emotional responses, performance standards) (L. K. Mitchell & Krumboltz, 1990). The work of Krumboltz and his colleagues is noteworthy as an attempt to describe the process of career development and in their acknowledgement of a broad range of contextual factors that influence career development.

Contemporary theories emerge

Reminiscent of the period of rapid change when vocational guidance was first conceptualised, the latter part of the 20th century and the early part of the 21st century also witnessed rapid change as society became increasingly complex and diverse. Despite the influence and valuable contributions of these foundational theories, by the late-20th century, theorists and researchers gathered together to consider the possible future directions of career theory (see Savickas & Lent,

1994). Questions were asked about the future of career (Collin & Young, 2000), and calls were made to renovate career psychology (Savickas, 2000). New theoretical formulations were beginning to emerge that were more holistic and integrative (e.g., cognitive information processing [CIP] theory [Peterson, Sampson, & Reardon, 1991]; social cognitive career theory [SCCT; Lent, Brown, & Hackett, 1994]; systems theory framework [STF] of career development [Patton & McMahon, 1999]).

Holism and complexity are more easily accommodated in theories informed by the constructivist worldview. Theories underpinned by constructivism de-emphasise reductionism (i.e., reducing things to their smallest components) and determinism (i.e., searching for specific causes of events), both key features of trait-and-factor theories, and emphasise the importance of language, context, history, and social interactions (Stead & Subich, 2017). Philosophical foundations in constructivism feature prominently in most career theories proposed in the latter part of the 20th century and the early part of the 21st century, as evidenced by the theories presented in subsequent chapters of this book.

Cultural considerations

Although career theory has provided a greater understanding of how the complex process of career development unfolds, it has not, however, been without critique. Such critique generally centres around understanding of the term career itself, from where the theories have originated, their focus, and whose career development they account for. Concerns about career theory have been brought more sharply into focus as the employment market has dramatically changed; the field has become internationalised and globalisation has resulted in more diverse societies. Reflecting Brewer's (1919) description of vocational guidance as an "agent of culture" (p. viii), many of these concerns exemplify cultural considerations that will be considered here.

The term career itself warrants consideration from a cultural perspective. Despite holistic understandings of career being theorised, in practice, career and career development predominantly focus on paid employment in Western labour markets. The middle-class connotations of 'career' also warrant consideration. Career development's emphasis on paid employment disenfranchises those whose careers concern voluntary work and work in the home, especially women (Richardson, 2012). The relevance of career theory to the careers of women has long been questioned despite women representing approximately one-half of the population (Patton & McMahon, 2014). Moreover, the Western notion of career is less appropriate in developing countries where work may be conceptualised differently. In the Indian context, for example, the teachings of Mahatma Ghandi offer different views of education and work and the relationship between them (Devika & Arulmani, 2008) from Western notions depicted in most career theory. The terms career and career development have generally less relevance to the almost two-thirds of the global workforce who work in the informal economy (Kumar, 2016) and who, in general, earn low wages in occupations with no job security, spend their lives in poor working and living conditions, can claim little or no social security provisions and worker rights, experience multiple forms of poverty, register low level of skill formation.

(Kumar, 2016, p. 53)

Thus, we are reminded that

all cultures have their own ways, grounded in tradition and experience, of engaging with the world of work. The need at hand is to draw upon these traditions and customs to create career guidance techniques and methods that would have contemporary relevance.

(Nag, Arulmani, & Bakshi, 2012, p. 2)

Cultural consideration also need to be given to the origins of career theory in Western, primarily American settings. Further, a number of career theories that remain influential to the present time were proposed in the mid-20th century, as reflected in the foundational theories presented in this chapter. Theories reflect the times and contexts in which they were developed, and their relevance in the present time has been questioned. For example, a common criticism of the foundational career theories is that they do not adequately accommodate the careers of women and groups other than white, middle-class males, as mentioned previously. In relation to career development in childhood, Bakshi (2017) explicates the experiences of children growing up in developing world contexts and emphasises the inadequacy of Western career theory in these contexts. Moreover, with the internationalisation of career development, concerns have been raised about the appropriateness of the Eurocentric nature of career theory that has been exported to and imported into countries with vastly different cultures and traditions from where the theories originated. This trend has led to concerns about career theory's focus on personal rather than cultural and contextual factors, the goals of career choice being related to self-actualisation and job satisfaction, free choice and the opportunity to make several career decisions across time, and resources and practices that are culture-based and not easily transported to or adapted in other cultures (Leung & Yuen, 2012). A noticeable difference in the contemporary theories presented in Part II of this book, compared with those presented in previous texts which featured foundational theories, is that contributions emanate from a range of country authors, including Australia, Austria, Canada, England, India, and the United States. The cultural considerations overviewed here suggest that career practitioners need to engage reflectively with their clients and consider the cultural nature of their interactions (Arthur, 2017).

Chapter summary

Career theory, as revealed in this chapter, has a long history. A theme that has emerged from this chapter and remains a major challenge for career development as it moves forward and attempts to remain relevant in 21st-century society is its siloed nature and resultant separation from other disciplines such as organisational psychology, sociology, and management. Where career development theory and research provide valuable insights into individual career development, they do not provide detailed insight into the broader social and contextual factors that enable or constrain individual career development. Thus, practitioners focus their work primarily on individuals and are generally not trained to consider and respond to the broader social issues facing individuals.

Another theme that has emerged is career development's origins in the social justice movement. In the 21st century, social justice remains a core value underpinning career development (Arthur, 2005). Career theory's relationship with social justice, however, is not always evident. Thus, there is little in some theories to guide practitioners in applying the theory through a lens of social justice (Arthur, Collins, McMahon, & Marshall, 2009).

A further theme that has emerged during this chapter is the Western, primarily middle-class origins of career development and the societal changes brought about by globalisation and internationalisation. Again, most theories provide little guidance to practitioners in the application of the theory in diverse settings and with diverse clients.

Conclusion

In concluding this chapter on the origins and history of career development theory, two points are worth making. First, theory is valuable for enabling us to interpret career development in various ways – theory and practice are inextricably connected. Second, the words of John Killeen (1996) caution us that "theories may blind us to what lies beyond their scope" (p. 41). He suggests that career development practitioners develop awareness of "*theory*, not merely of *a* theory – enabling them to test against alternatives the implicit theory they bring with them to the profession" (p. 41). Thus, career development practitioners are urged to have a sound understanding of career development theories that have historically provided a major contribution to the field as well as theories such as those included in this book that have been proposed in more contemporary times. In particular, practitioners are urged to critically reflect on the cultural and contextual origins of career theory, their focus, and the clients to whom they apply, as well as the cultural and contextual location in which their application is being considered.

Learning activities

Learning activity 1

Draw a lifeline from when you were born to your present age. List beside the relevant ages, your aspirations, courses you have studied, and occupations and roles you have held. Reflect on how these aspirations, courses, occupations, and roles came about (i.e., what or who influenced your thinking, and how you made decisions and transitioned between the roles).

Now think about the theories you have been introduced to in this chapter and consider how they may have accounted for your career development at various times in your life.

If possible, share your time line with a partner who has drawn a similar lifeline and discuss the relationships that you see between your career development and the theories you have been introduced to.

Learning activity 2

1   Read the following quotes:

> Sociologists are interested in career choice and development primarily because of their consequences for socioeconomic inequality and mobility. Occupation is a strong determinant of a person's status within the community, earnings, wealth, and style of life.
>
> (Johnson & Mortimer, 2002, p. 37)

> The sociological perspective on career choice and development becomes increasingly necessary as a vehicle for understanding the diverse societal, institutional, and microcontextual environments of the modern world that influence these processes, the mechanisms of intergenerational and intragenerational mobility, and the determinants of adult socioeconomic wellbeing. It is also necessary to inform social policies that will enable people to make satisfying occupational choices and to obtain fulfilling occupational careers that will extend throughout the lives.
>
> (Johnson & Mortimer, 2002, p. 69)

> Now that you have read these quotes, make notes of your reactions to and thoughts about them.

2.   Using your notes as background, with a colleague or fellow student discuss differences that you perceive between the psychological career theories that have been overviewed in this chapter and the sociological perspective outlined in these quotes. Consider the potential advantages and disadvantages of separate disciplines and also of potential collaboration between the disciplines.

Learning activities: reflective questions

1   How would you explain the role of career theory to a colleague who is new to the field?

2 How would you describe the relationship between career theory and practice?
3 What are the benefits and risks for practice of basing your career practice on only one career theory?

References

Ali, S. R., & Brown, S. D. (2017). Integration of theory, research, and practice: Using our tools to address challenging times. In J. P. Sampson, E. Bullock-Yowell, V. C. Dozier, D. S. Osborn, & J. G. Lenz (Eds.), *Integrating theory, research, and practice in vocational psychology: Current status and future directions* (pp. 73–76). Tallahassee: Florida State University. Retrieved from http://journals.fcla.edu/svp2016/

Arthur, M. B. (2009). Foreword: Rapprochement at last? In A. Collin & W. Patton (Eds.), *Vocational psychological and organisational perspectives on career: Towards a multidisciplinary dialogue* (pp. ix–x). Rotterdam, The Netherlands: Sense.

Arthur, N. (2005). Building from cultural diversity to social justice competencies in international standards for career development practitioners. *International Journal for Educational and Vocational Guidance, 5*(2), 137–149.

Arthur, N. (2017). Constructivist approaches to career counselling: A culture-infused perspective. In M. McMahon (Ed.), *Career counselling: Constructivist approaches* (pp. 54–64). London: Routledge.

Arthur, N., Collins, S., McMahon, M., & Marshall, C. (2009). Career practitioners' views of social justice and barriers for practice. *Canadian Journal of Career Development, 8*, 22–31.

Bakshi, A. (2017). Child career development in developing world contexts. In M. Watson & M. McMahon (Eds.), *Career exploration and development in childhood* (pp. 114–126). Abingdon, Oxon: Routledge.

Bandura, A. (1977). Self-efficacy: Toward a unifying theory of behavioral change. *Psychology Review, 84*, 191–215.

Brewer, J. M. (1919). *The vocational-guidance movement: Its problems and possibilities.* New York: MacMillan.

Collin, A. (2009). One step towards realising the multidisciplinarity of career studies. In A. Collin & W. Patton (Eds.), *Vocational psychological and organisational perspectives on career: Towards a multidisciplinary dialogue* (pp. 3–18). Rotterdam, The Netherlands: Sense.

Collin, A., & Patton, W. (Eds.). (2009). *Vocational psychological and organisational perspectives on career: Towards a multidisciplinary dialogue.* Rotterdam, The Netherlands: Sense.

Collin, A., & Young, R. A. (Eds.). (2000). *The future of career.* Cambridge, UK: Cambridge University Press.

Council of the European Union. (2004). Draft resolution of the Council and of the representatives of the Member States meeting within the Council on strengthening policies, systems and practices in the field of guidance throughout the life in Europe. Retrieved from http://register.consilium.europa.eu/doc/srv?l=EN&f=ST%209286%202004%20INIT

Crites, J. O. (1969). *Vocational psychology.* New York: McGraw-Hill.

Dawis, R. V. (2005). The Minnesota Theory of Work Adjustment. In R. W. Lent & S. D. Brown (Eds.), *Career development and counseling: Putting theory to work* (pp. 3–23). Hoboken, NJ: John Wiley.

Dawis, R. V., & Lofquist, L. H. (1984). *A psychological theory of work adjustment: An individual difference model and its application*. Minneapolis, MN: University of Minnesota.

Devika, V. R., & Arulmani, G. (2008). Mahatma Ghandi's ideas for work, career, and life. In G. Arulmani, A. Bakshi, F. Leong & T. Watts (Eds.), *Handbook of career development: International perspectives* (pp. 105–117). New York: Springer.

Ginzberg, E., Ginsberg, S. W., Axelrad, S., & Herma, J. L. (1951). *Occupational choice: An approach to general theory*. New York: Viking Penguin.

Gottfredson, L. S. (1981). Circumscription and compromise: A developmental theory of occupational aspirations. *Journal of Counseling Psychology, 28*, 545–579.

Gunz, H. (2009). The two solitudes: The vocational psychological/organisational gap as seen from the organisational perspective. In A. Collin & W. Patton (Eds.), *Vocational psychological and organisational perspectives on career: Towards a multidisciplinary dialogue* (pp. 19–27). Rotterdam, The Netherlands: Sense.

Holland, J. L. (1959). A theory of vocational choice. *Journal of Counseling Psychology, 6*, 35–44.

Holland, J. L. (1985). *The Self-Directed Search: A guide to educational and vocational planning*. Odessa, FL: Psychological Assessment Resources.

Holland, J. L. (1997). *Making vocational choices: A theory of vocational personalities and work environments* (3rd ed.). Odessa, FL: Consulting Psychologists Press.

Hoyt, K. B. (2001). A reaction to Mark Pope's 2000 "A brief history of career counseling in the United States". *The Career Development Quarterly, 49*, 374–379.

Hughes, E. C. (1958). *Men and their work*. Toronto, ON, Canada: Collier-Macmillan.

Jin, L. (2017). The current status of career services and professionals in Mainland China's educational settings. In H. Yoon, B. Hutchison, M. Maze, C. Pritchard, & A. Reiss (Eds.), *International practices of career services, credentials, and training*. Broken Arrow, OK: National Career Development Association. Retrieved from www. ncda.org/aws/NCDA/page_template/show_detail/139017?layout_name=layout_deta ils&model_name=news_article

Johnson, M. K., & Mortimer, J. T. (2002). Career choice and development from a sociological perspective. In D. Brown & Associates (Eds.), *Career choice and development* (4th ed.) (pp. 37–81). San Francisco, CA: Jossey Bass.

Killeen, J. (1996). Career theory. In A. G. Watts, B. Law, J. Killeen, J. M. Kidd, & R. Hawthorn (Eds.), *Rethinking careers education and guidance: Theory, policy and practice* (pp. 23–45). London: Routledge.

Killeen, J., & Kidd, J. M (1996). The careers service. In A. G. Watts, B. Law, J. Killeen, J. M. Kidd, & R. Hawthorn (Eds.), *Rethinking careers education and guidance: Theory, policy and practice* (pp. 155–172). London: Routledge.

Krumboltz, J. D., Mitchell, A. M., & Jones, G. B. (1976). A social learning theory of career selection. *The Counseling Psychologist, 6*, 71–81.

Kumar, S. (2016). Advocacy counselling for informal workers: A case for Indian Street vendors. *Indian Journal of Career and Livelihood Planning, 5*(1), 52–64.

Law, B. (1996). Careers work in schools. In A. G. Watts, B. Law, J. Killeen, J. M. Kidd, & R. Hawthorn (Eds.), *Rethinking careers education and guidance: Theory, policy and practice* (pp. 95–111). London: Routledge.

Lent, R. W., Brown, S. D., & Hackett, G. (1994). Toward a unifying sociocognitive theory of career and academic interest, choice and performance [Monograph]. *Journal of Vocational Behavior, 45*, 79–122.

Leung, S-M. A., & Yuen, M. (2012). The globalization of an ethnocentric career theory and practice. In M. Watson & M. McMahon (Eds.), *Career development: Global issues and challenges* (pp. 75–91). New York: Nova Science.

McMahon, M. (2014). New trends in theory development in career psychology. In G. Arulmani, A. Bakshi, F. Leong, & T. Watts (Eds.), *Handbook of career development: International Perspectives* (pp. 13–28). New York: Springer.

Mimura, T. (2016). The ideas and actions for social justice at the beginning of vocational guidance in Japan. Paper presented at the annual conference of the International Association of Educational and Vocational Guidance (IAEVG), UNED, Madrid, Spain, November 15–18.

Mitchell, A. M., Jones, G. D., & Krumboltz, J. D. (Eds.). (1979). *Social learning theory and career decision making.* Cranston, RI: Carroll.

Mitchell, L. K. & Krumboltz, J. D. (1990). Social learning approach to career decision making: Krumboltz's theory. In D. Brown & L. Brooks (Eds.), *Career choice and development: Applying contemporary theories to practice* (2nd ed., pp. 145–196). San Francisco, CA: Jossey-Bass.

Nag, S., Arulmani, G., & Bakshi, A. J. (2012). Editorial. Career counselling and livelihood planning: Challenges and opportunities. *Indian Journal of Career and Livelihood Planning, 1*(1), 1–3.

Nauta, M. M. (2013). Holland's theory of vocational choice and adjustment. In S. D. Brown & R. W. Lent (Eds.), *Career development and counseling: Putting theory and research to work* (2nd ed., pp. 55–82). New York: Wiley.

Osipow, S. H., & Fitzgerald, L. F. (1996). *Theories of career development* (4th ed.). Boston: Allyn & Bacon.

Parsons, F. (1909). *Choosing a vocation.* Boston, MA: Houghton-Mifflin.

Patton, W. (forthcoming). *Career development as a partner in nation building Australia: Origins, history and foundations for the future.* Rotterdam, The Netherlands: Sense (Brill).

Patton, W., & McMahon, M. (1999). *Career development and systems theory: A new relationship.* Palo Alto, CA: Brooks/Cole.

Patton, W., & McMahon, M. (2014). *Career development and systems theory: Connecting theory and practice* (3rd ed.). Rotterdam, The Netherlands: Sense.

Peterson, G. W., Sampson, J. P. Jr., & Reardon, R. C. (1991). *Career development and services: A cognitive approach.* Pacific Grove, CA: Brooks/Cole.

Pope, M. (2000). A brief history of career counseling in the United States. *The Career Development Quarterly, 48*, 194–211.

Porfeli, E. (2009). Hugo Münsterberg and the origins of vocational guidance [Special Issue]. *The Career Development Quarterly, 57*, 225–236.

Richardson, M. S. (2012). Counseling for work and relationship. *The Counseling Psychologist, 40*(2), 190–242.

Roberts, K. (2012). Career development among the lower socioeconomic strata in developed countries. In M. Watson & M. McMahon (Eds.), *Career development: Global issues and challenges* (pp. 29–43). New York: Nova Science.

Roe, A. (1956). *The psychology of occupations.* New York: Wiley.

Roe, A., & Lunneborg, P. (1990). Personality and carer choice. In D. Brown & L. Brooks (Eds.), *Career choice and development: Applying contemporary theories to practice* (2nd ed.) (pp. 68–101). San Francisco, CA: Jossey-Bass.

Savickas, M. L. (2000). Renovating the psychology of careers for the twenty-first century. In A. Collin & R. A. Young (Eds.), *The future of career* (pp. 53–68). Cambridge, UK: Cambridge University Press.

Savickas, M. L., & Lent, R. W. (Eds.). (1994). *Convergence in career development theories*. Palo Alto, CA: CPP Press.

Stead, G. B., & Subich, L. M. (2017). Career counselling practice. In G. B. Stead & M. B. Watson (Eds.), *Career psychology in the South African context* (3rd ed., pp. 119–135). Pretoria, South Africa: Van Schaik.

Super, D. E. (1953). A theory of vocational development. *American Psychologist, 8*, 19–34.

Super, D. E. (1957). *The psychology of careers*. New York: Harper and Row.

Super, D. E. (1990). A life-span, life-space approach to career development. In D. Brown & L. Brooks (Eds.), *Career choice and development: Applying contemporary theories to practice* (2nd ed., pp. 197–261). San Francisco, CA: Jossey-Bass.

Swanson, J. L., & Fouad, N. A. (2015). *Career theory and practice: Learning through case studies* (3rd ed.). Los Angeles, CA: SAGE.

Van Norman, M., Shepard, B. C., & Mani, P. S. (2014). Historical snapshots: The emergence of career development in Canada. In B. C. Shepard & P. S. Mani (Eds.), *Career development practice in Canada: Perspectives, principles, and professionalism* (pp. 11–34). Toronto, Canada: CERIC.

Watts, A. G. (1996a). Careers work in higher education. In A. G. Watts, B. Law, J. Killeen, J. M. Kidd, & R. Hawthorn (Eds.), *Rethinking careers education and guidance: Theory, policy and practice* (pp. 127–141). London: Routledge.

Watts, A. G. (1996b). International perspectives. In A. G. Watts, B. Law, J. Killeen, J. M. Kidd, & R. Hawthorn (Eds.), *Rethinking careers education and guidance: Theory, policy and practice* (pp. 366–379). London: Routledge.

Wolfe, D. M., & Kolb, D. A. (1980). Career development, personal growth, and experiential learning. In J. W. Springer (Ed.), *Issues in career and human resources development* (pp. 1–11). Madison, WI: American Society for Training and Development.

2 The reciprocal relationship of career theory and practice

Mark Watson

Learning objectives

The purpose of this chapter is to:

- consider the interrelationship of career theory and career practice,
- identify classical criteria for the evaluation of career theory,
- suggest contemporary criteria for the evaluation of career theory, and
- consider career theory in relation to career practice in differing cultural contexts.

Introduction to the chapter

A starting point for a chapter that explores the role of career theory in relation to career practice is to consider whether there is a need for career theory. Since the inception of Frank Parsons's (1909) pioneering work at the beginning of the last century, the discipline of career psychology has developed theories in an attempt to explain the realities of making career decisions within the world of work evident at a particular time. Career theories have been developed for the same reason as the development of theories in other disciplines – they can provide logical explanations and principles that help us to understand phenomena (Sharf, 2013). They can also act as "interpretative filters" (Bakshi, 2014, p. 43) that enable us to make sense and meaning of the complexities that are evident in our discipline. But, of course, those complexities change over time. Indeed, individual career development in the world of work has become an increasingly complex process. Individuals can no longer consider the choice of career within a stable, predictable and indeed linear world of work (Savickas, 2005; Watson, 2016). Career theories that explain career behaviour as if that work world still exists lose relevance and application in the fluid, evolving work world of today. Indeed, Roberts (2012) argued that the world of work towards the middle of the last century was highly atypical of the history of Western industrial societies.

The nature of the world of work in contemporary times challenges and outdates "the comfort zones of career development theories that have guided us for much of the second half of the last century" (Watson, 2016, p. 13). Thus, there has been a need to constantly revise or create career theories in order to make sense of changing macrosystemic factors whether these are political, economic or social. This has led in recent decades to the development and redevelopment of career theories and practice that focus on nonlinear career concepts such as adaptability, resilience and chaos (Watson, 2016). There is reciprocity here between evolving change in macro-contexts and changing definitions of theoretical concepts such as 'career' and 'career development' (Watson & Stead, 2017). The changing nature of career theories is a consequence of the changing nature of the world of work and with that reciprocal change comes the need to also change the way we practice.

The response to the proliferation of career theories, particularly since the latter part of the last century and the first two decades of this century, has been mixed. Athanasou and Van Esbroeck (2008), for instance, queried whether there is a need for so many career theories and called for normative guidelines in order to better understand contextually individual career development. Arulmani, Bakshi, Leong, and Watts (2014), on the other hand, see the development of career theories as being robust and believe that the calls for development and redevelopment of career theory augur well for the discipline of career psychology. Implicit in both viewpoints is the need to critically evaluate contemporary career theories and there are subsequent sections of this chapter that describe classical and contemporary criteria that are useful in such an evaluation.

The reciprocity of career theory and practice

Before considering evaluative criteria for career theory it is important to consider the reciprocal interaction between career theory and practice; such a consideration emphasises that a critical criterion in evaluating career theory is whether or not it can be applied in contemporary times. The value of any career theory lies largely in whether it can be used within career counselling practice, career theory and career education. Indeed, the history of career theory development reflects career theorists' responses to the practical realities of career practice. A classic example of this reciprocity between theory and practice would be Frank Parsons's (1909) development of theoretical principles to address the realities of poverty and unemployment and the consequent social justice issues that arose from such conditions (Watson, 2016). Contemporary career theory has revisited these social justice issues in the present century as is evident in David Blustein's (2006, 2013) psychology of working theory.

The reciprocity of career theory and practice raises the question of what influences what; it is the old conundrum of which comes first, the chicken or the egg. Perhaps a more relevant question however would be whether this matters, whether the critical issue is rather that there needs to be a reciprocal relationship between career theory and practice. Indeed, there needs to be a triangulated relationship that includes the role of research both within theory and practice and between theory and practice. Reardon, Lenz, Sampson, and

Peterson (2011), amongst other questions they posed for the discipline of career psychology to consider, asked how career theory and research should find their way into practice. Perhaps we also need to ask how career practice finds its way into theory and research. Clearly, theory without practical application and research remains conceptual in nature, while career practice without theory and research remains unsubstantiated application. As Arulmani et al. (2014) state "one without the other would only partially address felt needs" (p. 3). On the other hand, a strong reciprocity between career theory, research and practice could lead to what McMahon (2014) believes would be the construction of a "richer and more sustainable discipline of career psychology that is culturally relevant in contexts beyond its traditional Western base" (p. 24). The challenge of cultural validation to career development theory is a topic discussed later in this chapter.

Although there is recognition in the career literature of the need for a stronger relationship between theory, research and practice, there is less clarity as to how to achieve this relationship. The role of research in validating both career theory and practice is described, but there is also a need to consider the role players who develop career theory, or who practice in the field in relation to their social context and worldview. In this regard, Watson (2006) focuses on the role of career practitioners and argued that the dominant, often prescriptive role of career theory is a consequence in part of the passive role adopted by career practitioners in accepting rather than challenging theoretical tenets and assumptions. Career practitioners could play a more activist role in informing career theorists of what works and does not work in the contemporary world within which they practice. Thus, there is a need for career practitioners not to simply adopt contemporary theory but also to call for adaptation of such theory based on its application within their career practice.

Is there a need to improve career theory and practice? Athanasou and Van Esbroeck (2008) are outspoken about the proliferating literature on career theory, bemoaning the fact that contemporary career theory, and in particular career practice, is often unscientific or based on common sense principles. Sharf (2013) too believes that, while the role of theory in other disciplines is well defined, "when applied to career development, theory becomes cruder and less precise" (p. 4). There is also the long-standing criticism that the validity and relevance of career theory is compromised by its lack of contextualisation (McMahon, Watson & Patton, 2014). The latter authors raise two pertinent issues for the further development of contemporary career theory. One issue is the need for greater contextualisation of the many influences on individual career development while, at the same time, not losing sight of established career theory's focus on the individual. Thus, these authors call for a move from "the present focus on decontextualized individuals to a focus on contextualized individuals" (p. 30). Implicit in such a call is the recognition that career theory's focus on intraindividual variables resulted in a predominantly psychological perspective of career development (McMahon & Watson, 2012). The second issue reflects the concerns raised by other authors at the start of this paragraph about the proliferation of career theory. McMahon, Watson and Patton (2014) call for the development of career theories that can accommodate change rather than changing career theories constantly to meet changing times, that theories are needed that "provide us with a way of understanding and adapting to such change" (p. 30).

One way to improve career theory and practice is to test both (Sharf, 2013), and a major means for such testing is research. This is particularly the case with contemporary theories that emphasise a more qualitative understanding of individual career development. Stead and Davis (2015) are of the opinion that qualitative forms of assessment and intervention still need to prove the efficacy of what they propose. Another way to improve career theory, in particular, is to consider such theory against established and emerging evaluative criteria. The next two sections describe such criteria.

Classical criteria for evaluating career theory

There is a need to consider established criteria that have been proposed to evaluate career theory. For instance, Watson and Stead (2017) believe that the operational inadequacy of some career theories make their validation difficult to establish. They point to the subjectivity of theoretical concepts, the retrospective data that some theories rely on and the lack of instrumentation to evaluate career theory. These authors have considered the issue of seeking quality in the quantitative emergence of career theories that has occurred since the pioneering theorists of the earlier part of the last century. Watson and Stead reviewed classical evaluative criteria that are evident in the career literature and themed them, resulting in four core classical criteria. These are described in no particular priority order in the following section.

The first criterion concerns the structure or framework of the theory, specifically its terms and constructs. Brown (2002) states that these terms and constructs must explain what happens and why it happens, in other words they should speak to the purpose of the theory. McMahon (2014) points out further the need for career theories to establish greater uniformity in the constructs they define. The second criterion concerns the need for theories to acknowledge their conceptual focus as well as the populations they focus on. As Sharf (2013) states, "It is important to understand what the subject of the theory is" (p. 4). This second criterion raises the point that a career theory needs to recognise the limits and indeed the limitations of its scope. For instance, career theories developed in the second half of the last century usually focused on middle-class, Westernised samples. Coupled with this second criterion is the tendency of theories to generalise the applicability of their theory across a wide diversity of contexts but with little substantive research evidence to support such assumptions.

The third criterion reflects a concern described earlier, the need for theory to test their hypotheses and the viability of their constructs. This calls for research and for theories to develop measurable constructs. The fourth criterion emphasises the inherent structure of a theory, the consistency with which the theoretical tenets are described. Sharf (2013) points, for instance, to the need for theory to develop constructs that are logically interrelated. This can be achieved by limiting the number of theoretical constructs, with Sharf arguing that the broader the theory "the more difficult it is to be specific about the terms that are used" (p. 4). Similarly, Brown (2002) describes a theory as parsimonious if it uses the "smallest number of constructs possible to explain the phenomena being addressed" (p. 9). While these themed evaluative criteria arise from the historical development of career theory, there is a need to consider criteria for the evaluation of contemporary career theory.

Contemporary criteria for evaluating career theory

Just as career theories change to reflect changing macro-contexts, so too is there a need to consider whether classical criteria are useful in evaluating contemporary career theory. More specifically, the issue goes beyond the relevance of classical criteria and explores whether classical criteria are sufficient for the evaluation of contemporary career theory. There is literature that considers classical criteria in relation to contemporary career theory. For example, McMahon (2014) concludes that no contemporary theories at present fit these classical criteria. McMahon expresses concern about the cultural and contextual relevance of contemporary career theory. There is a need, then, to retain classical criteria but also to move on and explore additional criteria or to expand on existing classical criteria in order to evaluate contemporary career theory. The discussion in this chapter now turns to six criteria that could be considered in the evaluation of contemporary career theory. These six criteria reflect present concerns in the career literature about theory building in the 21st century.

Six contemporary criteria

Given the concern that career theories continue to proliferate, perhaps the first contemporary evaluation criterion could be that the development of a specific theory should be positioned in relation to other theory development. In short, what is new about this theory, what makes it contemporary, what makes it able to address issues relevant to career development in the present times? Or is the practitioner faced with reformulated and redefined career theory lexicon? The latter question reflects an earlier call in this chapter for career theories to establish some common language. Hartung (2012) also calls for a common international language for career theory and practice and believes that this could stimulate "career development's continuing viability, validity and value" (p. 21). Sharf (2013) suggests that a second contemporary evaluation criterion could be established by considering career practitioners themselves. These intraindividual criteria call for career practitioners to consider whether they have confidence in a theory, whether it is suitable for the clientele with whom they work, whether it is congruent with their own personal philosophy, and whether they find the theory personally manageable within their practice.

Related to the issue of manageability is a third contemporary evaluation criterion, the conciseness of a theory in terms of the limited number of concepts that it employs. Although parsimony of career theories has been broadly noted under the fourth classical criterion, this contemporary criterion explicitly operationalises the construct in providing a quantitative guideline for concept development. In the last analysis a career practitioner needs to be able to apply a career theory and Sharf (2013) argues that theories with more than eight or nine concepts are difficult to remember within the practical realities of a counselling session or intervention.

A fourth contemporary evaluation criterion is to consider whether a career theory acknowledges the diverse contexts of clients. Contemporary career theory needs to recognise and accommodate these diverse contexts within which individual career development can occur. There is a need to apply this criterion for Watson (2009) suggests that career psychology itself is a cultural enterprise that seeks application in diverse cultural contexts without sufficiently acknowledging or understanding those contexts. Naidoo, Pretorius and Nicholas (2017) call for career psychology to critically engage with the diversity within the national contexts in which it would apply itself. Further, Watson (2010) suggests that this criterion could be addressed by career practitioners asking what their theory base should be, as well as whether the contemporary career theories they rely on are contextually sensitive in terms of cultural, socioeconomic and social conditions (Watson, 2013).

Such questions sensitise career practitioners, particularly those who work with what the literature refers to as 'non-career' populations, to the relevance and generalisability of career theory when working with people who are "the underprivileged, the disadvantaged, the disaffected" (Watson, 2013, p. 8). They call for theories that are sufficiently robust in their formulation for career practitioners to be able to deconstruct and reconstruct the theories within the realities of their career practice (Watson, 2017). In so doing, flexible theories encourage a more activist role from the career practitioners who apply them.

A fifth possible contemporary evaluation criterion relates to a term that is presently popular in the career literature, that of 'adaptability'. As an evaluative criterion this implies that the constructs of a career theory themselves need to be flexible and adaptable so that they can accommodate the constant change that they seek to theorise about. This criterion reflects McMahon, Watson and Patton's (2014) earlier suggestion that we need theories that can reflect change rather than constantly seek to change our theories.

Finally, a sixth possible contemporary evaluation criterion might be that of social justice. This criterion returns us to the foundations of career theory development and calls for career theory to be evaluated in terms of its exclusivity/inclusivity. While this criterion relates to the fourth criterion of contextualisation, it calls for a critical examination of the theory's constructs as well. For example, it has been argued that the term 'career' itself may suggest social exclusivity (Blustein, 2013; Watson, 2010).

Most of the classical criteria for evaluation described earlier are enmeshed with several of the contemporary evaluation criteria. However, an underlying theme of the suggested contemporary evaluation criteria is their focus on inter-systemic factors influencing individual career development. Certainly they also retain an intra-theory focus on the structure of a theory and its conceptual soundness but there is a greater recognition that contemporary theories should also focus on ensuring the contextual sensitivity of what they propose. Failure to do so traps a career theory within a narrow population band in terms of its applicability and reinforces the image of career psychology as elitist and serving a limited and privileged population. This latter statement logically leads to the next subsection which expands further on the need for contemporary career theory to be valid across cultural contexts.

Cultural considerations for career theory

Underlying several of the classical and contemporary criteria for evaluating a theory is the relevance and applicability of a career theory in relation to culture. This consideration is explicit in classical evaluation criterion two and con-temporary evaluation criterion four. The term culture is used in this chapter to refer to a diversity of specific population, be they ethnic, social, socio-economic or socio-political. A consistent criticism of established and contemporary career theories has been their insufficient consideration of contextualisation, specifi-cally in relation to diverse populations (Watson & Stead, 2017). The latter authors state that much of career theory remains cocooned and thus insular in its theoretical formulations; indeed much of career theory has been described as contextually blind and contextually bound (Stead & Watson, 2002; Watson, 2009). The evaluative criteria suggested earlier become harder to apply the fur-ther a career theory generalises to population groups on which it was not founded. Perhaps there is a need for a career theory to declare itself in terms of who it was developed for, and its consequent constraints in terms of global application. Such theoretical introspection could prevent what Arulmani (2014) refers to as "cultural imperialism" (p. 87) in which dominant cultures transfer their concepts and norms unilaterally on less dominant cultures.

Certainly prominent career theorists and practitioners continue to struggle with the seeming lack of cultural validity of career theory. Thus, Leong and Yuen (2012) criticise contemporary career theory for its almost exclusive emphasis on individual career development and its description of a more idea-lised Westernised cultural context. As a consequence, these authors query the-oretical transferability to other cultural contexts. Similarly, others have been concerned about the different meanings that individuals from differing cultural contexts have of what are considered standard terminology in most career the-ories (Stead & Watson, 2017) and that culturally constructed terms cannot be exported to other cultural contexts (Ratner, 2008).

An example of the latter concern is the pivotal term 'career' which has been considered debatable for use in relation to individuals' experiences of both employment and unemployment (Arthur, 2017). Similarly, Arulmani et al. (2014) believe that the term career should be seen as existing along a continuum with its fully developed meaning at the one end and an absence of the concept ("culturally alien", p. 4) at the other end. The latter authors believe that career theory terminology has been prescriptively applied to cultures other than those for whom the theory was original formulated. Thus, Arulmani et al. state that individuals in developing world contexts struggle to understand their career development with "constructs and ideas that do not equip them to effectively address felt needs" (p. 3). To the extent that contemporary career theory attempts to be generally applicable, there may need to be the simple starting point of defining what 'career' means in the context in which the theory would be applied.

Summary and conclusion

This chapter has explored contemporary career theories in terms of the reciprocal relationship with career practice. The role of career research in this relationship has also been considered. Underlying this triadic relationship is the critical issue of quality, particularly given the quantitative expansion of career theories in recent decades. The discussion in this chapter considers how a career theory could be evaluated in terms of its validity and its relevance. Classical evaluative criteria were described that have been established in the literature. However, given the constant nature of change in the world of work and the corresponding development of career theories, consideration was given to reformulating classical evaluative criteria and suggesting new contemporary evaluative criteria that would assist career practitioners to consider the quality of contemporary career theories. Nowhere is such an evaluation more critical than in the consideration of the applicability of contemporary career theory to diverse populations. Career theories founded on limited Westernised and middle-class populations are not representative of the vast majority of individuals. There are individuals who want to work but suffer from chronic unemployment given limited opportunity. For such individuals subsistence is more critical than finding meaning in a potential work role. There are also adults who perform multiple roles, some of which are paid and some unpaid.

The reciprocal relationship between career theory, research and practice continues to be a focus of concern within the literature. Lent (2016), for instance, while acknowledging that it is not a prerequisite of career theory to explore and research the practical implications of their theories, urges career theorists and researchers to speculate, hypothesise, or provide case examples of how their theories may apply in practice. According to Lent, failure to do so could result in a situation where "career practitioners do not see the practice light at the end of the research tunnel" (p. 22). A necessary and obvious solution lies in increased communication between career theorists, researchers and practitioners. Lent calls for more "routine" (p. 24) dialogue and the bringing together of these three groups of role players in settings such as conferences. This suggestion reinforces Sampson, Bullock-Yowell, Dozier, Osborn, Lenz and

Ross's (2016) recognition of a collective need for greater reciprocity between these three role players. The latter author's analysis of a book devoted to the issue of the integration of career theory, research and practice concluded that the most commonly identified challenge was the lack of communication, while the most commonly mentioned recommendation was the need for such communication through the literature and through interfacing at an organised level. This echoes Watson's (2006) earlier call for career practitioners to accept their role in the integration of career theory, research and practice, to make sure that their voice is heard.

Blustein (2016) considers the issue of reciprocity between career theory, research and practice within the historical context of career theory development and concludes that a central issue facing the discipline today is the fact that marginalised populations have now become a mainstream concern. Thus, the reciprocity between career theory, research and practice needs to be considered sensitively. Further, the future development of career theory needs to be considered qualitatively in that it needs to be critically evaluated in terms of its potential application. No one is more ably positioned to do this than career practitioners who must apply the theory of their choice to the realities of their practice. That career practitioners may have become part of the problem in the decontextualised use of career theory is explored in this chapter. Career practitioners need to recognise that their relationship to theory is reciprocal; they can help shape theory through their contextualised application of it. Thus, a more activist role is suggested for the career practitioner in ensuring genuine reciprocity between career theory and practice.

Learning activities

1   Consider the career theory/theories that you identify with in terms of their strengths and weaknesses for the applied contexts within which you practice.
2   Apply the contemporary evaluation criteria described in this chapter to the career theory/theories of your choice.

Learning activities: reflective questions

1   To what extent do the contemporary career theories described in this book relate to the classical evaluation criteria described in this chapter?
2   To what extent do the contemporary career theories described in this book relate to the contemporary evaluation criteria described in this chapter?
3   To what extent is there a reciprocal relationship between the realities of career practice and the contemporary career theories described in this book?

References

Arthur, N. (2017). Constructivist approaches to career counselling: A culture-infused perspective. In M. McMahon (Ed.), *Career counselling: Constructivist approaches* (2nd ed., pp. 54–64). Abingdon, Oxon: Routledge.

Arulmani, G. (2014). The Cultural Preparation Process Model and career development. In G. Arulmani, A. J. Bakshi, F. T. L. Leong, and A. G. Watts (Eds.), *Handbook of career development: International perspectives* (pp. 81–103). New York: Springer.

Arulmani, G., Bakshi, A. J., Leong, F. T. L., & Watts, A. G. (2014). The manifestation of career: Introduction and overview. In G. Arulmani, A. J. Bakshi, F. T. L. Leong, & A. G. Watts (Eds.), *Handbook of career development: International perspectives* (pp. 1–10). New York: Springer.

Athanasou, J. A., & Van Esbroeck, R. (2008). An international and social perspective on career guidance. In J. A. Athanasou & R. Van Esbroeck (Eds.), *International handbook of career guidance* (pp. 695–709). Dordrecht, The Netherlands: Springer.

Bakshi, A. J. (2014). Life span theory and career theories: Rapprochement or estrangement? In G. Arulmani, A. J. Bakshi, F. T. L. Leong, & A. G. Watts (Eds.), *Handbook of career development: International perspectives* (pp. 43–66). New York: Springer.

Blustein, D. L. (2006). *The psychology of working: A new perspective for counseling, career development, and public policy*. New York: Routledge.

Blustein, D. L. (2013). (Ed.). *The Oxford handbook of the psychology of working*. New York: Oxford University Press.

Blustein, D. L. (2016). Integrating theory, research and practice: Lessons learned from the evolution of vocational psychology. In J. P. Sampson, E. Bullock-Yowell, V. C. Dozier, D. S. Osborn, & J. G. Lenz (Eds.), *Integrating theory, research and practice in vocational psychology* (pp. 179–187). Tallahassee: Florida State University Libraries.

Brown, D. (2002). Introduction to theories of career development and choice. In D. Brown and Associates (Eds.), *Career choice and development* (4th ed., pp. 3–23). San Francisco, CA: Jossey-Bass.

Hartung, P. J. (2012). Career development in a global context: History, status and prospects. In M. Watson & M. McMahon (Eds.), *Career development: Global issues and challenges* (pp. 11–26). New York: Nova Science.

Lent, R. W. (2016). Integration of theory, research, and practice: A social cognitive perspective. In J. P. Sampson, E. Bullock-Yowell, V. C. Dozier, D. S. Osborn, & J. G. Lenz (Eds.), *Integrating theory, research and practice in vocational psychology* (pp. 20–27). Tallahassee: Florida State University Libraries.

Leong, S-M. A., & Yuen, M. (2012). The globalization of an ethnocentric career theory and practice. In M. Watson & M. McMahon (Eds.), *Career development: Global issues and challenges* (pp. 75–91). New York: Nova Science.

McMahon, M. (2014). New trends in theory development in career psychology. In G. Arulmani, A. J. Bakshi, F. T. L. Leong, & A. G. Watts (Eds.), *Handbook of career development: International perspectives* (pp. 13–27). New York: Springer.

McMahon, M., & Watson, M. (2012). Career development: 21st century global issues and challenges. In M. Watson & M. McMahon (Eds.), *Career development: Global issues and challenges* (pp. 1–10). New York: Nova Science.

McMahon, M., Watson, M., & Patton, W. (2014). Context-resonant systems perspectives in career theory. In G. Arulmani, A. J. Bakshi, F. T. L. Leong, & A. G. Watts (Eds.), *Handbook of career development: International perspectives* (pp. 29–41). New York: Springer.

Naidoo, A. V., Pretorius, T. B., & Nicholas, L. (2017). The emergence of career psychology in South Africa: A socio-historical perspective. In G. B. Stead & M. B. Watson (Eds.), *Career psychology in the South African context* (3rd ed., pp. 1–20). Pretoria, South Africa: Van Schaik.

Parsons, F. (1909). *Choosing a vocation.* Boston, MA: Houghton Mifflin.

Ratner, C. (2008). *Cultural psychology, cross-cultural psychology, indigenous psychology.* New York: Nova Science.

Reardon, R. C., Lenz, J. G., Sampson, J. P. Jr., & Peterson, G. W. (2011). Big questions facing vocational psychology: A cognitive information processing perspective. *Journal of Career Assessment, 19,* 240–250.

Roberts, K. (2012). Career development among the lower socioeconomic strata in developed countries. In M. Watson & M. McMahon (Eds.), *Career development: Global issues and challenges* (pp. 29–43). New York: Nova Science.

Sampson, J. P.Jr., Bullock-Yowell, E., Dozier, V. C., Osborn, D. S., Lenz, J. G., & Ross, N. T. (2016). The state of the art in integrating theory, research, and practice in vocational psychology. In J. P. Sampson, E. Bullock-Yowell, V. C. Dozier, D. S. Osborn, & J. G. Lenz (Eds.), *Integrating theory, research and practice in vocational psychology* (pp. 188–192). Tallahassee: Florida State University Libraries.

Savickas, M. L. (2005). The theory and practice of career construction. In S. D. Brown & R. W. Lent (Eds.), *Career development and counseling: Putting theory and research to work* (pp. 42–70). Hoboken, NJ: John Wiley.

Sharf, R. S. (2013). *Applying career development to counseling* (6th ed.). Pacific Grove, CA: Brooks/Cole.

Stead, G. B., & Davis, B. L. (2015). Qualitative career assessment: Research evidence. In M. McMahon & M. Watson (Eds.), *Career assessment: Qualitative approaches* (pp. 21–30). Rotterdam, The Netherlands: Sense.

Stead, G. B., & Watson, M. B. (2002). Contextualising career psychology in South Africa: Bringing it all back home. *Journal of Psychology in Africa, 12,* 147–160.

Stead, G. B., & Watson, M. B. (2017). Indigenisation of career psychology in South Africa. In G. B. Stead & M. B. Watson (Eds.), *Career psychology in the South African context* (3rd ed., pp. 209–220). Pretoria, South Africa: Van Schaik.

Watson, M. (2006). Voices off: Reconstructing the stage of career theory and practice for cultural diversity. *Australian Career Practitioner, 17,* 5–9.

Watson, M. (2009). Transitioning contexts of career psychology in South Africa. *Asian Journal of Counselling, 16,* 133–147.

Watson, M. (2010). Career psychology in South Africa: Addressing and redressing social justice. *Australian Journal of Career Development, 19,* 24–29.

Watson, M. (2013). Deconstruction, reconstruction, co-construction: Career construction theory in a developing world context. *Indian Journal of Career and Livelihood Planning, 2,* 1–12.

Watson, M. (2016). Career development in changing world contexts: Reconstructing the wheels of theory and practice. *CEAV Journal, 43,* 13–18.

Watson, M. (2017). Career constructivism and culture: Deconstructing and reconstructing career counselling. In M. McMahon (Ed.), *Career counselling: Constructivist approaches* (2nd ed., pp. 43–53). Abingdon, Oxon: Routledge.

Watson, M. B., & Stead, G. B. (2017). An overview of career theory. In G. B. Stead & M. B. Watson (Eds.), *Career psychology in the South African context* (3rd ed., pp. 21–47). Pretoria, South Africa: Van Schaik.

3 Stasis and change

The paradox in theories of career development

Wendy Patton

Learning objectives

The purpose of this chapter is to:

- provide an overview of career theory,
- identify longstanding challenges within the field's knowledge base and extant work, and
- overview current and future approaches to address these challenges.

Early theory development

From early theorising in the 1800s (Carlyle, 1833/1884), career theory has been beset by propositions in relation to vocational decision-making and behaviour that have been derived from different epistemological underpinnings. For example, Carlyle's work demonstrated an early example of person-environment fit theory. Although, Parsons' (1909) work was described similarly, McMahon (2008) noted that it embraced early constructivist thinking in its emphasis on broader client interpersonal and external contexts and the encouragement for clients to take an active role in the decision-making process. In contrast, Munsterberg's theory of vocations developed at around the same time as Parsons' work (Porfeli, 2009) and has been acknowledged as an important precursor to trait-factor thinking.

The critique of Ginzberg, Ginsburg, Axelrad, and Herma (1951), as to the atheoretical nature of vocational guidance, heralded an era of vocational theory building (Savickas, 2008). Indeed Savickas and Baker (2005) noted that following the work of Ginzberg and colleagues (1951), there was an explosion of career theories; "almost one theory per year was published for the next 20 years" (p. 41). Updating and development, and extending particular constructs or processes, have led to a continual expansion of multiple theoretical formulations in the literature.

Current status of the field of career theory

The proliferation of career theories emphasises an issue that continues to be a challenge for the field. Although theoretical propositions and models have been developed to various levels of sophistication, several authors have noted that theorisation remains inadequate and incomplete and lacking in comprehensiveness and coherence (e.g., D. Brown, 2002; S. D. Brown & Lent, 2005, 2013; McMahon, 2014). In particular, the field continues to be critiqued for (a) its overemphasis on Western middle-class, predominantly male populations (Blustein, 2006; McMahon, Watson, & Patton, 2014); (b) its lack of attention to social justice (Blustein, 2006; McMahon, 2014); and (c) failure to attend to roles other than paid work, such as the growing demands for unpaid care work (Richardson, 2017; Richardson & Schaeffer, 2013). In addition, it has been criticised for focusing on intraindividual issues to the detriment of contextual issues (Patton & McMahon, 2014). This chapter addresses the proliferation of career theories, with a critique of the apparent contradictory parsimony in relation to theories that are perceived as mainstream. The central arguments to be made are that this position is, at the very least, confusing and, at its worst, dividing and limiting. Despite a number of attempts at integration, both within vocational psychology and across related disciplines, a disparate field remains. Herein lies the contradiction.

This chapter's aim is not to review theories in depth but to examine four key ongoing challenges in the field. First, new or revised theories continue to be developed, contributing to an ongoing proliferation and lack of coherence in the field; second, there remains a mainstream focus on traditional theories with a narrow focus; third, repeated attempts at convergence/integration, including the development of metatheories and multidisciplinary perspectives, continue to struggle to find a place in the mainstream theoretical literature. Finally, there remains a theoretical concentration on narrow populations. Although an expanding literature focuses on applicability to diverse populations and contexts, such a topic is beyond the focus of this chapter. The present chapter focuses on the traditional North American and Western influences evident in many career theories (Athanasou & Van Esbroeck, 2008; McMahon, 2014).

Proliferation: growth in number of theories

The proliferation of career theories (McMahon, 2014) continues, although it is acknowledged that this has been in response to broad social changes, in addition to responding to a need for a theory base that is more accommodating of complexity. However, as has been the case since early theorising, the proliferation is also partly due to different branches of psychology influencing explanations for vocational behaviour. For example, the two key theories which were developed following the critique of Ginzberg et al., (1951) included that of Holland (1959) and Super (1957). Each was derived from different psychological branches (differential and developmental psychology), each attended to different vocational concerns (relating interests to vocational environments, and in Super's case moving emphasis from occupations to careers), and each was relevant to the time and context. For example, trait-factor approaches (Holland) were appropriate to returning soldiers to work after WWII, and the notion of career development was still possible in the second half of the 20th century within stable occupations and workplaces. Each of these theories was subject to modification (Holland, 1997; Super, 1990; Super, Savickas, & Super, 1996). In addition, Ginzberg developed a theory of occupational choice (Ginzberg, 1972), and a focus on self and self-concept emerged (Lent, Brown & Hackett, 1994; Super, 1990).

As the structure of work and its social organisation changed, with attendant uncertainty, theories also began to change (Savickas, 2008). Constructivist and social constructionist epistemologies grew in influence (McMahon, 2014; Young & Collin, 2004). For example, Young and Collin (2004) suggested that there are more similarities than differences between these philosophies, and that the differences primarily centre on whether construction is a cognitive process or a social process. The emphasis on these philosophies in career theory led to a special issue of the *Journal of Vocational Behavior* (Young & Collin, 2004) and a monograph devoted to constructivism and social constructionism in vocational psychology and career development (McIlveen & Schultheiss, 2012). However, as discussed as follows, a focus on positivism remains in career theory.

As noted previously, theories were derived from different branches of psychology, and were repeatedly refined, contributing to an extensive literature. These include the social learning theory of career decision-making (Krumboltz, 1979; L. K. Mitchell & Krumboltz, 1990), a social cognitive theory–based model (Lent, 2005; , Brown, & Hackett, 1994, 2002) and models based on cognitive processing theory (Peterson, Sampson, & Reardon, 1991; Peterson, Sampson, Lenz & Reardon, 2002; Reardon, Lenz, Sampson, & Peterson, 2009, 2011). Savickas (2013) updated and advanced Super's (1957) theory to publish a theory of career construction designed to enhance the relevance and applicability of Super's work for 21st century. Along with Guichard's (2009) self-construction theory, career construction has informed the life-design paradigm (Savickas et al., 2009).

Two additional theoretical models have been derived from action theory and lifespan and human development theory. These include the developmental-contextual approach of Vondracek, Lerner and Schulenberg (1986; Vondracek & Porfeli, 2008) and the contextualist approach to career (Young, Valach, & Collin, 2002; Young, Domene, & Valach, 2015). More recently, Vondracek, Ford, and Porfeli (2014) incorporated living systems theory into a theoretical framework of vocational behaviour.

To meet challenges about the relevance of the construct of career in changing times, a number of authors have extended theorising about career to incorporate broader understanding about the role of work in individuals' lives. Blustein and colleagues (2006; Duffy, Blustein, Diemer, & Autin, 2016; Blustein, 2017) have developed an inclusive and integrative psychology of working theory, emphasising that much of our work has been developed in relation to understanding work lives of a small proportion of the population, those that live in relative affluence. This multidisciplinary framework emphasises that vocational psychology must draw theoretical concepts from a number of areas of psychology.

For example, Schultheiss (2013) centred culture within the relational cultural paradigm, providing a central place for a more inclusive study of career incorporating culture, race, gender, sexualities and social class.

The theoretical work of Richardson (1993, 2017) argues for the refocusing of career theory, research and practice on all work and thereby addressing the lives of those ignored with the existing limited construct of career. Within this framework, voluntary and unpaid work, and new understandings of care work, are included in individuals' understandings or work and career. In particular, Richardson (2017) advocated for a practice-driven theoretical approach, arguing that "a useful theory is one that translates into and helps develop practices that are effective in fostering desired change" (p. 40).

New theoretical developments for a changing context have focused on the constructs of chance and chaos. First conceived in 1999 as planned happenstance (K. E. Mitchell, Levin, & Krumboltz, 1999), Krumboltz further extended social learning theory to develop happenstance learning theory (Krumboltz, 2009; Krumboltz, Foley, & Cotter, 2013). Additionally, Pryor and Bright's (2003, 2011) chaos theory of careers "seeks to understand individuals as complex, dynamic, non-linear, unique, emergent, purposeful open systems, interacting with an environment comprising systems with similar characteristics" (2003, p. 123). These authors emphasised that their theoretical formulation is not necessarily concerned with content, but with the development of structures within which theoretical frameworks can be located.

The contradiction of proliferation and parsimony: holding on to traditional theories

Another criticism of the career theory literature is the embracing of traditional theories and lack of attention to new and emerging theories. For many years, reviews and major textbooks published in the United States focused on the same theories (e.g., Osipow, 1990; Brown & Brooks, 1996; Brown & Assoc, 2002). The text by S. D. Brown and Lent (2005) included the theories of Dawis, Holland, Savickas, Gottfredson and Lent and colleagues. The second edition of this text (Brown & Lent, 2013) included these theories but not the work of Gottfredson.

In 2008, Leung identified the following theories as the "big five", acknowledging that they are all theories developed in the US: that of Dawis and Lofquist; Holland, Super, and Savickas' update; Gottfredson; and Lent and colleagues. Betz's review (2008) focused on Holland; Lent and colleagues; Dawis and Lofquist; Gottfredson; and Vondracek, Lerner and Schulenberg's developmental-contextual theories. Similarly, Hartung and Subich (2011) focused on person–environment fit (P–E fit), developmental, socio-cognitive-behavioral, and constructionist theories. This selective focus on theories in major texts was also noted in Walsh, Savickas, and Hartung's (2013) fourth edition of the *Handbook of Vocational Psychology*.

This continuing focus on traditional theoretical formulations has drawn a number of criticisms. For example, Reardon, Lenz, Sampson, and Peterson

(2011) commented that "there appears to be an inherent bias or selectivity regarding which knowledge or theories merit attention in the field of vocational psychology" (p. 243). Patton and McMahon (2014) asserted that students working with key textbooks, primarily written in and for the North American population, would be presented with a narrow view of the body of theory available for understanding career behaviour. It is evident that theorists with new formulations need to continue to press their place in the literature to emphasise the insights that they can bring to our understanding of vocational behaviour. In a possible sign of change, Sampson, Bullock-Yowell, Dozier, Osborn, and Lenz (2017) recently focused on theories that were contributing to integration of theory, research and practice, namely person–environment fit, counselling for work and relationship, systems theory framework, and socio-cognitive and cognitive information–processing theories.

Continued segregation and integrative frameworks

Critiques about the segmented nature of career theories, and the lack of comprehensiveness and coherence began to appear from the early 1990s (Osipow, 1990; Super, 1992). Each theory provided information about different parts of vocational behaviour, but "none of the theories perfectly (or even adequately) explains and predicts all the pertinent career phenomena" (Osipow, 1994, p. 223). Reflecting on this endeavour within developmental psychology, Ford and Lerner (1992) commented that

> Without the construction of more integrative and comprehensive frame-works than those that presently exist, we are likely to be increasingly overwhelmed by mountains of data and empirical generalizations. . . . They continue to accumulate as a pile of 'bricks' of knowledge. . . . The role of integrative theorizing is to help decide how to combine those 'bricks' in a way that represents a more accurate and less mechanistic view of ourselves.
>
> (p. 231)

Recognition of the proliferation of disparate theories led to a call for integration and convergence, and a meeting of invited scholars to focus on the problem (see Savickas & Lent, 1994). This recognised challenge in the field led to the development of the systems theory framework (STF; McMahon & Patton, 1995; Patton & McMahon, 2014, 2017), which remains the first attempt to present a comprehensive metatheoretical framework of career development. The STF is not a theory of career development and is not designed to be so; rather, systems theory is introduced as the basis for an overarching, or metatheoretical, framework within which all concepts of career development described in the plethora of career theories can be usefully positioned and utilised in theory and practice. With the individual as the central focus, constructing his or her own meaning of career, constructs of existing theories are relevant as they apply to each individual. In short, systems theory provides the framework for a macrolevel analysis of theory, and also facilitates a microlevel analysis of an individual's career development.

A number of attempts to demonstrate new patterns of relationships between existing theories, therefore advancing conceptual unity, have been stimulated by the STF. For example, Patton (2007) presented a discussion of the potential for the STF in theory integration with respect to relational theories. McIlveen (2007) and McIlveen and Patton (2007) proposed the integration of dialogical theory with both career construction theory and the STF. Patton (2008) discussed similarities and differences between the STF and career construction theory, and more recently, Patton (2015) discussed the interconnections between constructs within the STF and contextual action theory.

Other integrative frameworks include the work of Blustein (2001, 2006; Duffy et al., 2016), Guichard (2009), Hartung and Subich (2011) and Vondracek, Ford, and Porfeli (2014). In addition, Savickas (2013) asserted that career construction theory tied together the segments of developmental, self and contextual segments in Super's life-span life-space theory. As these examples illustrate, to date there has been both an ongoing proliferation of new paradigms as well as ongoing attempts to develop theoretical connections and metaframeworks. However, it is evident that issues identified in the 1990s remain.

Division across disciplines

In addition to division within the disciplinary field, career theory has been criticised for being segmented across disciplinary branches (M. Arthur, 2008; Collin & Patton, 2009a). This segmentation has occurred within psychology, however, it is important to note that psychological theory has dominated the field and sociological contributions have received minimal attention. The recent emphasis on context has provided the opportunity to revisit these contributions (see Patton & McMahon, 2014).

The description of developing theories earlier in this chapter demonstrated their derivation from different branches of psychology and this work has contributed to greater bifurcation of the field of career development. Attempts to integrate disciplinary camps have been occurring for some time (e.g., Savickas, 2001), however Van Esbroeck and Athanasou (2008) noted that "the situation did not really improve and led to even larger divergence" (p. 4). Collin and Patton (2009a) drew writers from vocational psychology and organisational psychology to assess the extent of the divide and to propose ways toward dialogue. Authors in this volume used a range of "divide" metaphors such as "two tributaries", "lost twin", "separate islands", "parallel streams", and "Balkanisation of fields". Collin and Patton (2009b) noted that there was a "greater-than-expected degree of similarity between the perspectives" (p. 210), and proffered specific and concrete suggestions to develop a synergy and indeed proposed a new field to be named "career studies" (Collin, 2010).

Cultural considerations

Athanasou and Van Esbroeck (2008) noted that "much of the influence [in career development] has been Western and decidedly North American" (p. 698). This dominance remains (McMahon, 2014) and has emphasised the lack of applicability of the career theory literature within and across cultures. Although a number of recent works have contributed to change, for example Stead and Watson (2017), Mkhize (2012), and Maree and Molepo (2017) in South Africa; Malik and Aguado (2005) in Europe; and Arulmani (Arulmani, 2017; Arulmani, Bakshi, Leong, & Watts, 2014) in India; McMahon (2014) is adamant that "there remains an urgent need to encourage and privilege voices from non-Western cultures" (p. 24).

In addition to these and other writers presenting accounts of career behaviour for their specific countries, other authors have presented approaches to counter this narrow picture. For example, N. Arthur (2017) discussed the relevance of the culture-infused perspective, noting the irrelevance of many traditional theories as guides for this work. Similarly, Arulmani (2017) emphasised what he termed a cultural preparation process to career development. Watson (2017) argued that "we need to deconstruct existing career theory . . . in order to reconstruct them within the realities of the clients we serve" (p. 47). Each of these authors argue that constructivism provides an important underpinning to broaden traditional perspectives and constructs in career theory.

The importance of theorising to address the lives of diverse populations and recognising the relationships between dimensions of peoples' identities seems paramount. Although there has been some attention paid to gender, age, and social class, particularly in the contributions from sociological and contextual perspectives, the discussion of diversity needs to be expanded along a number of continua, including ability, sexuality, religion, and their intersections. Richardson (2017) argues that the stories of our clients need to be our starting point in developing theory.

Chapter summary and conclusion

The career theory field continues to be challenged by a contradictory proliferation and parsimony. New theories continue to be developed, and additional new theoretical discussions aim to provide a greater conceptual unity. Efforts to provide conceptual convergence and integration within the career theory field, and across the disciplines which have influenced the field for decades, continue. However major, and it must be noted primarily US-based texts that cover a large consumer market, continue to provide limited coverage to new developments. A decade ago, Betz (2008) concluded that "although we are not at a point of full theoretical integration or convergence . . . we definitely have *theoretical co-mingling*. Researchers have realized that there are useful concepts in vocational psychology, not all associated originally with a single theoretical model" (p. 369). More recently Vondracek, Ford, and Porfeli (2014) asserted that integration has remained an "elusive goal" (p. 10), although progress has been made.

As the structure of work and its social organisation have changed, with attendant uncertainty, and a greater internationalisation of the field has emerged, so too have theories begun to change. At the heart of this change is the need for theories relevant to an increasingly uncertain world of work and constructivist, person-centred approaches to understanding career behaviour (McMahon, 2017). These approaches need to embrace diversity of the individual, and diversity of possible experience.

In conclusion, the field of career theory is paradoxically in a state of stasis and change. As Vondracek and Porfeli (2008) commented:

> Quitting the pursuit of human truth because it is too complex or obscured would be a tragic failure of . . . vocational psychology. Theoretical formulations that come ever closer to the true complexity of the world and the varying perspectives that humans share continue to be sought.
>
> (p. 217)

While it is evident is that theorists, researchers and practitioners continue to actively work to develop a literature that is relevant and applicable to challenging times, this chapter has argued that the field holds on too much to the past. Much more needs to be done to ensure that the voices of theorists with new and diverse perspectives are included in theorising about career behaviour.

Learning activities

1   Choose two theories and identify major similarities in their attention to particular concepts or in their epistemological underpinning.

2   Identify current challenges in the world of work which are (or are not) addressed by existing career theories, for example, planning in uncertain times.

3   Choose two theories and apply them to your own career development. What do they account for/not account for? Which elements of your own career development are not adequately accounted for by these theories?

Learning activities: reflective questions

1   What might be some reasons for resistance in the field to embrace new and emerging theories?

2   Reflect on your own career decision-making processes. Which theoretical approaches were (would have been) useful for you?

References

Arthur, M. (2008). Examining contemporary careers: A call for interdisciplinary inquiry. *Human Relations*, 61, 163–186.

Arthur, N. (2017). Constructivist approaches to career counselling: A culture-infused perspective. In M. McMahon (Ed.), *Career counselling: Constructivist approaches* (2nd ed., pp. 54–64). London: Routledge.

Arulmani, G. (2017). Contexts and circumstances: The cultural preparation process approach to career development. In M. McMahon (Ed.), *Career counselling: Constructivist approaches* (2nd ed., pp. 79–90). London: Routledge.

Arulmani, G., Bakshi, A., Leong, F., & Watts, T. (2014). (Eds.). *Handbook of career development: International Perspectives*. New York: Springer.

Athanasou, J. A., & Van Esbroeck, R. (2008). International and social perspectives on career guidance. In J. A. Athanasou & R. Van Esbroeck (Eds.), *International handbook of career guidance* (pp. 695–709). Dordrecht, The Netherlands: Springer Science + Media.

Betz, N. E. (2008). Advances in vocational psychology. In S. D. Brown & R. W. Lent (Eds.), *Handbook of Counseling Psychology* (pp. 357–389). Hoboken, NJ: John Wiley.

Blustein, D. L. (2001). Extending the reach of vocational psychology: Toward an inclusive and integrative psychology of working. *Journal of Vocational Behavior*, 59, 171–182.

Blustein, D. L. (2006). *The psychology of working: A new perspective for career development, counseling, and public policy*. Mahwah, NJ: Erlbaum.

Blustein, D. L. (2017). Integrating theory, research and practice: Lessons learned from the evolution of vocational psychology. In J. P. Sampson Jr., E. Bullock-Yowell, V. C. Dozier, D. S. Osborn, & J. G. Lenz (Eds.), *Integrating theory, research and practice in vocational psychology: Current status and future directions* (pp. 179–187). Tallahassee: Florida State University.

Brown, D. (2002). Status of theories of career choice and development. In D. Brown & Associates, *Career choice and development* (4th ed., pp. 510–515). San Francisco, CA: Jossey-Bass.

Brown, D. & Assoc. (2002). *Career choice and development* (4th ed.). San Francisco, CA: Jossey-Bass.

Brown, D., & Brooks, L. (1996). (Eds.). *Career choice and development: Applying contemporary theories to practice* (3rd ed.). San Francisco, CA: Jossey-Bass.

Brown, S. D., & Lent, R. W. (2005). *Career development and counseling: Putting theory and research to work*. New York: Wiley.

Brown, S. D., & Lent, R. W. (2013). *Career development and counseling: Putting theory and research to work* (2nd ed.). New York: Wiley.

Carlyle, T. (1833/1884). The tailor retailored. In *Carlyle's Complete Works* (Vol. 1, Chap. 4). Boston, MA: Cambridge University Press. (Original work published in 1833).

Collin, A. (2010). The challenge of career studies. *Career Research and Development*, 23, 12–14.

Collin, A., & Patton, W. (2009a). (Eds.). *Vocational psychological and organisational perspectives on career: Towards a multidisciplinary dialogue*. Rotterdam, The Netherlands: Sense.

Collin, A., & Patton, W. (2009b). Towards dialogue and beyond. In A. Collin, & W. Patton (Eds.), *Vocational psychological and organisational perspectives on career: Towards a multidisciplinary dialogue* (pp. 209–226). Rotterdam, The Netherlands: Sense.

Duffy, R. D., Blustein, D. L., Diemer, M. A., & Autin, K. L. (2016). The psychology of working theory. *Journal of Counseling Psychology, 63*(2), 127–148.

Ford, D., & Lerner, R. (1992). *Developmental systems theory: An integrative approach.* Newbury Park, CA: SAGE.

Ginzberg, E. (1972). Toward a theory of occupational choice: A restatement. *Vocational Guidance Quarterly, 20,* 169–176.

Ginzberg, E., Ginsburg, S. W., Axelrad, S., & Herma, J. L. (1951). *Occupational choice: An approach to general theory.* New York: Columbus University Press.

Guichard, J. (2009). Self-constructing. *Journal of Vocational Behavior, 75,* 251–258.

Hartung, P. J., & Subich, L. (2011). (Eds.). *Developing self in work and career: Concepts, cases and contexts.* Washington, DC: American Psychological Association.

Holland, J. L. (1959). A theory of vocational choice. *Journal of Counseling Psychology, 6,* 35–44.

Holland, J. L. (1997). *Making vocational choices: A theory of vocational personalities and work environments* (3rd ed.). Odessa, FL: Consulting Psychologists Press.

Krumboltz, J. D. (1979). A social learning theory of career decision making. In A. M. Mitchell, G. B. Jones, & J. D. Krumboltz (Eds.), *Social learning and career decision making* (pp. 19–49). Cranston, RI: Carroll Press.

Krumboltz, J. D. (2009). The happenstance learning theory. *Journal of Career Assessment, 17*(2), 135–154.

Krumboltz, J. D., Foley, P. F., & Cotter, E. W. (2013). Applying the Happenstance Learning Theory to involuntary work transitions. *The Career Development Quarterly, 61*(1), 15–26.

Lent, R. W. (2005). A social cognitive view of career development and counseling. In S. D. Brown & R. W. Lent (Eds.), *Career development and counseling: Putting theory and practice to work* (pp. 101–127). Hoboken, NJ: John Wiley.

Lent, R. W., Brown, S. D., & Hackett, G. (1994). Toward a unifying sociocognitive theory of career and academic interest, choice, and performance [Monograph]. *Journal of Vocational Behavior, 45,* 79–122.

Lent, R. W., Brown, S. D., & Hackett, G. (2002). Social cognitive career theory. In D. Brown & Associates, *Career choice and development* (4th ed., pp. 255–311). San Francisco, CA: Jossey-Bass.

Leung, S. A. (2008). The big five career theories. In J. A. Athanasou & R. Van Esbroeck (Eds.), *International Handbook of Career Guidance* (pp. 115–132). Dordrecht, The Netherlands: Springer Science & Media.

Malik, B., & Aguado, T. (2005). Cultural diversity and guidance: Myth or reality? In B. A. Irving & B. Malik (Eds.), *Critical reflections on career education and guidance* (pp. 56–71). London: Routledge Falmer.

Maree, K., & Molepo, M. (2017). Implementing a qualitative (narrative) approach in cross-cultural career counselling. In M. McMahon (Ed.), *Career counselling: Constructivist approaches* (2nd ed., pp. 65–78). London: Routledge.

McIlveen, P. (2007). A test for theoretical integration: Systems theory and dialogical self. *Australian Journal of Career Development, 16*(3), 31–37.

McIlveen, P., & Patton, W. (2007). Dialogical self: Author and narrator of career life themes. *International Journal for Educational and Vocational Guidance, 7*(2), 67–80.

McIlveen, P., & Schultheiss, D. E. (2012). (Eds.). *Social constructionism in vocational psychology and career development.* Rotterdam, The Netherlands: Sense.

McMahon, M. (2008). Qualitative career assessment: A higher profile in the 21st century? In R. Van Esbroeck & J. Athanasou (Eds.), *International handbook of career guidance* (pp. 587–601). Dordrecht, The Netherlands: Springer.

McMahon, M. (2014). New trends in theory development in career psychology. In G. Arulmani, A. Bakshi, F. Leong, & T. Watts (Eds.), *Handbook of career development: International perspectives* (pp. 13–27). Dordrecht, The Netherlands: Springer.

McMahon, M. (2017). (Ed.). *Career counselling: Constructivist approaches* (2nd ed.). London: Routledge.

McMahon, M., & Patton, W. (1995). Development of a systems theory framework of career development. *Australian Journal of Career Development, 4*, 15–20.

McMahon, M., Watson, M., & Patton, W. (2014). Context-resonant systems perspectives in career theory. In G. Arulmani, A. Bakshi, F. Leong, & T. Watts (Eds.), *Handbook of career development: International Perspectives* (pp. 29–42). New York: Springer.

Mitchell, L. K., & Krumboltz, J. D. (1990). Social learning approach to career decision making: Krumboltz's theory. In D. Brown & L. Brooks (Eds.), *Career choice and development: Applying contemporary theories to practice* (2nd ed., pp. 145–196). San Francisco, CA: Jossey-Bass.

Mitchell, K. E., Levin, A. S. & Krumboltz, J. D. (1999). Planned happenstance: Constructing unexpected career opportunities. *Journal of Counseling and Development* 77(2),115–124.

Mkhize, N. (2012). Career counselling and indigenous populations: Implications of worldviews. In M. Watson & M. McMahon (Eds.), *Career development: Global issues and challenges* (pp. 125–141). New York: Nova Science.

Osipow, S. H. (1990). Convergence in theories of career choice and development. *Journal of Vocational Behavior, 36*, 122–131.

Osipow, S. H. (1994). Moving career theory into the twenty-first century. In M. L. Savickas & R. W. Lent (Eds.), *Convergence in career development theories: Implications for science and practice* (pp. 217–224). Palo Alto, CA: CPP Books.

Parsons, F. (1909). *Choosing a vocation.* Boston, MA: Houghton Mifflin.

Patton, W. (2007). Connecting relational theory and the Systems Theory Framework: Individuals and their systems. *Australian Journal of Career Development, 16*(3), 38–46.

Patton, W. (2008). Recent developments in career theories: The influence of constructivism and convergence. In J. A. Athanasou & R. Van Esbroeck (Eds.), *International Handbook of Career Guidance* (pp. 133–156). Dordrecht, The Netherlands: Springer Science.

Patton, W. (2015). Career counselling: Joint contributions of Contextual Action Theory and Systems Theory Framework. In R. A. Young, J. Domene, & L. Valach (Eds.), *Counseling and action: Toward life-enhancing work, relationships and identity* (pp. 33–50). Dordrecht, The Netherlands: Springer Science and Media.

Patton, W., & McMahon, M. (2014). *Career development and systems theory: Connecting theory and practice* (3rd ed.). Rotterdam, The Netherlands: Sense.

Patton, W., & McMahon, M. (2017). The Systems Theory Framework of career. In J. P. Sampson Jr., E. Bullock-Yowell, V. C. Dozier, D. S. Osborn, & J. G. Lenz (Eds.), *Integrating theory, research and practice in vocational psychology: Current status and future directions* (pp. 50–61). Tallahassee: Florida State University.

Peterson, G. W., Sampson, J. P. Jr., Lenz, J. G., & Reardon, R. C. (2002). A cognitive information processing approach to career problem solving and decision making. In D. Brown & Associates, *Career choice and development* (4th ed., pp. 312–372). San Francisco, CA: Jossey-Bass.

Peterson, G. W., Sampson, J. P. Jr., & Reardon, R. C. (1991). *Career development and services: A cognitive approach*. Pacific Grove, CA: Brooks/Cole.

Porfeli, E. J. (2009). Hugo Munsterberg and the origins of vocational guidance. *The Career Development Quarterly, 57*, 225–236.

Pryor, R. G. L., & Bright, J. E. H. (2003). The chaos theory of careers. *Australian Journal of Career Development, 12*(3), 12–20.

Pryor, R. G. L., & Bright, J. E. H. (2011). *The chaos theory of careers: A new perspective on working in the 21st century*. Hoboken, NJ: Taylor & Francis.

Reardon, R. C., Lenz, J. G., Sampson, J. P., & Peterson, G. W. (2009). *Career development and planning: A comprehensive approach* (3rd ed.). Pacific Grove, CA: Brooks/Cole.

Reardon, R. C., Lenz, J. G., Sampson, J. P., & Peterson, G. W. (2011). Big questions facing vocational psychology: A cognitive information processing perspective. *Journal of Career Assessment, 19*, 240–250.

Richardson, M. S. (1993). Work in people's lives: A location for counseling psychologists. *Journal of Counseling Psychology, 40*, 425–433.

Richardson, M. S. (2017). Counseling for work and relationship: A practice driven theoretical approach. In J. P. Sampson Jr., E. Bullock-Yowell, V. C. Dozier, D. S. Osborn, & J. G. Lenz (Eds.), *Integrating theory, research and practice in vocational psychology: Current status and future directions* (pp. 40–49). Tallahassee: Florida State University.

Richardson, M. L., & Schaeffer, C. (2013). Expanding the discourse: A dual model of working for women's (and men's) lives. In W. Patton (Ed.), *Conceptualising women's working lives: Moving the boundaries of discourse* (pp. 23–50). Rotterdam, The Netherlands: Sense.

Sampson, J. P. Jr., Bullock-Yowell, E., Dozier, V. C., Osborn, D. S., & J. G. Lenz, J. G. (2017). (Eds.). *Integrating theory, research and practice in vocational psychology: Current status and future directions*. Tallahassee, FL: Florida State University.

Savickas, M. L. (2001). The next decade in vocational psychology: Mission and objectives. *Journal of Vocational Behavior, 59*, 284–290.

Savickas, M. L. (2008). Helping people choose jobs: A history of the guidance profession. In J. A. Athanasou & R. Van Esbroeck (Eds.), *International handbook of career guidance* (pp. 97–113). Dordrecht, The Netherlands: Springer Science.

Savickas, M. L. (2013). Career construction theory and practice. In S. D. Brown & R. W. Lent (Eds.), *Career development and counseling: Putting theory and research to work* (2nd ed., pp. 147–186). New York: Wiley.

Savickas, M. L., & Baker, D. B. (2005). The history of vocational psychology: Antecedents, origin, and early development. In W. B. Walsh & M. L. Savickas (Eds.), *Handbook of vocational psychology* (3rd ed., pp. 15–49). Mahwah, NJ: Lawrence Erlbaum Associates.

Savickas, M. L., & Lent, R. W. (Eds.). (1994). *Convergence in career development theories: Implications for science and practice*. Palo Alto, CA: CPP Books.

Savickas, M. L., Nota, L., Rossier, J., Dauwalder, J-P., Duarte, M. E., Guichard, J., Soresi, S., Van Esbroeck, R., & van Vianen, A. E. M. (2009). Life designing: A paradigm for career construction in the 21st century. *Journal of Vocational Behavior, 75*, 239–250.

Schultheiss, D. E. (2013). A relational cultural paradigm as a theoretical backdrop for considering women's work. In W. Patton (Ed.), *Conceptualising women's working lives: Moving the boundaries of discourse* (pp. 51–62). Rotterdam, The Netherlands: Sense.

Stead, G. B., & Watson, M. B. (2017). *Career psychology in the South African context* (3rd ed.). Pretoria, South Africa: Van Schaik.

Super, D. E. (1957). *The psychology of careers.* New York: Harper and Row.

Super, D. E. (1990). A life-span, life-space approach to career development. In D. Brown & L. Brooks (Eds.), *Career choice and development: Applying contemporary theories to practice* (2nd ed., pp. 197–261). San Francisco, CA: Jossey-Bass.

Super, D. E. (1992). Toward a comprehensive theory of career development. In D. H. Montross & C. J. Shinkman (Eds.), *Career development: Theory and practice* (pp. 35–64). Springfield, IL: Charles Thomas.

Super, D. E., Savickas, M. L., & Super, C. M. (1996). The life-span, life-space approach to careers. In D. Brown & L. Brooks, (Eds.), *Career choice and development* (3rd ed., pp. 121–178). San Francisco, CA: Jossey-Bass.

Van Esbroeck, R., & Athanasou, J. A. (2008). Introduction. In J. A. Athanasou & R. Van Esbroeck (Eds.), *International handbook of career guidance* (pp. 1–19). Dordrecht, The Netherlands: Springer Science + Media.

Vondracek, F. W., & Porfeli, E. J. (2008). Social context for career guidance throughout the world: Developmental-contextual perspectives on career across the lifespan. In J. A. Athanasou & R. Van Esbroeck (Eds.), *International handbook of career guidance* (pp. 209–225). Dordrecht, The Netherlands: Springer Science & Media.

Vondracek, F. W., Ford, D. H., & Porfeli, E. J. (2014). *A living systems theory of vocational behavior and development.* Rotterdam, The Netherlands: Sense.

Vondracek, F. W., Lerner, R. M., & Schulenberg, J. E. (1986). *Career development: A life-span developmental approach.* Hillsdale, N.J.: Erlbaum.

Walsh, W. B., Savickas, M. L., & Hartung, P. J. (2013). (Eds.), *Handbook of vocational psychology* (4th ed.). New York: Routledge.

Watson, M. (2017). Career constructivism and culture: Deconstructing and reconstructing career counselling. In M. McMahon (Ed.), *Career counselling: Constructivist approaches* (2nd ed., pp. 43–53). London: Routledge.

Young, R. A., & Collin, A. (2004). Introduction: Constructivism and social constructionism in the career field. *Journal of Vocational Behavior, 64*(3), 373–388.

Young, R., Domene, J., & Valach, L. (2015). (Eds.). *Counseling and action: Toward life-enhancing work, relationships and identity.* Dordrecht, The Netherlands: Springer Science.

Young, R. A., Valach, L., & Collin, A. (2002). A contextual explanation of career. In D. Brown & Associates, *Career choice and development* (4th ed., pp. 206–250). San Francisco, CA: Jossey-Bass.

Part II

Contemporary theoretical perspectives

Empirical evidence and cross-cultural applications

Part II of the book presents 13 chapters that each detail a contemporary theory and illustrate its practical application through a case study and analysis. The section contains well established theories as well as emerging theories that intentionally link applications beyond the individual to organizations and broader social systems.

4 Social cognitive career theory
Empirical evidence and cross-cultural applications

Hung-Bin Sheu and Laura Phrasavath

Learning objectives

The purpose of this chapter is to:

- identify key SCCT variables and hypotheses regarding the process of career choice and development,
- describe the validity of SCCT models with individuals of diverse backgrounds and cultural identities,
- apply SCCT in case conceptualisation for working with people who have career-related issues, and
- gain knowledge regarding how to design SCCT-based career interventions.

Introduction to the chapter

Since the introduction of social cognitive career theory (SCCT) by Lent and colleagues nearly 25 years ago, several SCCT models have been proposed to account for predictors of important vocational outcomes, including interest development, career choice and action, performance and persistence, and work and educational satisfaction (Lent, Brown, & Hackett, 1994; Lent & Brown, 2008). These four models (i.e., interest, choice, performance/persistence, satisfaction) have received attention from researchers and practitioners in the United States and other countries. Meta-analytical findings have demonstrated the validity of SCCT across different career domains, and gender and racial/ethnic groups (Lent et al., 2018; Sheu et al., 2010). Although the fifth model of career self-management was recently added to this constellation of SCCT frameworks (Lent & Brown, 2013), it is excluded from this chapter due to limited space and the small number of studies conducted so far on this new model. In this chapter, we provide an overview of SCCT and its empirical evidence, focus on practical applications of the first four SCCT models, and introduce activities that can be used to facilitate the learning of this theory.

Overview of SCCT

Building upon Bandura's (1986) social cognitive theory, SCCT presents a unifying approach that integrates variables hypothesised in Bandura's triadic reciprocal causation into interlocking, segmental models for predicting people's vocational outcomes. These variables include person inputs (e.g., gender, race/ethnicity, social class, personality predispositions), person-cognitive variables (e.g., self-efficacy, outcome expectations, goals), environmental factors (e.g., distal and proximal contextual affordances), and behavioural outcomes (e.g., career choice and action, performance and persistence). This theoretical integration not only provides a thorough view of the factors that are posited to contribute to successful career development but also offers directions for designing intervention and outreach programs.

Figure 4.1 shows the first three SCCT models (interest, choice, performance/persistence; Lent et al., 1994). The fourth model (satisfaction; Lent & Brown, 2008) shares a similar configuration in which self-efficacy and expected or received outcomes are postulated to partially mediate the effects of personality traits and contextual factors on goal progress and satisfaction in a given career domain as well as global life satisfaction. Essentially, these models deem these two person-cognitive variables (i.e., self-efficacy and outcome expectations) as central psychological mechanisms through which personal agency is exercised as the individual develops and pursues his or her career paths. Next, we will highlight each key variable and discuss how they are integrated in SCCT.

Key variables

At the core of SCCT models are the signature variables of social cognitive theory – self-efficacy and outcome expectations. The former is defined as "a

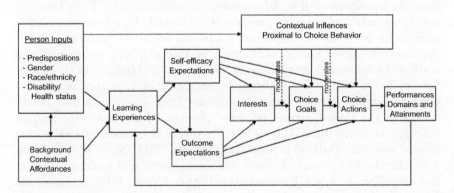

Figure 4.1 Model of personal, contextual and experiential factors affecting career-related choice behaviour.
Note: Direct relations between variables are indicated with solid lines, moderator effects (where a given variable strengthens or weakens the relations between two other variables) are shown with dashed lines.
Source: Copyright 1993 by R. W. Lent, S. D. Brown, and G. Hackett. Reprinted with permission.

judgment of one's capability to accomplish a certain level of performance", whereas the latter is referred to as "a judgment of the likely consequences such behaviour will produce" (Bandura, 1986, p. 391). While self-efficacy has been studied as a trait-like variable (i.e., general self-efficacy) by some scholars, SCCT conceptualises both self-efficacy and outcome expectations as task-specific or domain-specific constructs, for example, in the fields of science, technology, engineering, and mathematics (STEM). Self-efficacy and outcome expectations are primary change mechanisms through which individuals exercise control over their career choice and development. Research has shown that these two person-cognitive variables can be modified through four types of learning experiences: performance accomplishments, vicarious learning or modelling, verbal persuasion, and physiological/affective states (see Sheu & Lent, 2015 for a review). Depending on the exposure to and nature of these experiences, people may develop varying levels of confidence in and expect different outcomes associated with carrying out vocational behaviours, such as learning math, choosing a college major, and entering or persisting in an occupation.

As one of the three vertices of triadic determinism, environmental factors are conceptualised in SCCT to include both proximal and distal contextual affordances (Lent et al., 1994; Lent, Brown, & Hackett, 2000). Proximal contextual influences, such as emotional supports from family and friends or financial barriers, are posited to have direct, immediate impacts on individuals' intention to enter a career, as well as how they perform and persist in and feel satisfied with the chosen occupation. Existing studies have demonstrated the direct effects of environmental supports and barriers on career choice and action and academic satisfaction, as well as their indirect effects on such outcomes via self-efficacy, outcome expectations, and interests (Lent et al., 2018; Sheu et al., 2010). It should be noted that these proximal contextual factors could also determine whether individuals translate their interests into career choices and whether they act on such intentions by entering chosen careers. However, these moderation hypotheses have received limited empirical attention.

Contextual affordances also include factors that are more removed from the individual's current choice-making process or performance/persistence in a career (Lent et al., 1994). These distal contextual affordances may include resources and training opportunities in the community, shifts in the economy and labour force, socio-political contexts, and other influences. While these contextual factors may not directly or immediately affect the individual's career choice, they can shape the learning experiences available to the individual, which would later become sources of his or her efficacy beliefs and outcome expectations. In other words, these factors constitute larger societal and cultural backdrops that, over time, influence the person's education and training, career options and decisions, as well as performance and persistence in the chosen career. Distal contextual affordances and their long-term effects have rarely been studied in the field of vocational psychology; nevertheless, they have practical implications for career interventions, especially for people who are oppressed or marginalised and who struggle with discrimination and limited resources and opportunities for their career development.

Another group of SCCT variables pertains to person inputs, such as predispositions, biological sex, gender, disabilities, and race/ethnicity. These tend to be stable traits or characteristics which are less malleable to external forces. However, they could, by themselves or the interactions with contextual factors (e.g., discrimination, cultural norms), influence learning experiences and resources available to an individual and/or affect his or her career outcomes. Personality traits and affective variables (e.g., positive affect) have been found to positively correlate with academic satisfaction and intended persistence in engineering majors among college students (Lent et al., 2015; Navarro, Flores, Lee, & Gonzalez, 2014). Demographic person-input variables, such as gender and race/ethnicity, have also been studied as moderators for testing the cross-gender and cross-racial/ethnic validity of SCCT models (e.g., Sheu, 2017; Sheu, Mejia, Rigali-Oiler, Primé, & Chong, 2016). Effects of person-input variables are discussed in case studies.

SCCT as a unifying framework

The most important contribution made by SCCT is the integration of person-cognitive, contextual, and person-input variables into one coherent framework for predicting vocational outcomes (Figure 4.1). A person's demographic background and resources available in the larger cultural and societal context are hypothesised to contribute to his or her learning experiences. These experiences may include successful or failure performance, access to role models, encouragement from significant others, or anxiety or excitement, which give rise to the person's confidence in and expected outcomes associated with performing specific academic and career behaviours. It is assumed that those who have higher confidence levels in and/or expectations of desirable outcomes regarding a vocational domain are more likely to develop interest in, express intention to pursue, as well as perform better and persist longer (in the face of obstacles) in careers of the same domain. Similarly, higher self-efficacy and more favourable expected or received work conditions/outcomes are posited to jointly facilitate progress made toward a career goal, and these variables would predict higher levels of satisfaction with the chosen career path.

Person inputs and proximal contextual factors play slightly different roles across different SCCT models. In the first three overlapping models (Figure 4.1), person inputs are posited to predict interest development and career choice indirectly via their effects on learning experiences and proximal contextual factors. For instance, individuals with certain attributes (e.g., outgoing, sociable) or backgrounds (e.g., membership of the dominant group) might have access to more resources and be exposed to different experiences, which could then cultivate interests in and pave the way to entering an occupation. Proximal contextual factors also function as moderators which may encourage or deter the individual from developing interests into choice intentions and from turning intentions into career actions. On the other hand, in the SCCT satisfaction model, personality traits and affective variables directly contribute to educational and work satisfaction in addition to their indirect influence on satisfaction outcomes via other variables in the model, including environmental supports and obstacles, self-efficacy, outcome expectations, and goal progress. In spite of these minor differences, all four SCCT models (interest, choice, performance/persistence, satisfaction) share the same mechanisms that underlie the process of career choice and development.

The integrative nature of SCCT models offers researchers and practitioners a comprehensive framework in designing interventions for facilitating the development of vocational outcomes. Given the central roles that person-cognitive variables play in SCCT, it is no surprise that most intervention research has focused on improving self-efficacy and outcome expectations of middle-school and college students via exposing them to sources of efficacy information (Sheu & Lent, 2015). Positive performance accomplishments and access to role models who share similar demographic backgrounds have received strong empirical support for their effects on boosting confidence and obtaining information about possible outcomes in a given career domain. Several studies also investigated how modifying self-efficacy, outcome expectations, and perceptions of contextual affordances could influence participants' interest in and intentions to pursue different career paths (e.g., Dahling & Thompson, 2010; Weisgram & Biger, 2006). These experimental findings suggest the benefits of including person-cognitive and contextual affordance variables in vocational interventions, and demonstrate how different theory-based interventions could be integrated into career outreach programs using SCCT.

Cultural validity of SCCT

The cultural validity of SCCT models has received increasing attention from scholars in different countries. In the U.S., SCCT models have been tested across different racial/ethnic groups, such as between White/European Americans and Latino/a Americans (Navarro, Flores, Lee, & Gonzalez, 2014) and across White/European, Asian, and Latino/a Americans (Sheu et al., 2016), as well as in single minority or majority samples including Black/African Americans (Ezeofor & Lent, 2014; Gainor & Lent, 1998), Asian Americans (Hui, Lent, & Miller, 2013), and White/European Americans (Sheu, 2017). Some of these studies also examined gender differences. These U.S.-based findings offer evidence for the cross-racial/ethnic and cross-gender validity of SCCT.

A recent review further shows that different SCCT models have been examined with student and adult samples in Asia, Europe, and other parts of the world, such as United Arab Emirates and Turkey (Sheu & Bordon, 2017). A few of these investigations directly compared participants across different countries (e.g., Taiwan vs. Singapore, Angola vs. Mozambique) on their pursuit of academic and overall life satisfaction, offering rigorous evidence for the cross-country validity of the SCCT satisfaction model (Lent et al., 2014; Sheu, Chong, Chen, & Lin, 2014). Together, findings derived from diverse samples in the United States and different countries demonstrate the relevance of key

SCCT variables and the applicability of SCCT hypotheses across various cultural contexts and languages.

We next showcase a recent SCCT meta-analysis and present hypothetical case scenarios and analyses. Reflection questions are also offered to facilitate the learning of empirical evidence and practical utilities of SCCT.

Research in brief

An example of SCCT research and its practical utilities

Lent et al. (2018) evaluated the SCCT interest and choice models in STEM-related fields by meta-analysing 143 studies conducted over a thirty-year period in the United States. Based on all samples, a key finding showed that environmental supports were positively associated with self-efficacy and outcome expectations, both of which were in turn predictive of interest and choice goals. Supports and barriers had stronger effects on the two person-cognitive variables for racial/ethnic majority samples than for minority samples. Additionally, outcome expectations produced a larger path to interest for racial/ethnic majority samples but were a stronger predictor of choice goals for minority samples, whereas self-efficacy had similar effects on interest and choice goals across both groups. However, barriers produced a larger and negative path to self-efficacy for male samples while supports and barriers were more strongly and negatively related to each other among female samples. This large-scale, multivariate meta-analysis demonstrates the validity of SCCT while offering suggestions for designing career interventions for different racial/ethnic and gender groups.

Research in brief: reflective questions

1   How would you present findings of this meta-analysis to help clients understand the importance of self-efficacy and outcome expectations?
2   Given that self-efficacy produced similar effects while those of outcome expectations on interest and choice goals differed by race/ethnicity, how would this finding inform your career interventions with racially/ethnically diverse clients?
3   Given that the relation between supports and barriers differed by gender and that effects of these two contextual factors on interest and choice goals were mostly mediated by self-efficacy and outcome expectations, how would you apply these findings when working with male versus female clients?
4   This meta-analysis was based on data gathered in STEM-related fields. What do you think about its relevance to other vocational domains (e.g., advertising, graphic design)?

Case study

Case scenario 1: Denise

Denise (pseudonym) is a 19-year-old woman of Black American and Latina American heritage. Currently a sophomore in college, Denise was referred to the career counselling centre by her academic advisor. As the first in her working-class family to attend college, Denise expressed feeling overwhelmed in school and pressured to choose a major. While her academic advisor recommended that she explore multiple career fields, Denise's parents believed that choosing one career path as early as possible would "waste less time and money". Denise was initially interested in attending law school, but her parents discouraged her from pursuing graduate education as that would prevent Denise from "finding a good husband and caring for a family". Because her college major remained undeclared, she had become increasingly anxious and withdrawn in her classes. Denise soon began to feel apathetic toward everything; she was then placed on academic probation. She contemplated leaving school to work in her neighbourhood until she decided on a college major. Meanwhile, Denise resented not being able to explore different classes and majors the way that some of her peers were able to. "I have to either choose my major really soon or just drop out for a while," remarked Denise. "Those families on TV that tell their kids that they can be anything they want? We can't afford that."

Case scenario 2: David

David (pseudonym) is a 35-year-old male who has lived in the United States since migrating with his family from China two decades ago. He has worked for the same IT company after receiving a master's degree in computer science. While enjoying his work (e.g., developing software programs, fixing computer hardware), David has begun to feel unhappy and isolated on the job. He noticed that several of his coworkers, who entered the company around the same time, had been promoted to higher positions or taken on important projects whereas he continued to work in the same position. David debated working for a different company and even considered changing careers altogether. However, he hesitated to make a move because he worried about disappointing his parents, who expected him to have a stable job and income and wanted him to marry soon. As the only child, David felt pressured to have his own family. Recently, he became more anxious and less confident in performing work-related tasks. While employees of the company had diverse cultural backgrounds, with several coworkers also from Asia, David kept mostly to himself and had no contact with them after work. He liked working with computers but had become more dissatisfied with his current job.

Case analyses

Like any other type of counselling, a solid therapeutic relationship is foundational to successful career counselling. In addition to assessing Denise's and

David's career concerns, the counsellor should prioritise developing a strong working alliance from the beginning. Given these clients' unique cultural, racial/ethnic, and socio-economic backgrounds, the counsellor should be mindful of power dynamics and imbalance, differences in communication styles, and perceived stigma of seeking mental health services, all of which could affect the development of the alliance. Furthermore, risk assessments should be conducted to ensure clients' safety. Explanations of the counselling process and limitations of confidentiality will also help clients make informed decisions and become active participants.

SCCT presents a useful approach and language that allow Denise and David to describe their challenges and dissect problems into smaller and more manageable components, which can reduce their feelings of confusion and being overwhelmed. It is important to help them recognise that career concerns can be caused by a host of different factors. For example, Denise's struggle with selecting a college major and staying in school (i.e., the choice model) could be related to the lack of opportunities for exploring different career interests, low self-efficacy in performing schoolwork, an unclear picture of favourable outcomes associated with a college degree, discouragement from parents, or her depressive symptoms. Once these obstacles are identified, actionable plans can be developed to cope with the barriers and build a solid ground for making informed career choices.

As a working adult, David seems to know his career interests (e.g., working with computers and software programs) and possesses the skills and knowledge to continue a career in IT. His drop in job satisfaction could be the result of decreased performance or progress at work, uncertainty about what he can gain from his current job, an undesirable work environment, or feeling less efficacious in carrying out work-related tasks. Anxiety and isolation may also contribute to David's dissatisfaction with his job and overall life. SCCT persistence/performance and satisfaction models offer an appropriate framework to organise and discuss these concerns.

In addition to person-cognitive variables, SCCT also emphasises the importance of contextual and cultural factors. For instance, gender role expectations seem relevant to Denise (e.g., women should value family and relationships over careers) and David (e.g., men need stable jobs to be a good provider), and these expectations could limit both clients' career options. Cultural values, such as emotional self-control and conformity to norms, could dictate how David and Denise react to or cope with crises. Furthermore, a client's socio-economic status could interact with aforementioned cultural factors. Given her working-class background, Denise's decision about taking leave versus staying in school could be influenced by both her family's financial situation and gender role expectations. However, close ties with members of immediate or extended families could also serve as sources of practical or emotional support. It is therefore important to help these two clients understand how larger cultural contexts shape their career aspirations and how proximal environmental factors promote or hinder the resolutions of their career issues. A deeper understanding of these intersecting contextual factors and person-cognitive variables will help Denise and David avoid self-blame and empower them to take actions.

Assessment and intervention for Denise

Although Denise expressed intention to pursue a law career, this goal was built on shaky ground. Her career interests seem somewhat undifferentiated and loosely defined, which could be associated with low self-efficacy in and unclear outcome expectations about possible career options. Because career exploration is the primary task at this developmental stage, an assessment of her career interests and self-efficacy will be beneficial. Objective assessment tools, such as the *Strong Interest Inventory* (Harmon, Hansen, Borgen, & Hammer, 2005) and the *Skills Confidence Inventory* (Betz et al., 2003), can provide an overview of Denise's interest and confidence in different vocational domains. A thorough examination and comparison of her interest and self-efficacy profiles are likely to spark crucial discussion about career directions Denise wants to pursue or avoid. Tapping into Denise's prior experiences (or lack thereof) in various career, academic, or leisure activities will provide substance to and confirm or disconfirm the findings of objective assessments.

To consolidate her career interest and choice in law or other fields, career counselling should include building up self-efficacy in and clarifying outcome expectations associated with selected career paths. Interventions can be guided by sources of efficacy information, such as performance accomplishments (e.g., review Denise's grades in different academic subjects, discuss prior or current job experiences, participate in student clubs) and vicarious learning (e.g., identify and contact role models, shadow a professional in the field of her interest). Additionally, it will be beneficial to obtain accurate occupational information, and online tools like O*Net are often useful. How Denise interacts with her parents and perceives their expectations should also be processed, which can inform the development of coping strategies for gathering supports or managing pressure from her family. Finally, the extent to which Denise's psychological distress hinders her progress in career counselling should be assessed, and a referral to another mental health professional for dealing with emotional issues should be arranged if necessary.

Assessment and intervention for David

To facilitate the development of intervention strategies, information should be gathered about David's job satisfaction, performance, and work conditions. This can be done through using formal assessment tools or assigning homework (e.g., work diary). Interpretations of assessment results should be aided with specific work examples and in-depth discussion regarding both positive and negative aspects of his job. Clarification of work values and expected or received outcomes will be beneficial, and techniques such as vocational card sort can be useful. Along with David's expressed career interests and self-efficacy in an IT career, presentation of assessment findings can be organised according to SCCT persistence/performance and satisfaction models to gain insights into his career challenges.

Given that David possesses the skills and knowledge to work in the IT industry, perceived work conditions and outcome expectations are likely to play a key role in his decision to persist on the current job, find another job in the same field, or switch to a different career. If the IT field continues to interest David, career interventions can focus on helping David prioritise and balance what he wants to get out of his work (e.g., doing what he likes, opportunities for advancement, stable income) and important things in his personal life (e.g., meeting parents' expectations, getting married and starting a family). It will be important to brainstorm how to create a better work environment where he can improve his professional growth and well-being. Coping strategies, such as goal-setting, assertiveness training, and interpersonal and communication skills, will be useful in revitalising his work motivation as well as improving his sense of accomplishments and job satisfaction.

Denise and David are each facing a multitude of career issues within their unique cultural contexts. SCCT offers them a tool to appreciate the complexity of career development and identify areas for growth. With a solid working alliance, career counsellors can help them understand the limitations of their environments and personal characteristics, identify and secure resources for achieving career goals, and exercise control over their vocational behaviours (e.g., claim a college major) and outcomes (e.g., improve job satisfaction) by boosting self-efficacy and developing favourable outcome expectations or work conditions. Through knowledge about themselves, occupations, and change processes delineated in SCCT, Denise and David will become active participants in counselling sessions and the architects in building their careers.

Case study: reflective questions

1   Assuming this is the first time that Denise and David are seeking career counselling, how would you introduce SCCT and explain its relevance to their career issues in ways that are easy to understand and allow them to participate in setting counselling goals and tasks?

2   According to SCCT, interventions suitable for Denise and David include improving self-efficacy and/or developing positive outcome expectations of their vocational behaviours. Write down or brainstorm with your peers ideas and activities that could help these clients improve on these two person-cognitive variables in and outside of career counselling sessions.

3   Economically disadvantaged or financially constrained clients like Denise and David tend to have limited resources or less freedom to change careers. How would you help these clients cope with such environmental barriers and gather supports for achieving their career goals?

4   These two case scenarios cover different cultural, racial/ethnic, gender, and socio-economic backgrounds. For working with members of other nondominant groups, such as the LGBT population, how would you adopt or modify SCCT to meet their career needs?

Summary and recommendations

SCCT interest, choice, performance/persistence, and satisfaction models provide a unifying view of how person inputs, contextual affordances, human cognition, and behaviour interact with each other in shaping one's career choice and development. Based on robust empirical evidence, these models offer useful tools for assisting clients of diverse backgrounds at varying developmental stages and with different career concerns. Each key variable represents a target for career counsellors to intervene. Particularly, one's self-efficacy and outcome expectations are malleable and responsive to specific situations and performance domains, making them prime candidates for designing treatment plans. As an empirically supported framework, SCCT offers a roadmap for individuals to develop, change, and regulate their academic and career behaviour.

Despite the practical utilities of SCCT, examining the complex interactions between different factors could be overwhelming to clients who prefer less sophisticated approaches. Therefore, presenting the theory in a clear way with less technical jargon will be helpful to these individuals. Also, for some clients, their difficulties could be isolated in an area, such as lacking specific career information, which may not require the introduction of the whole theory. Given its focus on specific career domains, measurement of SCCT variables can be tricky because there may not be generic measures that are applicable to all clients. In addition to formal assessments, career counsellors should also utilise their interview skills and consider informal assessment tools (e.g., vocational card sort, work diary) to gather information and increase clients' awareness. Applications of SCCT should be tailored to fit each client's needs to bring about positive counselling outcomes.

The SCCT literature can be further strengthened with empirical evidence in three areas. First, longitudinal designs can help ascertain the temporal order of SCCT variables (self-efficacy, outcome expectations, choice intention and action, goal progress). Longitudinal findings will provide guidelines for how to prioritise treatments. Second, researchers and practitioners should team up to examine the effectiveness of SCCT-based interventions in diverse populations, especially among individuals of marginalised groups. Finally, although SCCT models have been tested in different countries, direct cross-cultural comparison studies remain relatively rare. Researchers should continue to devote their attention to gather evidence for the cultural validity of this theory.

In conclusion, SCCT represents an integrative approach that brings together demographic, environmental, cognitive, and behavioural variables to account for vocational development of individuals with diverse backgrounds and needs. After discussing SCCT's theoretical foundation, empirical evidence, and practical utilities, this chapter ends with two experiential exercises that are designed to deepen the learning of this theory.

Learning activities

Learning activity 1

Interview and shadow a professional who has been working in the field of your interest for one workday. Gather the following information:

1 What kinds of education and training did this person have before entering the current occupation?
2 What makes this person feel confident in performing job-related tasks?
3 What are those important things that he or she is getting out of the job?
4 What does this person like or dislike about the job? How would you apply SCCT variables in describing the information you have collected from this person?

Learning activity 2

Attend a job fair or browse job listings on local newspapers or websites. Read the description of a job that interests you, and think about the following:

1 How confident are you that you can successfully perform one or two specific tasks included in the job description?
2 What would improve or decrease your confidence in carrying out these tasks?
3 What are the important outcomes that this job can offer to you?

Next, select a job that you have not considered before, and think about the following:

1 What kinds of resources might you need to prepare yourself for entering this occupation?
2 What are the barriers that could prevent you from being successful in this career?

References

Bandura, A. (1986). *Social foundations of thought and action.* Englewood Cliffs, NJ: Prentice Hall.

Betz, N. E., Borgen, F. H., Rottinghaus, P., Paulsen, A., Halper, C. R., & Harmon, L. W. (2003). The Expanded Skills Confidence Inventory: Measuring basic dimensions of vocational activity. *Journal of Vocational Behavior, 62,* 76–100.

Dahling, J. J., & Thompson, M. N. (2010). Contextual supports and barriers to academic choices: A policy-capturing analysis. *Journal of Vocational Behavior, 77,* 374–382.

Ezeofor, I., & Lent, R. W. (2014). Social cognitive and self-construal predictors of well-being among African college students in the U.S. *Journal of Vocational Behavior, 85*, 413–421.

Gainor, K. A., & Lent, R. W. (1998). Social cognitive expectations and racial identity attitudes in predicting the math choice intentions of Black college students. *Journal of Counseling Psychology, 45*, 403–413.

Harmon, L. W., Hansen, J. C., Borgen, F. H., & Hammer, A. C. (2005). *Strong Interest Inventory: Applications and technical guide.* Palo Alto, CA: Consulting Psychologists Press.

Hui, K., Lent, R. W., & Miller, M. J. (2013). Social cognitive and cultural orientation predictors of well-being in Asian American college students. *Journal of Career Assessment, 21*, 587–598.

Lent, R. W., & Brown, S. D. (2008). Social cognitive career theory and subjective well-being in the context of work. *Journal of Career Assessment, 16*, 6–21.

Lent, R. W., & Brown, S. D. (2013). Social cognitive model of career self-management: Toward a unifying view of adaptive career behaviour across the life span. *Journal of Counseling Psychology, 60*, 557–568.

Lent, R. W., Brown, S. D., & Hackett, G. (1994). Toward a unifying social cognitive theory of career and academic interest, choice, and performance. *Journal of Vocational Behavior, 45*, 79–122.

Lent, R. W., Brown, S. D., & Hackett, G. (2000). Contextual supports and barriers to career choice: A social cognitive analysis. *Journal of Counseling Psychology, 47*, 36–49.

Lent, R. W., Miller, M. J., Smith, P. E., Watford, B. A., Hui, K., & Lim, R. H. (2015). Social cognitive model of adjustment to engineering majors: Longitudinal test across gender and race/ethnicity. *Journal of Vocational Behavior, 86*, 77–85.

Lent, R. W., Sheu, H., Miller, M. J. Cusick, M. E., Penn, L. T., & Truong, N. N. (2018). Predictors of science, technology, engineering, and mathematics choice options: A meta-analytic path analysis of the social-cognitive choice model by gender and race/ethnicity. *Journal of Counseling Psychology, 65*, 17–35.

Lent, R. W., Taveira, M., Pinto, J. C., Silva, A. D., Blanco, Á., Faria, S., & Gonçalves, A. M. (2014). Social cognitive predictors of well-being in African college students. *Journal of Vocational Behavior, 84*, 266–272.

Navarro, R. L., Flores, L. Y., Lee, H.-S., & Gonzalez, R. (2014). Testing a longitudinal social cognitive model of intended persistence with engineering students across gender and race/ethnicity. *Journal of Vocational Behavior, 85*, 146–155.

Sheu, H. (2017, August). Well-being of college students: Gender difference and impacts of cultural orientations. Poster presented at the 2017 Annual Conference of the American Psychological Association. Washington, DC.

Sheu, H., & Bordon, J. J. (2017). SCCT research in the international context: Empirical evidence, future directions, and practical implications. *Journal of Career Assessment, 25*, 58–74.

Sheu, H., Chong, S. S., Chen, H., & Lin, W. (2014). Well-being of Taiwanese and Singaporean college students: Cross-cultural validity of a modified social cognitive model. *Journal of Counseling Psychology, 61*, 447–460.

Sheu, H., & Lent, R. W. (2015). A social cognitive perspective on career intervention. In P. J. Hartung, M. L. Savickas, & W. B. Walsh (Eds.), *APA handbook of career intervention: Vol. 1. Foundations* (pp. 115–128). Washington, DC: American Psychological Association.

Sheu, H., Lent, R. W., Brown, S. D., Miller, M. J., Hennessy, K. D., & Duffy, R. D. (2010). Testing the choice model of social cognitive career theory across Holland themes: A meta-analytic path analysis. *Journal of Vocational Behavior, 76*, 252–264.

Sheu, H., Mejia, A., Rigali-Oiler, M., Primé, D. & Chong, S. S. (2016). Social cognitive predictors of academic and life satisfaction: Measurement and structural equivalence across three racial/ethnic groups. *Journal of Counseling Psychology, 63*, 460–474.

Weisgram, E. S., & Biger, R. S. (2006). Girls and science careers: The role of altruistic values and attitudes about scientific tasks. *Journal of Applied Developmental Psychology, 27*, 326–348.

5 Cognitive information processing theory
Applications of an empirically based theory and interventions to diverse populations

Debra S. Osborn, Casey Dozier, Gary W. Peterson, Emily Bullock-Yowell, Denise E. Saunders, and James P. Sampson, Jr.

Learning objectives

The purpose of this chapter is to:

- identify the key elements of the CIP pyramid and the career readiness model;
- describe the steps of a CIP-based decision-making model;
- discuss how to apply the CIP pyramid, CASVE cycle and career readiness model to a case example; and
- explore the relevancy of CIP theory to various cultural contexts.

Introduction to the chapter

Cognitive information processing (CIP; Sampson, Reardon, Peterson, & Lenz, 2004) theory has been in existence for nearly five decades. During this time, the theory has kept the key elements of the pyramid of information processing and a decision-making model called 'domains and the CASVE cycle' (communication, analysis, synthesis, valuing, and execution), but has expanded to include a readiness model and new tools to increase its applicability to practitioners. In the following sections, the origin and key tenets of CIP theory are presented, followed by empirical support for and evidence of cultural validity of the theory. A case example demonstrates how an international student with a career concern might be approached, career concerns conceptualised, and interventions chosen from the CIP perspective. Finally, strengths and weaknesses as well as future directions for CIP theory are discussed.

Cognitive information processing theory

Origins of theory

The theoretical paradigm of cognitive information processing (CIP) can be traced to theorists and researchers of the cognitive revolution of the 70s and

80s, including Hunt (1971); Newell and Simon (1972); and Lackman, Lackman, and Butterfield (1979). The application of CIP to career problem solving and decision-making (Peterson, Sampson, & Reardon, 1991) involves two fundamental structures, (a) the pyramid of information processing domains (see Figure 5.1), which consists of the knowledge domain at the base with the elements of self-knowledge and options knowledge, the decision-making skills domain in the middle, and the executive processing skills domain at the apex; and (b) the CASVE cycle (see Figure 5.2) within the decision-making skills domain, which transforms information in a five-step recursive process from the identification of a problem to the implementation of a solution. The cognitive memory structures within self-knowledge (episodic memory) and options knowledge (semantic memory) domains were formulated from the works of Tulving (1972). The five information transformation skills involved in career decision-making were formulated by Peterson, who drew from works identifying the outcomes of baccalaureate education (Peterson & Swain, 1978; Peterson & Watkins, 1979). The works of Flavell (1979) and Meichenbaum (1977) were instrumental in formulating the components, referred to as metacognitions, of the executive processing domain, which consists of self-talk, self-awareness, and monitoring and control.

The antecedents of the application of CIP to career counselling practice go as far back as 1972 with the creation of the Curricular Career Information Service (CCIS) at Florida State University where career counselling and advising satellite centers were implemented across campus. Clients accessed career information with the assistance of career advisors in an open-space library context and had access to computer delivery systems (Reardon, 1977). This approach ushered in a learner-centered environment, dramatically different from the traditional one-on-one career counselling session scheduled in a private office. CIP,

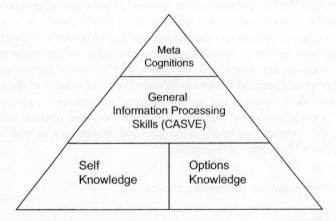

Figure 5.1 The Pyramid of Information Processing domains.
Source: Reprinted from *The Career Development Quarterly, 41,* 1992, p. 70, copyrighted NCDA. Reprinted with permission of the National Career Development Association. Used with permission.

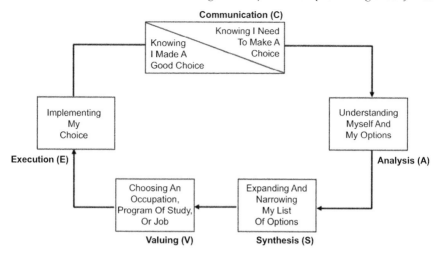

Figure 5.2 The CASVE cycle.
Adapted from: Sampson, J. P., Jr., Peterson, G. W., Lenz, J. G., & Reardon, R. C. (1992). A cognitive approach to career services: Translating concepts into practice. *The Career Development Quarterly, 41,* 67–74. Copyright National Career Development Association. Used with permission.

as an approach to career problem solving and decision-making, was integrated into the training of career counsellors and advisors, and into the delivery of career counselling services in the 90s (Sampson et al., 2004) The ultimate goal of career counselling using the CIP theory and delivery approach is the enhancement of career problem-solving and decision-making skills, which entails growth and development in all four domains of the pyramid of information processing domains (Peterson, Sampson, & Reardon, 1991; Peterson, Sampson, Lenz, & Reardon, 2002; Sampson et al., 2004).

Key theoretical principles

CIP is comprised of three key theoretical principles, including the pyramid of information processing domains, the CASVE cycle, and the career decision-making readiness model. CIP theory has also been applied to a seven-step service delivery sequence resulting in a differentiated model of service delivery (Sampson et al., 2004), and career assessments such as the *Career Thoughts Inventory* (CTI; Sampson, Peterson, Lenz, Reardon, & Saunders, 1996), the *Decision Space Worksheet* (DSW; Peterson, Leasure, Carr, & Lenz, 2010), and the *Career State Inventory* (CSI; Leierer, Peterson, Reardon, & Osborn, 2017) to explore career decision-making readiness.

CIP theory posits that effective career decision-making consists of four key elements divided into three domains and represented visually in a pyramid (See Figure 5.1). The knowledge domain is the foundation, consisting of self and options knowledge. Self-knowledge includes aspects of self, and can include interests, skills, values, personality, spirituality, employment preferences, cultural experiences, and so forth. Options knowledge addresses what a person knows about the occupational, educational, training, or employment options they are considering, as well as the organisational schema they use to manage that knowledge. The second domain is the decision-making domain, and includes factors that influence decision-making such as whether a person leans more toward independent, dependent, or interdependent decision-making approaches, decision-making styles such as rational or emotional, and the decision-making process. CIP offers a detailed decision-making model, known as the CASVE cycle (see Figure 5.2).

The CASVE cycle comprises five steps, ending with repeating the first step. *Communication* is the first step during which a person identifies the gap between his or her real and ideal career decision. For example, individuals may say they are undecided about a career (real) and would like to make an informed career decision by the conclusion of career counselling (ideal). Internal and external cues that are presently encouraging them to make a career decision are also explored. In *analysis*, clients explore, organise, and build on what they currently know about themselves and their options. This might include completing a standardised or nonstandardised assessment and sharing their thoughts about the options they are considering. *Synthesis* contains two steps: *synthesis-elaboration*, where options are increased, followed by *synthesis-crystallisation*, where this list is narrowed as clients learn about each option and evaluates how well that option fits with their self-knowledge. The desired outcome of this step is to identify three to five attractive options. In *valuing*, a cost-benefit analysis of each option to oneself, one's significant other, family, community, and society is conducted and a preliminary first choice is made. In *execution*, a preferred option is reality tested, a preparation program is created if needed, and paid or unpaid employment is sought, which is followed by revisiting the first step in the process, *communication-revisited*, to determine whether the gap has been closed or steps in the process need to be repeated.

The final domain in the pyramid of information processing is executive processing, located at the apex of the pyramid, includes the identification and management of self-talk. Sometimes self-talk can be helpful, but at other times, it can be dysfunctional. Dysfunctional career thoughts, defined as "thoughts that impair an individual's ability to solve a career problem or make a career decision" (Sampson et al., 2004, p. 91), are included in this domain, and have a negative influence on the other domains. Often these negative thoughts focus on decision-making confusion, commitment anxiety, and external thoughts, subscales on the CTI (Sampson et al., 1996), a CIP tool designed to measure dysfunctional career thoughts. When working with clients from a CIP-theory base, a practitioner tries to place a client on the CIP pyramid and locate where they are in the CASVE cycle, both for case conceptualisation and for determining interventions. In addition, the career practitioner is trying to determine how ready a client is to engage in the career decision-making process.

CIP readiness model

Readiness for career decision-making is the "capability of an individual to make appropriate career choices, taking into account the complexity of family, social, economic, and organisational factors that influence an individual's career development" (Sampson et al., 2004, p. 68). The model is composed of two key elements, capability and complexity. Capability, an internal measure, refers to a person's cognitive and emotional states that might impact their ability to see themselves and their options accurately, while complexity is external, involving factors outside a person (e.g., poverty, discrimination, familial demands). If placed on a two-dimensional axis, the combination of low or high capability and complexity yields four possible outcomes (see Figure 5.3), and provides a picture of client decision-making readiness as well as a suggestion on the service delivery model that might be best suited to meet his or her individual needs. The next section describes the counselling process.

CIP seven-step sequence and differentiated service delivery model

In 2004, Sampson et al. created a seven-step sequence for applying CIP theory. The steps are: (1) initial interview, (2) preliminary assessment, (3) define the problem and analyse the causes, (4) formulate goals, (5) develop an individual learning plan, (6) execute the individual learning plan, and 7) summative review and generalisation. These steps are somewhat fluid, in that goals may be clarified or deleted altogether depending on what the client discovers during career counselling. In the initial interview, the career practitioner

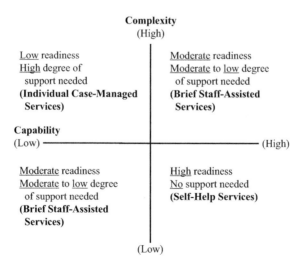

Figure 5.3 A two-dimensional model of readiness for career decision-making.
Source: Sampson, Peterson, Reardon, & Lenz, 2000.

talks with the client to gain an understanding of career concerns, and during the preliminary assessment, focuses on determining the client's readiness to engage in career decision-making. A screening instrument such as the CTI might be used at this point. As a result of this screening and determination of a client's level of career readiness, the client may be referred to self-help, brief staff-assisted, or individual case-managed services (Sampson et al., 2004).

Self-help services would be indicated for individuals with high capability and low complexity; they know how to make effective decisions and have few outside barriers to decision-making. They may need to be pointed to information resources or guides, but can manage the process by themselves. Those with either low capability and low complexity or high capability and high complexity would benefit most from brief staff-assisted career services. They are likely to have substantial gaps in one or two areas of the CIP pyramid, or require several steps to complete their goals, and thus having a career practitioner 'check in' with them would be helpful. Clients with low capability and high complexity require an individual case-managed approach given the likely gaps across multiple domains and the combination of internal and external pressures along with the presence of dysfunctional career thoughts. A slower process with ample support from a career counsellor is recommended for individuals in this category. It is also possible for individuals to shift between service delivery models. For example, someone in an individual case-managed approach might move to the brief-assisted model upon return to career counselling at a later date, and someone in the self-directed model may find that while that model worked for writing a résumé, determining where to send the résumé is a more difficult process and may require some brief discussions with a career practitioner.

The third step includes defining the problem and analysing the causes. This aligns with the *communication* step in the CASVE cycle, in which fuller exploration of the gap occurs, along with internal and external cues that a problem exists that needs to be addressed. The career counsellor gathers information to gain a full picture of the client's situation, including his or her cultural context and worldview, because from this discussion, goals for career counselling are formulated (step 4). In steps five and six, a co-constructed plan is construed and acted on, and in cases in which more than one goal and step have been determined, a written ILP is recommended. The final step involves both client and counsellor regularly reviewing the client's progress in executing the individual learning plan and addressing his or her goals. This discussion includes how the skills, knowledge, and process the client used for this decision might generalise to future career decisions. In this section, we reviewed the basic tenets of CIP theory as well as its practical application in career counselling. In the next section, we review evidence of the cultural validity of CIP theory.

Cultural validity of CIP theory

While CIP theory has seen the majority of its application in the United States, it has also been applied internationally (Fairweather, Govan, & McGlynn, 2006;

Northern Ireland Department for Employment, 2008; Sampson et al., 2000; Teuscher, 2003). In their development of a career services website, one of the recommendations by the joint partnership between the Department of Education and Department of Employment and Learning in Northern Ireland (2008) was to use the differentiated CIP model for service delivery. Similarly, Scotland's framework for improving and redesigning career information and advising proposes the CIP-differentiated model (The Scottish Government, 2011). Teuscher (2003) suggested the decision-making aides for 64 Swiss adolescents applied to the CASVE cycle, a process that was deemed acceptable and helpful for their career decisions. In addition, about 17 per cent of CIP-focused articles were published by international authors (Sampson, Peterson, Reardon, & Lenz, 2018). Beyond international appeal, CIP research has been conducted with diverse populations, including people with disabilities and people who are homeless, and in a variety of settings, including schools and in prisons (Sampson et al., 2018).

Empirical support for CIP theory

CIP theory, with nearly 300 citations, is a well-researched theory (Brown, 2015; Sampson et al., 2004). In reviewing the CIP bibliography (Sampson et al., 2018) for works that inform evidence-based practice, 158 works (57.4 per cent) were identified in which 25 consisted of pretest–posttest designs, which isolate effect sizes of CIP interventions; 32 describe CIP process and application, many of which are case studies; and 101 document validity of CIP theory–based measures. Moreover, of 132 published refereed research articles, 60 (45 per cent) were authored by Florida State University faculty and students; 50 (38 per cent) articles were authored by non-FSU researchers in the United States; and 22 (17 per cent) articles were published by international authors, including those from South Korea, Australia, Finland, Portugal, Iceland, Iran, Greece, Turkey, and Malaysia. Most (98 per cent) of the contributions by national and international authors were after 2000, underscoring recent growth trends in dissemination of CIP theory.

The effectiveness of the brief-assisted model was recently supported in a study by Osborn, Hayden, Peterson, & Sampson, (2016) with 138 drop-in clients who completed pre- and posttests regarding their knowledge of their next steps, confidence in taking the next step, and anxiety surrounding their choice. After a brief (15–30 minute) meeting with a career advisor, significant gains were found in knowledge and confidence, and a significant decrease occurred with anxiety. In addition, these clients were asked about their preferences for additional services. True to the differentiated model, the majority (67 per cent) stated that they could best be served by a brief walk-in model, about a quarter (26 per cent) stated that self-directed services would suffice, and 6 per cent preferred extended one-on-one individual career counselling. This differentiated model allowed for 19,000 individuals to receive walk-in career services at this university career center (Osborn et al., 2016).

Research in brief

A major focus of CIP-related research has explored the nature of dysfunctional career thoughts. Career indecision has repeatedly been correlated with dysfunctional career thoughts and multiple mental health indicators such as life stress, depression, hopelessness, anxiety, and perfectionism (see CIP bibliography for specific studies). Bullock Yowell, Peterson, Reardon, Leierer, & Reed, (2011) found that negative thinking correlated with increases in career and life stress and decreases in decidedness and career choice satisfaction for 232 college students. When the researchers partitioned off negative career thoughts in their model, the relationships between career and life stress and career indecision and dissatisfaction decreased. In a recent qualitative study examining five career counselling clients with highly elevated dysfunctional career thoughts, as measured by the CTI, along with MMPI-2 profiles, Finklea (2016) found repeated evidence of accompanying mental health concerns, including somatic symptoms, obsessive-compulsive concerns, and severe anxiety and depression.

Research in brief: reflective questions

1   Given repeated links among career indecision, dysfunctional career thinking, and mental health concerns, what implications might there be for training career practitioners? For mental health practitioners?
2   Given these results, when a career client demonstrates high negative thinking, what else might a counsellor need to attend to and how?
3   If a client demonstrated both career and mental health concerns, how would a career counsellor structure the session? Would one area be explored first, and if so, which area? Should a counsellor expect that changes in one area would affect changes in the other? Should both be addressed at the same time?

Case study

"Rustum" (pseudonym) initially entered the career services office for drop-in career advising, and he was asked the same question all clients are asked, "What brings you in today?" In response to this question, Rustum simply shrugged his shoulders and kept signing in on the computer without any eye contact. The lack of response was an initial indicator to the counsellor that Rustum might need more assistance, and a referral to individual career counselling might be warranted. When conceptualising clients, two main factors to consider are capability and complexity. Capability consists of internal factors such as motivation, ability to think clearly, and honest exploration. Complexity includes external influences including family, social, economic, and organisational factors (Sampson et al., 2004).

Once Rustum and the drop-in career advisor sat down, they began a discussion that focused on Rustum's goals. Here is an example interaction that might occur during drop-in advising:

CAREER ADVISOR (CA): What brings you in today?

RUSTUM: (shoulder shrug with no eye contact)

CA: Tell me more about what brought you here today.

RUSTUM: I don't know. I am planning to go to medical school, but I'm not doing well in my classes.

CA: Tell me more about what "*not doing well*" means to you.

Note: Grades might give information about interests and skills, which can be linked to one's self-knowledge in the pyramid. It is also important to clarify if 'not doing well' indicates whether the student might be at risk for not being admitted into graduate school. Lower grades can limit options, increasing the complexity of one's situation.

RUSTUM: Well, I don't think my GPA is high enough. I don't know what I'm going to do.

CA: I sense some hesitation about your next steps. What makes you say you're GPA is not 'high enough'?

RUSTUM: I have a 2.5 and I know many medical schools want a minimum of 3.0.

CA: I hear your concerns. That can be scary to think you might not get admitted. What about extracurricular activities or other things you have done while you've been in school?

RUSTUM: (chuckles and says) Well, my parents wanted me to focus on school, so I haven't done anything. I haven't worked, I haven't been involved in any clubs or anything.

CA: It sounds like that's why you are coming into our office now. The good news is that you are coming in now, and I think we have a lot of information and resources that can be useful.

Analysis linking to theoretical principles

Here is a summary of the complexity and capability factors indicated so far in Rustum's situation. The factors in Table 5.1 contribute to higher complexity and lower capability because they decrease the likelihood that Rustum will gain admittance into medical school:

In assessing Rustum's career readiness, the counsellor and the client agreed that an individual case-managed service delivery model was appropriate. After beginning individual career counselling, some additional information was learned about Rustum. He is a 19-year-old male from Pakistan in his second

Table 5.1 Complexity and capability factors

Complexity: contextual factors	Capability: how a client thinks and feels
Indicators of high complexity: • Low GPA (2.5) • No extracurricular activities • No prior work experiences It is unclear if family influences are causing any additional stress or if the family might be a positive and supportive influence.	Indicators of low capability: • Limited self-knowledge • Statements such as "I don't know what I'm going to do" • Lack of eye contact? • Lack of motivation? Lack of eye contact could be a cultural norm or it could be an indicator of depression or anxiety. Both hypotheses could be considered at this time. There might be a lack of motivation if he has not been involved in other extra-curriculars, but that could also be related to family influences.

year enrolled at a large public university in the United States. His initial goal in individual career counselling is to gain admittance into medical school because he is receiving pressure to take over the family medical practice, however, he has no extracurricular activities, no work experience, and his grade point average is a 2.5. His current major is biological science, but he is uncertain if he even wants to go to medical school. He reports difficulty sleeping, lack of appetite, recurring periods of poor motivation, and ongoing suicidal ideation. He continues to express concerns about his lack of skills and feels that he is "not good at anything," and that he "has no skills."

Theoretical implications summary

When Rustum entered the Career Center, he knew he needed to explore options, but he had limited awareness about his values, interests, skills, and employment preferences. He was in the communication phase of the CASVE cycle because he knew he needed to make a decision, but he had not yet begun to explore his self-knowledge or his options knowledge. He reported that he was prompted to visit the Career Center primarily due to his family's recent inquiry about his future plans. He was concerned that many of his roommates and other friends were already seeking internships and felt like he could fall behind if he did not explore his options now. Rustum reported that he felt easily influenced by his family and made most of his career decisions on the basis of what his family wanted, not necessarily on what he wanted. Rustum reported that the CASVE cycle helped him think about next steps that would allow him to make a more informed choice.

Many interventions with this client focused on reframing negative thoughts. An occupational card sort was utilised to further understand how Rustum made sense of the world of work. The sorting task suggested a limited organising schema to sort his options. A discussion followed encouraging openness to expanding options under consideration and challenging a more rigid "would choose" and "would not choose" schema. An additional intervention, the *Decision Space Worksheet* (DSW, Peterson et al., 2010), was incorporated into the counselling process listing all the factors impacting his decision and ranking their importance. This activity was useful in highlighting two main concerns: what his family thought of his occupational choice and financial stress including a desire to avoid significant student loan debt.

Cultural implications

In addition to theoretical considerations, cultural considerations are also important to acknowledge. The United States is often viewed as an individualistic society focusing on individuals leading and making their own decisions (Coon & Kemmelmeier, 2001). However, many other cultures make decisions more collectively, as a family, or may have different values. For example, many individuals and cultures value continuing education, but that is not necessarily the case for Rustum or for every client, so it is important for counsellors to be aware of their own personal values and avoid imposing these (or assuming clients also ascribe to the same values) on clients. Striving to understand the client's values associated with the decision-making process aids in validating the client's needs while also helping the client work toward an informed decision.

Another cultural consideration is potential stigma associated with counselling. This is particularly relevant for Rustum since he indicated mild and passing suicidal ideations and previous counselling experiences that he felt focused too much on his thoughts. He was informed of resources and supports available to him that offer assistance for personal or mental health concerns. Learning about Rustum's previous counselling helped the counsellor implement more behavioral techniques. While many sessions still focused on reframing thoughts such as "I'm not good at anything", the focus was more behavioral than cognitive behavioral.

Working alliance implications

The foundation for therapeutic change often begins with a strong working alliance. Norcross (2011) cited several factors that contribute to building a strong working alliance. Some of the factors emphasised by Norcross (2011) that were utilised in building rapport with this client included building a collaborative relationship and the use of empathy. Additionally, the counsellor integrated humour to help Rustum recognise how negatively his thoughts were affecting his decision-making process.

The counselling relationship was collaborative in that Rustum was continually involved in the interventions chosen during career counselling. For example, he was given a choice to begin exploring options first or begin exploring more about himself. He chose to explore more about himself, and he expressed a specific desire to know more about his skills. Results of the assessments utilised during career counselling were clearly explained so that Rustum understood what his scores meant and how to use the information. This dialogue between the counsellor and the client encouraged transparency in the counselling process. Empathic statements focusing on Rustum's feelings were made throughout counselling. For example, the pressure he was feeling from family, stress about not getting admitted to medical school, and worry about falling behind his peers were all noted. Humor was used to illustrate the extreme nature of thoughts like "I am not good at anything". He quickly realised that it was unfair to say he was "not good at *anything*". The counsellor then collaborated with Rustum to decide on a new, more accurate phrase. The new phrase was "I feel that I want to learn some new skills and I am concerned I may fall behind my peers if I don't learn more about myself and what I am good at. I came to career counselling to learn more about myself and to further explore my options". Rustum agreed that this statement was more accurate than simply saying that he was "not good at anything".

Case study: reflective questions

The case described provides an application of cognitive information processing theory and illustrates the use of the pyramid of information processing, the CASVE cycle, and career readiness that were used to help inform the client about themselves and the process of making a career choice.

1　How might the career counselling approach be altered if the client's complexity and capability were higher, increasing career readiness?
2　Consider that the client came from a more collectivist culture. Would that affect your case conceptualisation and interventions?
3　Given the client's previous counselling experience and awareness of mental health concerns, how might you help to normalise stress associated with uncertainty in the decision process? Could this be integrated into self-knowledge?

Chapter summary

This chapter reviewed key CIP theory elements and provided steps and an example for integrating CIP into service delivery. CIP has an impressive body of conceptual and empirical work that supports its premises and demonstrates its applicability to various settings, clients, and environments. In addition, CIP provides theory-based and research-supported assessments and tools for use with clients, and annually generates research. Still, there are some groups for which limited or no CIP-related research has been conducted, such as Native Americans, immigrants, people with refugee backgrounds, people from other countries, internationals, people with emotional or cognitive deficits, and the chronically unemployed. Further, CIP theory has not been applied to corporate settings such as facilitating career decision-making within human resource management. In addition, while research has focused on the apex of the pyramid, additional research is needed on the remainder of the pyramid of information processing domains, the CASVE cycle, the CTI workbook, and the readiness model. Specifically, within the pyramid of information processing domains, additional research could focus on factors that influence clients' knowledge and use of career information, the effects of social media on self and occupational knowledge and decision-making, culture's impact on the career decision-making process, and the differing needs of clients at each stage of the CASVE cycle. As an intervention, the CTI workbook offers many avenues for exploration. For whom is the workbook most and least useful? How do the workbook's activities compare to other interventions in reducing negative career thoughts? How well does the decision-making checklist in the workbook fit with where a client says they are experiencing confusion? Research on the readiness model could include constructing an instrument that measures both capacity and capability, identifying empirically based interventions for both components, and exploring how interventions aimed at one component affect both components.

Learning activities

Learning activity 1: Reframing negative thoughts

Activity Purpose: This activity helps practitioners or students relate to the client experience of thought reframing. It is important for practitioners to have a strong grasp of how to identify, alter, and challenge negative thinking before working with clients to act on new ways of thinking about personal career development. When negative career thinking is prevalent, the reframing process is a necessary step in the process toward acting on new ways of thinking and continuing in a productive decision-making process.

   Task: This task can be completed as an individual or with a group such as a class. A class could be broken into smaller groups with each group addressing a different negative career thought. Individuals or groups should be tasked with identifying several common negative career thoughts (e.g., *I will never make the right choice; I will never meet my parents' expectations for me*). Before engaging in the activity the thoughts should be written on paper or hanging posters. If desired, thoughts problematic for the group or individual could be identified through *Career Thoughts Inventory* (CTI) items to which the group or individual agreed or strongly agreed. After identifying relevant or common thoughts, the group or individual should work to reframe the thought. Avoid simplistic, positive reframes (e.g., *I can't decide on a career path, I can decide on a career path*). Encourage reframing that considers the concept in more realistic terms (rather than black and white) and acknowledges the emotional component of the thought. Considering actions that could help solve problems associated with the thought is likely to lead to next steps in working through thoughts currently blocking the career development or decision-making process.

An example of a more realistic, action focused reframe is provided here: ORIGINAL NEGATIVE CAREER THOUGHT: "I know what I want to do but I can't develop a plan for getting there." POSSIBLE REFRAME: "I am frustrated with how complicated it is to reach my goal and may need help to figure out a plan. Reaching out to experts in my field of choice may provide me with examples of how people achieved the goals I want to achieve."

Learning activity 2

Using the CASVE cycle to explore your personal career decision-making process

Activity Purpose: The CASVE cycle is the CIP-suggested decision-making approach. Enhanced understanding of CASVE cycle application with clients is best achieved by initially navigating the process personally. Engaging the process personally will provide insight into how to apply the cycle to client decisions and a greater appreciation for the challenge of making a quality decision.

Task: This task is best completed individually as each decision-making process is detailed and unique. Review the chapter information on the CASVE cycle before beginning the activity. If you are currently considering a career decision, attempt to use the CASVE cycle to assess your current decision-making status and move forward in your process. If you are not currently seeking a change, conduct a forensic analysis of your last career change (e.g., decision to go to graduate school, choice to change jobs or take a promotion) using the CASVE cycle. Follow the following phases and prompts to consider your current or recent career decision-making process. Consider whether you need more information at a phase in order to successfully move forward in the cycle. If an instructor, consider making this a paper assignment for the course or a self-reflection activity.

Communication

- Prompts: Describe the internal and external cues that led you to make a career change. Also describe those internal and external cues that were opposed to the decisions you have made or are making.
- Gap: Where are you now and where do you want to be?

- Goal(s): Include one or more goal statement(s) that clearly indicates an outcome or outcomes related to narrowing the identified gap.

Analysis

- Summarise your self-knowledge with regard to values, interests, skills, and other personal preferences.
- Occupational Knowledge: Review the information you have researched about at least two occupations or jobs you are considering.
- Consider how you typically make decisions and whether any negative thoughts are currently interfering with your decision-making process.

Synthesis

- Elaboration: Identify methods for generating occupational/job options and list at least five options for consideration.
- Crystallisation: Of the options listed in elaboration, identify no more than three occupational options to consider in valuing phase that follows. Use your previously identified self and occupational knowledge to narrow down to three or fewer.

Valuing

- Describe the relative costs and benefits of each of your occupational options identified in crystallisation. These costs and benefits should be in relation to yourself, your significant others, your cultural group, and your community and/or society.
- Prioritise or rank your occupational options and state your tentative, first choice.

Execution

- Include a list of steps you would need to take and goals that need to be accomplished in order to appropriately execute your top choice.

Communication

- Describe how the process of completing this activity affected you as a counsellor, person in training for a profession, and/or job seeker. Has it widened, better defined, and/or helped to close your "gap"? Do you need to revisit some phases? Speak to the specific metacognitions you experienced while engaging in this activity.

Learning activities: reflective questions

1   Self Knowledge: What are some new things I could do this year that would teach me more about myself to better prepare me to make a good career decision?

2   Decision-Making: What is the last big or complex decision I made? How did I go about making that decision? Is there anything I could learn from the CASVE cycle to improve that last big decision or my typical decision-making process?

3   Metacognitions: When I am considering what to do next for my job, career, or education, what positive and negative thoughts do I typically have?

References

Brown, S. D. (2015). Career intervention efficacy: Making a difference in people's lives. In P. J. Hartung, M. L. Savickas, & W. B. Walsh (Eds.), *APA handbook of career interventions* (pp. 61–77). Washington, DC: American Psychological Association.

Bullock Yowell, E., Peterson, G. W., Reardon, R. C., Leierer, S. J., & Reed, C. A. (2011). Relationships among career and life stress, negative career thoughts, and career decision state: A cognitive information processing perspective. *The Career Development Quarterly*, 59, 302–314.

Coon, H. M., & Kemmelmeier, M. (2001). Cultural orientations in the United States: (Re)Examining differences among ethnic groups. *Journal of Cross-Cultural Psychology*, 32, 348–364.

Fairweather, F., Govan, D., & McGlynn, M. (2006). *The development of Careers Scotland's service delivery framework*. Derby, UK: Centre for Guidance Studies, University of Derby. Retrieved from www.derby.ac.uk/research/icegs/

Finklea, T. J. (2016). The connection between psychopathology and dysfunctional career thoughts. (Unpublished doctoral dissertation). Florida State University, Tallahassee, Florida. Retrieved from http://diginole.lib.fsu.edu/islandora/search/finklea?type=edismax

Flavell, J. H. (1979). Metacognition and cognitive monitoring: A new idea of cognitive-developmental inquiry. *American Psychologist*, 34, 906–911.

Hunt, E. B. (1971). What kind of computer is man? *Cognitive Psychology*, 2, 57–98.

Lackman, R., Lackman, J. L., & Butterfield, E. C. (1979). *Cognitive psychology and information processing*. Hillsdale, N. J.: Erlbaum.

Leierer, S. J., Peterson, G. W., Reardon, R. C., & Osborn, D. S. (2017). The Career State Inventory (CSI) as a measure of readiness for career decision making: A manual for assessment, administration and intervention 7.0. Technical Report No. 57. Technical Report. Tallahassee, FL: Center for the Study of Technology in Counseling & Career Development.

Meichenbaum, D. (1977). *Cognitive-behavior modification*. New York: Plenum.

Newell, A., & Simon, H. (1972). *Human problem solving*. Englewood Cliffs, N.J.: Prentice-Hall.

Norcross, J. C. (2011). *Psychotherapy relationships that work: Evidence-based responsiveness*. New York: Oxford University Press.

Northern Ireland Department for Employment & Learning and the Department of Education (2008). Strategy and implementation plan for Preparing for Success: A joint strategy & implementation plan between the Department for Employment & Learning and the Department of Education. Retrieved from www.careersserviceni.com/ NR/ rdonlyres /249B3948-A023–046BD-8609–4382C017D998/0/CEIAGPfS.pdf

Osborn, D. S., Hayden, S. C., Peterson, G. W., & Sampson, J. P., Jr. (2016). Effect of brief staff-assisted career service delivery on drop-in clients. *The Career Development Quarterly*, *64*, 181–187.

Peterson, G. W., Leasure, K. K., Carr, D. L., & Lenz, J. G. (2010). The Decision Space Worksheet: An assessment of context in career decision making. *Career Planning and Adult Development Journal*, *25*, 87–100.

Peterson, G. W., Sampson, J. P. Jr., & Reardon, R. C. (1991). *Career development and Services: A cognitive approach*. Pacific Grove, CA: Brooks/Cole.

Peterson, G. W., & Swain, W. (1978, October). Critical appreciation: An essential element in educating for competence. *Liberal Education*, *64*, 293–301.

Peterson, G. W., & Watkins, K. (1979). Identification and assessment of competence. (Final report, Florida Competency-based Articulation Project). Tallahassee, FL.:ERIC Document Reproduction Service No. ED 169 839.

Peterson, G. W., Sampson, J. P. Jr., Lenz, J. G., & Reardon, R. C. (2002). A cognitive information processing approach to career problem solving and decision making. In D. Brown & Associates (Eds.), *Career choice and development* (4th ed.), pp. 312–369. New York: Jossey-Bass.

Reardon, R. C. (1977). Campus location and the effectiveness of a career information center. *Journal of College Student Personnel*, *18*, 240–241.

Sampson, J. P. Jr., Peterson, G. W., Lenz, J. G., & Reardon, R. C., & Saunders, D. E. (1996). *Career thoughts inventory*. Odessa, FL: Psychological Assessment Resources.

Sampson, J. P., Jr., Peterson, G. W., Reardon, R. C., & Lenz, J. G. (2000). Using readiness assessment to improve career services: A cognitive information processing approach. *The Career Development Quarterly*, *49*, 146–174.

Sampson, J. P., Jr., Reardon, R. C., Peterson, G. W., & Lenz, J. G. (2004). *Career counseling and services: A cognitive information processing approach*. Pacific Grove, CA: Brooks/Cole.

Sampson, J. P., Jr., Peterson, G. W., Reardon, R. C., & Lenz, J. G. (2018). *Bibliography: A cognitive information processing (CIP) theory-based approach to career development and services*. Retrieved from https://career.fsu.edu/sites/g/files/upcbnu746/files/ 20170323CIPBibliography.pdf

Tulving, E. (1972). Episodic and semantic memory. In E. Tulving & Donaldson (Eds.), *Organization of memory*, pp. 381–403. London: Oxford University Press.

Teuscher, U. (2003). Evaluation of a decision training program for vocational guidance. *International Journal for Educational and Vocational Guidance*, *3*, 177–192.

The Scottish Government. (2011). *Career information, advice and guidance in Scotland: A framework for service redesign and improvement*. Retrieved from https://education. gov.scot/Documents/CareerInformationAdviceGuidanceScotland.pdf

6 Contextual action theory
Concepts, processes, and examples

Richard A. Young and José F. Domene

Learning objectives

The purpose of this chapter is to:

- comprehend key concepts and processes of contextual action theory;
- understand career as goal-directed, intentional action over a significant period of life; and
- apply the theory in conceptualising the career development experiences of individuals in their social context.

Introduction to the chapter

In this chapter, we describe a theory of career based on goal-directed, intentional action. The chapter begins by addressing the central concepts and processes of the theory. We also explain how the meaning ascribed to career and the meaning ascribed to human action are linked, so that the latter can be used to understand the former. The chapter then pays particular attention to how this understanding of career captures cultural differences. We want to ensure that the theory could encompass different cultures and contexts in a meaningful way rather than isolate them as variables to be controlled. Finally, we provide an extensive illustration of how the theory is used to understand a case, based on the principle that our understanding and ultimately our theories begin with persons acting in context.

Central concepts of contextual action theory

Varieties of career theories exist, each with its own uniqueness and validity. One reason for this variation is the elasticity and flexibility of the term "career," which can refer to many different phenomena. When what is to be explained has different meanings, it is understandable that the theories themselves will differ. In developing contextual action theory (CAT), we were concerned about the meaning of the term career and wanted to ensure that it had consequence in the theory. We wanted to separate the close connection between career and specific economic systems that is often assumed.

Action theory has extensive roots in the social sciences and psychology, as well as in the humanities. Many approaches that rely on human action as an explanation of social phenomena emphasise the importance of meaning and the challenges of rationality of action. CAT is an application of action theory to career psychology. It emerged from von Cranach's (von Cranach, Ochsenbein, & Valach, 1986) description of human action. Von Cranach developed a notion of goal-directed action as conscious and intended behaviour, which was directed and controlled socially. Our elaboration of this approach over the past 20 years has resulted in an understanding of actions as "intentional, individual or joint process, oriented toward achieving a desired end state or goal" (Domene, Valach, & Young, 2015, p. 152). At the same time, we recognise that human action is not always rational or logical, and includes a manifestation of unconscious processes.

Career theories may vary because they have different purposes, including predicting outcomes, identifying processes, suggesting certain behaviours, or supporting intervention programs. The purpose of CAT is to seek explanations in terms of the goals of behaviour. It addresses the question, "Can this behaviour be understood through considering how it is goal-directed?" In this way, CAT is unlike theories that aspire to predict behaviour or explain outcomes in terms of causes. At the same time, CAT is based on the assumption that most human behaviour is goal-directed, even if the person acting is not fully conscious of the goals or the action is not fully rational. The notion of seeking explanations on the basis of goals fits nicely with career interventions and planning because career is often a goal. But rather than the model or theory as the starting point and the behaviour or action as that toward which it points, CAT begins with the action from which the explanation is generated.

The connection between action and career

Within CAT, "career" refers to what a person does in his or her life. It involves both personal and social meaning, and refers to doing, engaging, or carrying out. The term "action" has similar meanings – it refers to what one does and how one engages. Action is distinguished from behaviour because it involves intentionality and agency, which are also characteristics of career. Career not only depends on an understanding of action but also depends on actions themselves. Where career and action differ, is that action refers to a specific, time-limited phenomenon, for example, making breakfast this morning. In contrast, career includes a much longer time perspective and comprises many actions. For example, consider a person's career as a parent. Both the similarity and differences in common understandings of action and career contribute a fundamental premise of CAT. That is, there are systems of action that allow actions to be linked across time to construct career. People engage in specific, time-bound actions because they are seen as contributing to longer-term, more complex goals. For example, a person's career as a parent is made up of many actions, which change and evolve over time reflecting the child's age. Terms such as "occupational career," "marriage career," "parenting career," "patient career," or "illness career" have meaning for individuals in their social contexts and are supported by those social contexts.

In addition to action and career, "project" is another important construct in CAT. It allows the person who is engaging in the action, that is, the actor, and others to link actions over a mid-term length of time. Several related actions across a mid-term length of time are identified as a project. For example, consider the occupational career of dentist. Within that career, one can readily identify the project of being admitted to dental school. This project may be composed of actions such as completing the application, being interviewed, and deciding on an offer of admission. Often, people understand that many time-bound, limited actions are part of longer-term projects, even when these actions are habitually performed or engaged in without full awareness of the complexity of the goals a project may encompass. Similarly, people also attribute meaning to specific actions retrospectively because they fit with longer-term projects. The "project" construct is a strong heuristic is this era when work is shifting from long-term employment to an open talent market, as noted by the European Political Strategy Centre of the European Commission (2016). Specifically, it notes a "project-focused" approach to work. Although this approach may reflect the needs of businesses and changing technology, project also captures the important link between action and career. Briefly, people make meaning in the short, mid, and long term, but the ability to do that depends on the structures available in their societies and cultures.

Research in brief 1

Domene et al. (2012) explored romantic relationships as a key context of the transition to work. Specifically, the authors addressed the question of how young adult couples in committed romantic relationships constructed and pursued goals together during their transition into the world of work. The projects that emerged from the action project–method analysis included ones focused on pursuing future occupational and educational plans, balancing multiple priorities in the lives of both members of the couple, deciding where to live, and projects related to maintaining or advancing their relationship with each other. Most participants made substantive progress on achieving these projects over the six months of their research involvement. In most cases, both members of the couple were actively involved in each other's career development, and viewed their partner's work and school as being a part of their own future. Finally, the couples' actions and goals were found to be motivated by an overarching desire to support each other during the transition to work, highlighting the importance of considering romantic relationship contexts in understanding emerging adults' career development.

Research in brief: reflective questions

1   Given the focus of participants' projects, how might couples define successful achievement of those projects?
2   Besides CAT, what theories of career development can be used to understand how young couples work together to facilitate the transition to work?
3   How could the findings of this study be used to assist young adult couples to achieve a life-enhancing career?

Finally, we use the notion of joint action extensively in our work because most actions and virtually all projects and careers involve others. Joint actions in the form of conversations between persons significant to each other have been foundational in CAT research, for example, future-related conversation between parents and their adolescent children, between young adult friends, and between mothers and fathers of young adults with intellectual and developmental disabilities. Projects also typically involve multiple people, as illustrated by the study presented in Research in brief 1. Similarly, long-term careers depend on even greater networks of others, including institutions and social contracts. For example, marriage as a long-term career is constructed differently within cultures, but is possible as a career because of these social institutions and culturally imbued meanings.

The four terms – action, joint action, project, and career – represent the systems of action. Each represents a temporal period from the immediate moment to long time-spans in one's life. The complexity of what each system involves increases as one moves from action to career. Each system depends on the construction of meaning. Career represents how persons construct the links between their actions and projects over a long term. As one can readily imagine, careers involve a large range of actions and projects, and thus, reflect how the cultural embeddedness of action.

Organisation of action

CAT also describes the ways in which action is organised. Clearly, action involves behaviour, which relies on skills, habits, and the actor's internal and external resources. These are the elements of action. For example, the action of a conversation between a parent and a young adult family member involves specific verbal and nonverbal behaviours. It also requires that both parties have some level of conversational skill if the conversation is to be sustained. It also involves goals to be organised. Complex actions or constructed series of actions in the form of projects and careers rely substantially on resources including time, language, institutions, other people, and culture (Young, Domene, & Valach, 2015). Unconscious processes are represented in specific behaviours.

Functional steps represent the second way that action is organised. Understandably, most actions require several steps in reaching goals. Functional steps, then, refer to the contiguous elements that are the intentional means by which people move toward their goals. For example, a father, in conversing with his son about the son's future, may guide his son's decision rather than deciding for his son. The father may invite his son to share his ideas and explore the pros and cons of these ideas with his son as two functional steps in this conversation toward reaching his goal.

Finally, actions are organised in terms of their goals. Goals can be understood as the meaning of our actions and provide an important link to context and culture. The goal of a company team-building exercise provides certain actions with different meanings for the participating employees than the same behaviours would have in their private lives. We also recognise that these meanings are constructed socially, within language groups, cultures, and other groups. This understanding of action as a socially and subjectively co-constructed goal-oriented process is an important step in systematically analysing everyday processes and helpful to clients in facilitating change. The traditional view of describing action simply by the quantitative measures of elements, that is, specific behaviours, cannot capture the meaning of action.

Perspectives on action

CAT proposes and uses three perspectives to access and develop a full understanding of actions, projects, and career: manifest behaviour, internal processes, and goals. Action involves manifest behaviour that can be observed and recorded. A conversation between a counsellor and client is one in which certain things are said, nonverbal behaviours are present, and the conversation has a certain duration. During this conversation both counsellor and client experience many thoughts, emotions, and sensations. These are the internal processes that accompany action. Finally, action is seen in its social context by the actor and others who can answer the question, "What is this action about?" These three perspectives – the manifest, the subjective, and the social – reflect the way in which actions are experienced and understood in everyday life. None of these can be discounted or ignored if we want a comprehensive understanding of action.

Framing important issues in career theory

We propose CAT as a comprehensive and integrative framework for understanding career. As a framework, it must be able to address pertinent issues in the career field. For example, we recognise that constructionism is popular is the career theory and practice. CAT is founded on how actors and others construct their actions, projects, and career. Similarly, CAT's emphasis on joint action and the social embeddedness of projects and career reflect the relational nature of career. CAT also has important links to narrative and identity because the construction of narratives and identity are themselves action processes. CAT also highlights the intentionality by addressing the intention of the action rather than goals that exist outside of the action, and by extension, projects and career. Finally, CAT captures culture by asserting that culture is the field of action, as discussed later in this chapter.

Life-enhancing career

Everyone experiences some actions as more meaningful than others. We are more motivated in some projects than others. In addition, we experience our careers as life enhancing or not as life enhancing as we expected. For example, only 20 per cent of Canadians experience their occupational careers as very satisfying (life enhancing) (Statista, 2016). In CAT, we have identified 29 characteristics of meaningful actions, motivated projects, and life-enhancing careers (Young et al., 2015). For example, a life-enhancing career is often one that responds to an individual's needs for predictability and novelty. Similarly, projects cannot be successfully engaged in unless there are both personal and external resources available to engage in the project. Consider, for example, the external supports, such as available education and work programs, that a person with an intellectual disability may need in order to make the transition from secondary school to work. Emotion, emotional sensitivity, and emotional regulation are characteristics of meaningful actions, projects, and career. At the level of goals, actions and projects should be seen as leading to long-term meaning in life, and involve others in important ways. CAT allows for the identification of these and other characteristics that lead to life-enhancing careers and, when absent to a significant degree, lead away from careers that enhance our lives.

Cultural sensitivity

Career theories differ because they arise in different times and places, mirroring contextual and cultural factors. Arulmani (2014), for example, made a strong case for the connection between work, career, and culture. Virtually all career theories are highly reflective of the context and culture in which they emerged. This connection between the context and the theory is not a negative attribute of the theories. However, this characteristic can become problematic when a theory is assumed to be universal or used in cultures or contexts for which it was not developed as if it were a universal theory. In addition, a more explicit challenge of career theories is whether and how they address context. In the development of CAT, we wanted to ensure that the theory was able to encompass different cultures and contexts in a meaningful way rather than isolate them as variables to be controlled.

We have highlighted the importance of considering culture and cultural contexts in a number of places in our description of CAT. We contend that CAT is a culturally sensitive approach to understanding career, although we acknowledge that action theory generally has roots in Western psychology. Nonetheless, it is well recognised in the field of cultural psychology. Indeed, Eckensberger

(2015) proposed a culturally inclusive action theory, and human action as the unit of analysis, as the means to clarify the relationship between the individual and the culture. Such clarification is sorely needed when one considers that work and career are cultural phenomena (Arulmani, 2014).

Young, Marshall, and Valach (2007) argue that CAT is a way in which we can capture specific cultural phenomenon and at the same time be inclusive enough to "speak broadly across cultures" (p. 8). We begin by basing this approach on Boesch's (1991) definition of "culture," that is, "culture is the field of action" (p. 29). When Boesch states that culture is the field of action, he asserts that culture and action co-construct each other. Culture is also the field of projects and career. Both project and career involve more people over longer periods, so culture is represented in ways that are more complex and projects and careers serve to construct cultures in various ways. Cultural sensitivity in CAT is increased by recognising that actions are parts of ongoing processes, for example, understanding action in the larger context and over time, and by accepting that individuals will imbue action with personal meaning through their own narratives and folk explanations.

Case study

This fictitious case example explores the actions that occur between Perrine and her parents, Pierre and Manon, related to Perrine's process of deciding what post-secondary education options she should pursue. Perrine is a 19-year-old woman living in a French-speaking region of New Brunswick, Canada. French is the language spoken at home, as Pierre and Manon have limited English-language fluency.

Perrine is currently employed part time in the family's convenience store, where she works as a cashier and assists bookkeeping and inventory management. Perrine also volunteers as a tour guide at the local aquarium because she enjoys interacting with tourists and appreciates the opportunity to practice speaking English. Perrine maintains a strong social network, with several close friends whom she has known since childhood. In recent months, she has begun to worry that her friendship network is drifting apart, with friends moving away to pursue further education or employment. However, Perrine's primary source of social support is her parents; she considers her mother to be her "best friend."

Perrine's high school teachers had encouraged her to attend university because of her strong academic abilities. She delayed applying for financial reasons, and because she felt anxious about moving away from home. Although Pierre and Manon support the idea of their daughter pursuing higher education, neither of them attended university and, consequently, feel ill-equipped to guide her about this. Over the past few months, Perrine has realised that she enjoys many aspects of helping her father to run the family store and would like to pursue a career in business or entrepreneurship. The prospect of moving away from home has also become increasingly attractive to her as she transitions into adulthood. Consequently, she is currently thinking about post-secondary options that would allow her to learn more about the world of business and that would prepare her well for pursuing this career path.

One option Perrine is considering is a business administration degree in the province's largest university, which is an English-language institution located relatively far away from Perrine's hometown. She is attracted to this option because the program offers a specific focus on entrepreneurship, and because a university recruiter had told her that her chances of obtaining a scholarship were high. However, she is worried about her ability to complete coursework in English, and none of her friends attend that university.

In contrast, Perrine has two good friends who began attending the province's French-language university last year. They have encouraged Perrine to join them there. This university offers degrees in business administration. Although this option also requires her to relocate, Perrine believes that having friends who are already attending that university would help her to make the transition into university life. To complicate the situation, Perrine's mother recently found out that Perrine could complete the first two years of this degree at a satellite campus located in her hometown. This would allow Perrine to live at home and continue working at the family store. Perrine sees the financial merit in this option, but feels ambivalent about living at home for another two years. Furthermore, she does not want to tell her parents about her growing desire to move away, because she is concerned that this would hurt them emotionally. Privately, Perrine wonders whether the easiest way to avoid having this discussion would be to attend the English-language university instead.

Case analysis

When CAT is applied to Perrine's situation, it becomes evident that the task of planning for future education is occurring in a highly relational context; she is engaged in joint action and projects with her parents and friends. The central goal of one of these projects is figuring out where Perrine will pursue post-secondary education. This project is also intertwined with another project that she is beginning to undertake with her parents; the project of transitioning to adulthood. Although this latter project is still being formulated, the goal appears to be for the family to negotiate an appropriate balance between independence and closeness in their relationship as Perrine becomes an adult. The two projects are intertwined because actions taken with the intention to achieve one may have an impact on the other, and because Perrine is considering the goals of both projects together, as she pursues each one. For example, the possibility of moving out of the family home is a key aspect of both the transition to adulthood and the educational-choice projects.

The notion of goal-directed action undertaken in concert with others is evident throughout this case. Perrine is engaged in actions related to her educational-choice project with both her friends and her parents. She talks on the phone with her friends about their experience at the French-language university, and Perrine has visited them at school. Perrine also engages in ongoing discussions with her parents about her options for next year, discussions in which everyone feels free to share ideas and voice their hopes and doubts. Both she and Manon are actively involved in searching for information about the universities, with Manon extending this search to seeking advice and information about post-secondary education options from her own friends. Pierre's project-related joint actions with his daughter are more limited, consisting primarily of reassuring Perrine that he supports whatever choice is made. Pierre also discusses the possibility of Perrine continuing to work in the store over the summer tourist season, even if she moves away for school.

In analysing this case, it must also be understood that Perrine is unlikely to seek support from a career counselling professional: she is self-motivated and, when she is in need of assistance, would be more likely to seek support from her social network than from a stranger. Moreover, her opportunities to access career counselling are limited by her circumstances. She has graduated high school but is not yet in university, which prevents her from accessing school-based career services. Therefore, like many young people in Canada, Perrine would actually choose to make the decision about what educational path to pursue with assistance from friends and family. However, if Perrine did decide to seek career counselling, we believe that it would be useful to work with her using the CAT-informed approach to counselling that we have described in Young and colleagues (2015). This theory of counselling is integrated with but distinct from the theory of career development that we have described in this chapter and, as such, is beyond the scope of what we are able to discuss here.

Case study: reflective questions

1   What role do Perrine's family and friends play in her planning for future school and work?
2   To what degree are Perrine's linguistic and cultural background important factors in understanding her career development?
3   Perrine's volunteer work can be conceptualised as a joint project between herself and aquarium staff. What goals and actions are associated with this project?

Research in brief 2

Marshall et al. (2011) examined the career-related projects and actions of adolescents and their parents from Indigenous families living in an urban setting in Canada. The participants engaged in conversations (joint actions) about the adolescent's future, and subsequently had an opportunity to identify their joint project in light of the researchers' input. Four types of projects occurred. Some projects involved working toward a safe future. Some projects were designed to facilitate the adolescent completing their schooling, including exploring alternative schooling options. Some projects were oriented toward preparing adolescents to enter into the adult world as people who care for others. Finally, some families experienced the deaths of family members or friends, loss of secure housing, and deterioration of parents' health. In these cases, the project of "family survival" became top priority. This study not only confirms the importance of relationships to urban-residing Indigenous adolescents' career development, but also illustrates the ways in which career development actions are interwoven with cultural values and unexpected life circumstances.

Research in brief: reflective questions

1   What kinds of career goals appear to be informing the four types of projects in which these families were engaged?
2   In what ways could the participants' Indigenous culture have exerted an influence on the findings that emerged?
3   As a career counsellor, how would you respond to Indigenous adolescent clients whose career development projects were subsumed by a family survival project?

Summary

CAT has several strengths as a framework for understanding and describing how careers are constructed. As previously described, it is a culturally sensitive approach to career development that can be used in a wide range of socio-cultural contexts. Previous research grounded in CAT has successfully explored aspects of career development in Canadians of European ancestry, Chinese Canadians, and Indigenous people, among others. The research support behind CAT is another strength of the theory: There have been over 20 years of work elaborating the theory, and refining it based on the findings of studies conducted not only in the field of career psychology but also in the fields of human development, mental health, and nursing (Young et al., 2015). As such, it is well grounded in research evidence. Finally, CAT also has a systematic approach to practice associated with it; we have articulated five general tasks for counselling within a CAT framework (Domene et al., 2015): developing a working alliance, unpacking how actions are organised in the client's life, addressing specific problems and emotion, and establishing the connection with the client's daily life. Valach and Young (2012) also provided an extensive case illustration of the use of CAT in counselling. As this case shows, CAT can be integrated and used with other intervention approaches.

CAT offers an important and radically different way to understand how people construct life-enhancing careers and have meaningful lives. As with any emerging theory, its relative newness invites more empirical and theoretical work to extend and refine our understanding of these processes, including how career counsellors can work with them in practice. For example, one future direction is to continue exploring the implementation of the five tasks and the effectiveness of its uniquely designed interventions. Another direction is to investigate how CAT can inform counselling, as it is likely to be used in actual practice, in conjunction with other counselling modalities.

The strength of CAT's compatibility with interventions drawn from a variety of other approaches also leads to a limitation with the theory. The theory has relatively few distinct interventions of its own, and those are difficult to isolate for study. As such, the existing research support for CAT is based primarily on its merit for understanding clients' presenting problems in context. Research on specific CAT-based intervention strategies is only beginning to emerge. This limitation also reveals the most important future direction for CAT: developing and systematically studying CAT-based interventions. Consequently, the direction of our current work is aimed at expanding the evidence base for CAT-informed counselling.

To conclude, we have proposed CAT as a way to understand career development from the perspective of goal-directed action. In the theory we differentiate actions, projects, and careers in terms of their time span, describe how goal-directed action is organised (elements, functional steps, goals), and identify several perspectives required to understand the complexity of action (manifest, subjective, social). We also delineate the cultural sensitivity of the theory. As such, we argue that CAT provides a distinct and highly useful way to understand the way that goals for future work and life are jointly constructed and pursued by people in a diverse range of socio-cultural settings.

Learning activities

Learning activity 1: perspectives on projects

Think about something related to your home or work life in which you are currently engaged with at least one other person – that is, a joint project. Describe this project in terms of:

1   Social meaning (i.e., If you were to describe this project to someone else, how would you explain the meaning and purpose of the project?)
2   Subjective internal processes (i.e., What cognitions, emotions, and sensations that you and the other people who are part of the project may experience when the project is accomplished?)
3   Manifest behaviours (i.e., How would someone who is observing but not interacting with you be able to tell that all of you are engaged in this project together?)

Learning activity 2: a CAT understanding of action

Using the project that you described in Learning Activity 1 or another project of your choosing, keep a diary of your project-related actions for one week. Record actions taken towards achieving the project, specifying:

1 What were the behavioural elements of that action (e.g., introducing yourself to a prospective employer, describing how you could contribute to the company, responding to interview questions)?
2 What was the primary goal of that action (e.g., in contrast to a job interview, the primary goal of an informational interview may be to find out what it is like to work in a particular profession or company)?
3 Who, if anyone, else was involved in the action (e.g., the interviewer)?
4 What were your own thoughts and feelings as you engaged in these actions?

At the end of the week, review your diary to identify recurrent patterns in the elements and goals of your project-related actions: What do these patterns tell you about how you organise your actions and who are involved in the project with you?

Learning activities: reflective questions

1 CAT asserts that projects tend to be jointly undertaken with other people. To what degree have these assertions been evident in your own life?
2 How might the concepts of CAT help to expand your understanding of client experiences in your counselling practice?
3 Consider CAT in light of the other career development theories presented in this book: What concepts in this theory overlap with concepts from other theories, and what concepts are unique to CAT?

References

Arulmani, G. (2014). The cultural preparation process model and career development. In G. Arulmani, A. J. Bakshi, F. T. L. Leong, & T. Watts (Eds.), *Handbook of career development: International perspectives* (pp. 81–103). New York: Springer.
Boesch, E. E. (1991). *Symbolic action theory and cultural psychology.* New York: Springer-Verlag.
Castelleni, M. (2013). Alfred Schutz and Herbert Simon: Can their theories of action work together? *Journal for the Theory of Social Behavior, 43,* 383–404.

Domene, J. F., Nee, J. J., Cavanaugh, A. K., McLelland, S., Stewart, B. L., Stephenson, M., & Young, R. A. (2012). Young adult couples transitioning to work: The intersection of career and relationship. *Journal of Vocational Behavior, 18,* 17–25.

Domene, J. F., Valach, L., & Young, R. A. (2015). Action in counseling: A contextual action theory perspective. In R. A. Young, J. F. Domene, & L. Valach (Eds.), *Counseling and action: Toward life-enhancing work, relationships, and identity* (pp. 151–166). New York: Springer Science+Business Media.

Eckensberger, L. (2015). Integrating the emic (indigenous) with the etic (universal) – a case of squaring the circle or for adopting a culture inclusive action theory perspective. *Journal for the Theory of Social Behavior, 45,* 108–140.

European Political Strategy Centre. (2016). The future of work: Skills and resilience for a world of change. Issue 13, June 10, 2016, European Commission. http://ec.europa.eu/epsc/publications/strategic-notes/future-work_en Downloaded 21 June 2017.

Marshall, S. K., Young, R. A., Stevens, A., Spence, W., Deyell, S., Easterbrook, A., & Brokenleg, M. (2011). Adolescent career development in urban-residing Aboriginal families in Canada. *The Career Development Quarterly, 59,* 539–558.

Statista. (2016). How satisfied are you with your current employment situation overall? Retrieved from www.statista.com/statistics/683194/canadian-employmee-satisfaction. Retrieved 28 September 2017.

Valach, L., & Young, R. A. (2012). The case study of therapy with a Swiss woman. In S. Poyrazli, & C. E. Thompson (Eds.), *International case studies in mental health* (pp. 13–32). Thousand Oaks, CA: SAGE.

von Cranach, M., Ochsenbein, G., & Valach, L. (1986). The group as a self-active system: Outline of a theory of group action. *European Journal of Social Psychology, 16,* 193–229.

Young, R. A., Domene, J. F., & Valach, L. (Eds.) (2015). *Counseling and action: Toward life-enhancing work, relationships and identity.* New York: Springer.

Young, R. A., Marshall, S. K., & Valach, L. (2007). Making career theories more culturally sensitive: Implications for counseling. *The Career Development Quarterly, 56,* 4–18.

7 Career construction for life design
Practice and theory

Paul J. Hartung and Logan Vess

Learning objectives

The purpose of this chapter is to:

- discuss the origin and core principles of career construction theory and practice;
- explain the content and purpose of the career construction interview; and
- describe the processes of career construction interviewing, life portraiture, and action.

> Practice leads theory, not the other way around.
>
> M. L. Savickas (2015, p. 7)

Introduction to career construction theory

Evolved from over 40 years of counselling practice to address the complexities of 21st-century life, career construction comprises a theory of vocational behaviour (Savickas, 2013) and a system of career counselling (Savickas, 2011). Unique among career theories, career construction uses practice innovations to guide theory development. That is because career construction recognises that fluctuating client needs demand flexible counsellor responses untethered to strict theoretical principles (Savickas, 2015). Career construction counselling practice therefore leads career construction theory development in a reciprocal relationship of practice advances and theory building. This chapter overviews career construction: its origins, key principles, practice method, and validity for use in diverse contexts. A case study is then presented to demonstrate career construction counselling.

Origins

The roots of career construction (Savickas, 2011, 2013) can be traced to the early 20th-century vocational guidance movement and the advent of the matching model (Parsons, 1909). These roots spread to 20th-century advances in developmental (Super, 1990) and differential (Holland, 1997) career psychology. Today, career construction stands firmly rooted in 21st-century life design (Nota & Rossier, 2015; Savickas et al., 2009).

Career construction counselling originally derived from principles and practices of Adlerian psychotherapy, particularly the focus on early memory narratives and life-style assessment (Savickas, 2009). Later, career construction counselling used personal construct and biographical hermeneutic approaches to focus on meaning-making and life themes. Moving from psychological constructivism to firm grounding in social constructionism, career construction counselling (Savickas, 2011) assists clients to author and enact career stories that connect self-concepts to work roles, fit work into life, achieve self-completion, and make social contributions through work.

Theoretical principles

Career construction unifies and expands on the respective traditions of person–environment fit emphasising dispositional traits, life-span development emphasising developmental tasks, and narrative emphasising life themes (Savickas, 2013). This synthesis allows viewing individuals as (a) social *actors* who display personality types that fit corresponding work environments; (b) motivated *agents* who develop readiness to fit work into a constellation of life roles; and (c) autobiographical *authors* who use self-reflection to fashion their careers by constructing self-defining narratives (Savickas, 2011, 2015). Combined, these three perspectives offer a comprehensive and synergistic view on life-careers.

Traits – social reputation

Career construction uses the individual differences perspective to comprehend career choice *content* as a function of matching traits, or socially situated reputation to occupational environments. Career choice content reflects *what* specific job or occupation a person chooses and enacts. When reputation (i.e., traits like interests, abilities, and personality in the P–E fit lexicon) aligns with congruent job characteristics and requirements, one succeeds as an actor who fits a corresponding work role.

Tasks – career adaptability

Career construction uses the individual development perspective to comprehend career growth and change as a life-long *process*. Career choice process concerns *how* individuals manage life roles, navigate transitions, and meet social expectations about work across the life course. When individuals deal effectively with developmental tasks they succeed as agents in managing their careers and fitting work into their lives. Adapting to life-span developmental concerns readies self to more effectively manage work roles.

Themes – life project

Career construction uses the individual design perspective to construe the *meaning* individuals give to work as a reflection of their life projects. In an unstable and uncertain world, people often look within themselves to their own stories to create stability and certainty. Identity narratives in the form of self-defining stories convey life projects that carry meaning about *why* people move in different life-career directions. When individuals coherently narrate their life themes and enact them with purposeful engagement in vocational choice and adjustment they succeed as authors of work in their lives.

Practice method

Career construction counselling assists individuals to attain a clear sense of self, identity, and mission by narrating their life stories. A *Career Construction Interview* (CCI; Savickas, 2011) begins career construction counselling. Constructing a life portrait and action planning follow the CCI.

Career Construction Interview

The CCI contains six questions about counselling goals; role models; favourite magazines, TV shows, and web sites; favourite book or movie; favourite saying; and early recollections. These questions elicit, in turn, stories about the client's (a) counselling expectations, current problem, and the solution he or she already has in mind for it; (b) self-concept, or reputation as the lead actor in his or her own career story; (c) manifest vocational interests in places where the client wants to enact his or her self-concept; (d) script connecting his or her self-concept and interests into a life plan that can be authored; (e) self-advice in the form of the client's best inner wisdom and guidance for moving ahead; and (f) perspective on the current problem. As the client relates self-defining responses to CCI questions, the counsellor listens closely, asks follow-up questions, and makes reflective statements to clarify meaning. The counsellor and client then use the client's responses to all six CCI questions to co-construct a life-career portrait.

Life-career portrait

Using the answers to the CCI shapes a larger narrative, or portrait, that tells the career story with greater coherence, continuity, and clarity. Constructing a life-career portrait aims to promote understanding of the client's perspective on the problem (arc), chosen solution (actor), preferred stage (agent), workable script (author), and action plan (advice). Reflecting on the career story leads to setting goals and taking action for the next episode of the life-career.

Action

After constructing a life portrait, attention turns to action. This involves constructing a success formula and making a realistic action plan. Subsequently, counsellors encourage clients to tell their stories to valued audiences outside of the counselling context in their most cherished interpersonal relationships. Telling and talking about the career story and the conclusions drawn from the counselling process with valued audiences promotes making it more real and clear and feeling more confident in living it. Valued audiences typically include family members, friends, mentors, coaches, and teachers. Performing the story by identifying specific action to take increases exploration, commitment, and goal attainment.

Cultural validity

Evidence for the cross-cultural validity of career construction theory derives especially from work on career adaptability (for reviews, see Johnston, 2016; Rossier, 2015). Several published case studies support career construction counselling as an effective career intervention in the United States (e.g., Barclay & Stoltz, 2016; Savickas, 2009), South Africa (Maree, 2015, 2016), Italy (Hartung & Santilli, 2017), and other countries. The effectiveness of the CCI in these case study demonstrations underscores the usefulness of narrative interventions in helping people to create meaningful occupational futures. Meanwhile, qualitative studies indicate usefulness of the CCI for promoting client career awareness, self-confidence, sense of direction, and confirmation of their career path (Rehfuss, del Corso, Glavin, & Wykes, 2011) as well as identifying life themes and making meaningful career decisions (Rehfuss, Cosio, & del Corso, 2011). A process analysis supported prior research indicating the usefulness of career construction counselling for promoting self-reflective action (Hartung & Vess, 2016). Career construction counselling is further supported by several studies published in a *Journal of Vocational Behavior* special issue (Savickas & Guichard, 2016). A career construction workbook also has been initially supported by research (Hartung & Santilli, 2018) and has been translated in several languages, including Portuguese, Italian, Chinese, French, and German (see www.vocopher.com).

Research in brief

Career adaptability

Career adaptability denotes psychosocial resources for making changes in self and situation that involves:

concern about the future as a worker;
control over career decision-making and the future;
curiosity to explore possible selves and future work scenarios; and
confidence to pursue vocational aspirations and deal with barriers.

Career adaptability has become a topic of great interest for researchers around the world. Savickas and Porfeli (2012) introduced measurement of the construct of career adaptability through the *Career Adapt-Abilities Scale* (CAAS), validated by researchers across 13 different countries. The CAAS allows researchers to measure individuals' levels of career adaptability across the dimensions of concern, control, curiosity, and confidence. Career adaptability now offers a cross-nationally valid conceptual and practical frame for assisting individuals to manage their careers within changing world and local economies and job markets. This is due in large part to a wealth of literature that has accumulated to map the conceptual network and measurement of the construct (Rossier, 2015; Savickas, 2013; Savickas & Porfeli, 2012). For example, Zacher (2014) investigated the validity of the CAAS for indicating subjective career success beyond personality traits and self-evaluations. The heterogeneous sample included 1,732 employees living in Australia. Results indicated that overall levels of career adaptability positively predicted respondents' career satisfaction and self-rated career performance beyond personality traits and self-evaluations.

Research in brief: reflective questions

1   How would you broach the subject of career adaptability with your clients?
2   Of the four dimension of career adaptability (concern, control, curiosity, confidence), which do you believe is most salient for authoring the next chapter in one's career story?
3   How does career adaptability serve individuals in a world where work and jobs are less stable and continually changing?

Case study

Sonya (a pseudonym), a 24-year-old single White woman, sought career counselling. She held a bachelor's degree in architecture, and was currently pursuing a master's degree in architecture and urban design. Following is the client–counsellor dialogue containing Sonya's responses to the CCI questions, with the counsellor's clarifying questions and responses in italics and responses to the CCI items in bold.

1.   How can I be useful to you in constructing your career? I hope to accomplish a little more clarity in what I might want to do. *You said, 'a little more clarity,' so there are already some things you know. What are you thinking of?* Kind of what I figured out is that what I think I don't want to do is be an architect. I think I'm a little more interested in the urban design side. I've also had thoughts of even just teaching, maybe at the college level. I have a lot of other interests, even psychology.

2.   Who were your childhood role models? **Jane Goodall**. She did a lot of research and work that nobody had done before. She did all this traveling and

spent all this time studying. *Tell me one more thing when you think about her.* I think about her as a humanitarian. Just trying to do good for the world. **Second-grade teacher**. She was really fun, very positive, very upbeat, and caring. She always was very creative and interested in our well-being and our education. **Hermione Granger (*Harry Potter*)**. She was very committed to school and working hard. She was always keeping the other characters out of trouble and helping people. She always knew what to do. She was very committed and dedicated to her friends and family.

3.   What are your favourite magazines, TV shows, or websites? *Runner's World* (**magazine**). I ran cross-country and track in high school. *Parks and Recreation* (**television show**). It centers around this one character. She's really into government and politics and doing what's best for people and her community. It's about community and the relationships she has with her coworkers and friends. '**Manifesto**' (**a song by The City Harmonic**). They're a Christian band, the main chorus is: 'We believe in the one true God.' *What else does it say?* We believe in the father, spirit, son.

4.   What is your current favourite story from a book or movie? A story I always come back to is *The Shawshank Redemption*. It's about a man who gets convicted of murder. You find out he's innocent, but he gets sent to prison for a really long time. He never really gives up hope. He forms relationships and becomes this guy who sort of stands out from everyone else. Others kind of give up and give in to the fact that they are going to be in prison for the rest of their lives. He makes a lot of changes in the prison. He was really smart and he starts teaching people to get their GEDs and setting up the library and changes a lot of things. He escapes the prison. They find out he is innocent, but it's kind of a corrupt system.

5.   What is your favourite saying? I have a **favourite verse from the bible**: Let us run, with perseverance, the race marked out for us fixing our eyes on Jesus the author and perfecter of our faith. For the joy set before him, endured the cross, scorning its shame and sat down at the right hand at the throne of God. *What does that mean to you?* Fix my eyes on the goal ahead and the strength that Christ gives me to do that, to endure.

6.   What are your three earliest memories (with headlines)? '**Explore**.' I remember we had this bassinet. I have a memory of looking out. I'm lying on my back in there and I'm looking out. I'm seeing my mom and the people around me. *How did you feel as you were laying there looking out?* I think curious. A lot of curiosity and looking at the world around me.

'**Girl in Her Own Little World**.' I was maybe 3 or 4. I'm lying on the floor of my grandparents' house. My blanket is on top of me and I'm watching a show called *Arthur*. *What else happens?* I learned little lessons from watching the show. *You were snuggled up watching your shows. How did that feel watching your show?* Very cozy. It was a very comfortable thing.

'**Girl Ready to Go to Disney**.' I think I was 4. I went to Disneyworld. I remember being in the parking lot and having to put on my jacket. I had this pink jacket that had Minnie Mouse on it. I have this memory of putting the jacket on and walking toward the park, but we are still in the parking lot. It's not even really the fun part of the trip! *How did you feel?* I was excited because we were getting ready to go into the park. I think I was little bit annoyed that I had to put my jacket on. But it was a little chilly. *You were ready to go.* I was ready to roll.

Life portrait

In the second session, using Sonya's answers to the CCI questions, the counsellor worked with her to construct a life portrait as seen in Table 7.1. The client and counsellor used this life portrait to co-construct a new story leading Sonya to more intentional decision-making and action as supported in a process analysis of the case (Hartung & Vess, 2016). The client responses appear in italics. The following life portrait begins where client and counsellor ended:

Perspective

I am listening for how you construct and make sense of certain things and the last question I ask about the earliest recollections is the most important and the

Table 7.1 Sonya's life-career portrait

Perspective Early recollections	*I am concerned about: exploring, being curious, but being on my back, and getting ready to go.*
Self Role models	**I am/I am becoming a person who:** *does things no one ever did before, develops new theories, is very committed, creative, and an innovator, creates new things and goes places that haven't been explored before.*
Setting Magazines TV shows Websites	**I like being places where people do activities such as:** *government, politics, and doing what's best for people and the community. Build relationships with coworkers and friends, and have fun. Help people grow and change. Have a deeply religious commitment.*
Script Favourite story from book or movie	**The plot of my favourite book or movie is:** *maintaining hope, forming relationships, and corrupt systems; never giving up hope.* **Therefore, in these places I want to:** *fight against corrupt systems, make a lot of changes, teach people, and build communities.*
Success formula Self Setting Script	**I will be most happy and successful when I am able to be:** *a committed innovator who creates new things in places where people use government and politics to do what's best for communities, build relationships, have fun, and live their religious commitments so that I can fight against corrupt systems, make significant changes, teach people, and build communities.*
Self-advice Motto	**To apply my success formula now, the best advice I can give myself is:** *fix my eyes on the goal ahead and the strength that Christ gives me to endure.*

most personal. The reason I ask it last is so that we have already built a relationship. There is a reason you remember those memories out of thousands that you could remember, you recall the one that you need to hear yourself right now. Your inner authority and inner knowledge of who you are chose certain stories and it's my job to try and insist that you listen to you and hear what you said.

The theme of the first story is, 'I want to explore, but I am on my back.' You were curious, you were looking around at the world. Things were new to you. You were taking in information about the world. That is what you are doing right now. You are in the bassinet called 'a semester of architecture.' You became awfully curious about 'what do I want to do with this degree?' and 'what do I want to do with my life?' You are a very committed person—once you choose, you finish the race. You are not just going to bounce from thing to thing. You are telling yourself, you are lying on your back, a little bit helpless, but so curious. You are wondering what can you do with the training you have received. So, as I am saying this, what goes through your head? *I think that sounds right!*

The second story is 'Girl in Her Own Little World.' I am lying on the floor, but not trapped in the bassinet. I have a blanket on top, I am secure and I feel safe. So, I am in this architecture program. I am curious. I like to explore, but I am safe here. Does that sound like anybody you know? *Yes!*

'Girl Ready to Go,' that is why you are talking with me today. You are done lying around. You are ready to go. You are in the parking lot, you are not in the field exactly where you want to be. You are a little annoyed because you are still doing this stuff that you are not 100 percent committed to. You are excited because, 'I am getting ready to go.' You know that the degree program is ending in a year. You are in the parking lot now. You are ready to go. Does that feel right? *That definitely resonates. . . . Yes all of that.*

Self

So, where does Sonya go? A little more clarity would help. For the role model question: Who were the blueprints for the design of Sonya? She is part Jane Goodall, part her second-grade teacher, part Hermione. Here are some things that are very important to you: research, doing things that no one has done before. Developing new theories. Hermione was very committed to school, but creative. So, what I heard you say here is the creativity is very important to you. Part of urban design scares you, being stuck at a desk, because in your heart you are an innovator. You want to create new things and go places that haven't been explored before. Your biggest fear is your creativity being stifled. Between architecture and urban design, the design is important. You are a designer, an innovator, and a developer. What is happening for you as I say these words? *It all makes sense. These are things that I have come to recognise. But it is something different to hear someone else say it back to me. It gives a little more weight to hear somebody else say it. Not just like to read something I resonate with but . . . this is something you are pulling from things that I have said and pulling from what was shaped from the first interview. It gives more weight to these things that I have thought about.* When things are said out loud they become more true.

Script

Your favourite story is about what is happening now and next. It is like a preview of the next 5 to 10 years of your life. He's innocent, but they put him in jail anyway. He has to go to prison for a long time—that's called architecture school. But she never gives up hope that someday she will graduate. But while he's there, he makes changes in the prison. He thinks outside the box, and what does he set up? Do you remember? A school! He fought against a corrupt system. *Yeah.* Remember, I said you were not interested in personal pathology? You are interested in political pathology. Corrupt systems. What just went through your mind? *I think that makes sense. Even thinking about things that I am passionate about, like social justice. I feel pretty strongly about things like human trafficking. I actually worked for a nonprofit years ago that did international development work.* Social justice is a part of your next chapter, the next 5 to 10 years of your life as you grow in the roles that you take, you will be an advocate for people against corrupt systems. Sometimes you are going to speak up even at your own cost. One corrupt system will be anything rotten in the school where you teach. You grow and grow and you help communities, cities, and it might even be a national role. You know all these parts are there but you never made the step until now into integrating them into one beautiful thing. *Yeah.*

Setting

My question about television shows and magazines, that is my question of interests. Through your answers we found that you are interested in government, politics, doing what is best for the community, the importance of the community, and seeing how people grow. How does this happen? Through your personal manifesto. Remember I said we were looking for themes? This is why we are beginning to repeat ourselves. You can do all of this because you are bright, and more important than bright you are a hard worker. You are committed.

Self-advice

So, Sonya is saying, 'What do I have to do next?' The motto is now advice to the self. Here is what you said: 'Fix your eye on a goal and move ahead.' So, you need to explore, fix the picture, which is getting pretty clear. 'Let us run, with perseverance'—no problem, you have been doing that forever. Once you are committed, you learn to run through pain, run through rain, run through storms. You can get that done. Christ has marked a path for you, but you are complicit. There is also a co-author. Yes. There is also your freedom to be a saint or a sinner. So, the race I have set for myself, fixing my eyes on the goal, the author and perfecter of our faith. Sonya, you are the author and perfecter of your life, your career. You have done such great rehearsal. You did not do it alone. You did it with grandparents, parents, friends, teachers, and with a community of believers. They have helped you to this wonderful point where you now must make a commitment, a year from now. Author it, perfect it, and go forward. That's the gospel of Sonya. *I think that's pretty good.* How does it feel? *It feels like pieces that I already knew but are coming together more to frame a picture. It's got me starting to think, 'What does that look like?'* You told me how you are thinking about this, but how are you feeling? *A little bit excited, a little bit of fear. I have a feeling of a deeper understanding and confidence in all these pieces. I remember seeing them as pieces, but not recognising what that meant and how that came together. Before it felt like a lot of pieces and parts that I did not know what to do with.*

Action

The three feelings for today were (a) annoyed because I can't figure this out, (b) very curious, and (c) ready to explore. If we read it backwards, you can see this in your early recollections: explore, annoyed, curious! Now that you are more confident to admit to yourself the integrative possibilities—no longer questions of 'should I do architecture, should I do urban design, should I do psychology, should I teach, should I help build communities?' The answer is yes! Yes, yes, yes! You have known this for a long time in your soul. But, your spirit has not recognised it until now. You started doing this when you were a little girl. You have been rehearsing and rehearsing and now it comes together in the emergent truth. Not only do you believe in Christ, but now you can believe in Sonya. On the ride home, you will figure out step one, step two, and step three. You are made to be a professor. You are made to profess in the school, in the church, and in the community. So, who do you sit down with next to get that 'taking in information' and 'exploring'? There must be more people to talk to. *Yeah. I think some of the faculty, because they are doing what I am interested in. I want to know how they got there. Maybe even I could reach out to an architect who I worked with at the nonprofit. It's actually a Christian organisation. It all comes together! I guess that would be a place to start.* Who would you be comfortable admitting to that you would like to become a professor? *I think I would talk to the faculty about that. I think I have talked a little bit about it to my friends and family.* I'm wondering, is there anybody back in Indiana where you did your undergraduate degree who is worth a drive back and talking to? *I actually reached out to a guy who was on staff there that studied architecture and then went into ministry.* You have a network and resources there. I believe that you have the confidence to say this out loud. *Yes, I do.* When we sat down you weren't so sure. Now you are announcing, 'This is my coming out to the world. I am no longer an architecture major. This is unique to me. I resemble people in my class, but I am unique in this way.' *Yes.* How are your parents going to hear this? *I think they will be pretty open to it. I have already been having conversations about this. They already know I do not want to be an architect. So, I think when I first start talking about different things in under-grad it kind of scared them. But now they see there is this explorer side of me. I have done a lot of things that my siblings have not done.* She started off in the bassinet, and she was looking out saying 'I want to explore!' *Yeah! They have come to a point that they have recognised these things. I don't think they will be surprised.* Anything else we should talk about? *I don't think so.* Okay, I'd like to read back to you, what was our goal for today, what were we trying to achieve. You said, 'I'd like a little bit of clarity about my interests.' Did we do that? *Yes.* 'Figure out what I might do next.' Did we do that? *Yes, I believe so.*

Case study: reflective questions

1   After reading the case study about Sonya, how would you con-ceptualise her career adaptability at this point?
2   What did you notice that the counsellor did to foster critical moments for Sonya in conducting the *Career Construction Interview*?
3   How do Sonya's early memories give her some perspective on her current career problem?

Summary and conclusions

The case study outlined in this chapter adds to the growing literature about career construction for life-design counselling. Continuing research on the cru-cial elements of life design counselling is essential to aid both researchers and practitioners in understanding what leads to effective outcomes. An analysis of the case study (Hartung & Vess, 2016) provided critical insight into the factors that led to the desired outcomes of the *Career Construction Interview*, includ-ing reflexivity, career decision-making, and narratability. These factors also provide educators and counsellors-in-training with specific examples of how to foster the essential elements of life-design counselling in session.

A limitation of the Hartung and Vess (2016) study lies in its single-case-study design. Results from a single case study provide limited generalisability. Addi-tionally, the perspective of individuals conducting the analysis of life-design counselling could have inadvertently affected the questions and analysis of the session, leading to a bias in the results. To alleviate this, future research should consider using individuals who are unfamiliar with career construction coun-selling to conduct the analysis. As mentioned, future research could add to the previous case studies regarding life-design counselling and provide additional insight into the factors that lead to successful outcomes.

Steeped in years of practical and conceptual innovation, career construction theory and counselling offer a novel and useful approach for understanding and fostering work in people's lives. Rather than matching self to occupation or readying self to develop a career, career construction shifts the focus to constructing self in work. Career construction theory integrates person–environment fit, life-span development, and life-design traditions. Career construction counselling entails an interpersonal process of helping people author career stories that connect their self-concepts to work roles, fit work into life, and make meaning through work. Using the narrative paradigm, career construction counselling prompts a client–counsellor co-construction process that empowers individuals to author life-career stories that enhance their experiences of work as personally meaningful and socially useful.

Learning activities

A prevalent theme in the outcomes of the case study was the counsellor's ability to listen to and re-tell the client's story. This skill takes considerable practice and can be honed by listening for the important parts of an individual's story. To facilitate this process, instructors can use this two-part learning activity adapted from Lara and Vess (2014).

The goals for this learning activity are to assist learners' conceptualisation of the narrative nature of life-design counselling. Learners will develop an understanding of life design and narrative career intervention, which differ from the matching models of vocational guidance. Learners will hone their actively listening skills as they hear another individual's narrative, paying close attention to themes.

The instructional part of the lesson will take approximately 1 hour and 30 minutes to complete. The experiential component of the lesson and discussion can be completed in approximately 1 hour.

A personal narrative such as the case study presented in this chapter can be used. Alternatively, short audio narratives are available through Storycorps on the National Public Radio website (www.npr.org/series/4516989/storycorps/), or the instructor may request a colleague to share his or her career story.

Part I

First, the instructor emphasises the use of storytelling in counselling, highlighting the information covered in this chapter. Further, the instructor provides an overview of life design.

Part II

Next, the instructor emphasises the use of storytelling in counselling, highlighting the information covered in this chapter. The instructor may facilitate a brief discussion of how repeated words and verbs in one's narrative connect to that individual's life story. This can be achieved by asking learners open questions such as: 'What do you believe the significance of a storyteller using the verb "run" many times throughout their career story?'

Instructors should remind learners that it is not the place of the counsellor to interpret the narrative, only to ask clarifying questions to aid in the individual's development of their own personal career narrative. Clients are the experts on their own lives.

With the narrative materials selected (i.e., case study, audio narrative, or guest speaker), the instructor guides learners to create two columns on a sheet of paper, one for repeated words and the other for verbs. Learners are instructed to listen for examples, either while listening to or reading the narrative and write them down. If the story is being told live, the instructor may ask clarifying questions to the storyteller providing clarity as the information is shared. Once the narrative has reached its end, instructors may use the following questions for further discussion.

Learning activities: reflective questions

1   What words did you notice the storyteller repeating? How do these words connect with any themes present in the story?
2   What verbs did you notice the storyteller using? How might these verbs connect to action the storyteller will take to address his or her own potential career story challenges?
3   What is the significance of listening for a client's story in the context of his or her career narrative?

References

Barclay, S. R., & Stoltz, K. B. (2016). The life-design group: A case study assessment. *The Career Development Quarterly*, 64, 83–96.

Hartung, P. J., & Santilli, S. (2018). My Career Story: Description and initial validity evidence. *Journal of Career Assessment*, 26(2), 308–321.

Hartung, P. J., & Santilli, S. (2017). The theory and practice of career construction. In M. McMahon (Ed.) *Career counseling: Constructivist approaches* (2nd ed., pp. 174–184). Abingdon, Oxon: Routledge.

Hartung, P. J., & Vess, L. (2016). Critical moments in career construction counseling. *Journal of Vocational Behavior*, 97, 31–39.

Holland, J. L. (1997). *Making vocational choices* (3rd ed.). Odessa, FL: Psychological Assessment Resources.

Johnston, C. S. (2016). A systematic review of the career adaptability literature and future outlook. *Journal of Career Assessment*, 26(1), 1–28.

Lara, T. L., & Vess, L. R. (2014) Life trajectories: Teaching counselors how to assist clients with their working lives. *VISTAS 2014*. Retrieved from www.counseling.org/docs/default-source/vistas/article_47.pdf?sfvrsn=8

Maree, J. G. (2015). Career construction counseling: A thematic analysis of outcomes for four clients. *Journal of Vocational Behavior*, 86, 1–9.

Maree, J. G. (2016). Career construction counseling with a mid-career black male. *The Career Development Quarterly, 64*, 20–34.

NotaL., & Rossier, J. (Eds.). (2015). *Handbook of life design: From practice to theory, from theory to practice* (pp. 89–102). Göttingen, Germany: Hogrefe.

Parsons, F. (1909). *Choosing a vocation*. Boston, MA: Houghton-Mifflin.

Rehfuss, M. C., Cosio, S., & del Corso, J. (2011). Counselors' perspectives on using the career style interview with clients. *The Career Development Quarterly, 59*, 208–218. doi:10.1002/j.2161–0045.2011.tb00064.x

Rehfuss, M. C., del Corso, J., Glavin, K., & Wykes, S. (2011). Impact of the career style interview on individuals with career concerns. *Journal of Career Assessment, 19*, 405–419.

Rossier, J. (2015). Career adaptability and life designing. In L. Nota & J. Rossier (Eds.) *Handbook of life design: From practice to theory and from theory to practice* (pp. 153–167). Boston, MA: Hogrefe.

Savickas, M. L. (2009). Career-style counseling. In T. Sweeney (Ed.), *Adlerian counseling and psychotherapy: A practitioner's approach* (5th ed., pp. 183–207). Muncie, IN: Accelerated Development Press.

Savickas, M. L. (2011). *Career counseling*. Washington, D. C.: American Psychological Association Books, Inc.

Savickas, M. L. (2013). The theory and practice of career construction. In S. Brown & R. Lent (Eds.) *Career development and counseling: Putting theory and research to work* (2nd ed., pp. 147–183). New York: John Wiley.

Savickas, M. L. (2015). *Life-design counseling manual*. Rootstown, OH: Author.

Savickas, M. L., & Guichard, J. (Eds.). (2016). Special issue: Research on the process of narrative career counseling. *Journal of Vocational Behavior, 97*, 1–90.

Savickas, M. L., Nota, L., Rossier, J., Dauwalder, J., Duarte, M. E., Guichard, J., . . . van Vianen, A. E. M. (2009). Life designing: A paradigm for career construction in the 21st century. *Journal of Vocational Behavior, 75*, 239–250.

Savickas, M. L., & Porfeli, E. J. (2012). Career adapt-abilities scale: Construction, reliability, and measurement equivalence across 13 countries. *Journal of Vocational Behavior, 80*, 661–673.

Super, D. E. (1990). A life-span, life-space approach to career development. In D. Brown & L. Brooks (Eds.), *Career choice and development: Applying contemporary theories to practice* (2nd ed., pp. 197–261). San Francisco, CA: Jossey-Bass.

Zacher, H. (2014). Individual difference predictors of change in career adaptability over time. *Journal of Vocational Behavior, 84*, 188–198.

8 The systems theory framework of career development
Accommodating context, complexity, and culture

Mary McMahon and Wendy Patton

Learning objectives

The purpose of this chapter is to:

- provide a theoretical overview of the STF and its application to practice,
- illustrate the practical applications of the STF through a case study, and
- stimulate systemic thinking about career theory and practice.

Introduction to the chapter

The first publication of the systems theory framework (STF) in 1995 represented a landmark contribution to the career development field as the first metatheoretical framework. The STF is also one of the first theoretical contributions based on the constructivist worldview which emphasises holism, connectedness, meaning making, and individual agency. Since then, the influence of STF has manifested through its application to practice in diverse settings and with diverse clientele. The STF provides a "conceptual and practical map" (McMahon & Patton, 2017, p. 113) that can guide career practitioners in their day-to-day work and in their application of theory. Throughout its history, the authors of the STF have maintained connectedness between theory, research, and practice (see Patton & McMahon, 2017). This chapter first overviews the metatheoretical systems theory framework of career development and subsequently considers its cultural validity. A case example is provided in order to illustrate the theoretical principles in practice.

Overview of the systems theory framework

Origins of the theory

The STF has its origins in general systems theory. Until its application in career development through the STF, a number of authors (e.g., Collin, 1985; Collin & Young, 1986; Osipow, 1983) provided a rationale for the introduction of systems theory to career development and proffered theoretical applications. A brief introduction to general systems theory is provided followed by a broad consideration of systems theory in career development.

General systems theory

Attempts to view life as composed of systems appeared as early as 1925 (Whitehead, 1925). However, von Bertalanffy, acknowledged as the founder of the systems movement, published his first statement of general systems theory (GST) in 1968, having published previous discussions outlining principles of systems (1950a, 1950b). Additional understandings of the complexity of systems theory have come from many fields, including physics (Capra, 1975), psychology (Bateson, 1979), sociology (Berger & Luckmann, 1967), and the work of Lewin (1951). D. Ford (1987) and M. Ford and D. Ford (1987) developed an integrated framework of human development which furthered the development and understanding of systems theory in the human sciences. Developmental systems theory (DST; D. Ford & Lerner, 1992) and motivational systems theory (MST; M. Ford, 1992) have illustrated the applicability of systems theory principles to aspects of human behaviour. Although it is not possible to describe the work of these authors in detail in this chapter, readers may refer to Patton and McMahon (2014, 2017, in press) and to Chapter 15 for additional background reading.

Systems are essentially complex wholes comprising interacting parts referred to as subsystems. Examples include computer systems, transport systems, and education systems. The human system is viewed as purposive and constantly evolving. The individual system, itself a complexity of interrelated subsystems, interacts with other systems and subsystems, living and non-living. Human life consists of ongoing recursive processes involving disorganisation, adaptation, and reorganisation. Knowledge about self and the environment is an emergent process as the individual interacts with the world.

Systems theory in career development theory

Within the field of career development, theorists and researchers have drawn from systems thinking for many years. For example, Osipow (1983) commented that the application of systems theory to career development would allow linking and coherent inclusion of existing concepts, thereby not devaluing existing theoretical contributions. Collin and Young (1986) acknowledged the usefulness of systems theory as a framework for career, especially its capacity to understand complex, interrelated events. Collin (1985) identified the need for an overarching theory to join together disparate and incomplete theoretical constructs, and suggested that "an open system model of 'career' could generate a comprehensive, appropriate and grounded theory" (p. 48).

Several theoretical conceptualisations designed to further understand career behaviour have drawn on frameworks derived from systems theory. In particular, the work of Vondracek and his colleagues (Vondracek, Ford, & Porfeli,

2014; Vondracek & Kawasaki, 1995; Vondracek, Lerner, & Schulenberg, 1986) highlights elements of systems theory in understanding career behaviour. These authors emphasised the importance of the context in human development, and their life-span orientation allowed for change over time. Further, the concepts of embeddedness of relevant systems within each other, and dynamic interaction of these systems with each other, are clearly derived from the worldview which informs systems theory. The chaos theory of careers (Pryor & Bright, 2011) has also drawn extensively from systems theory. More recently, Vondracek and his colleagues (2014) proposed a living systems theory of vocational behaviour and development (LSVD) as an integrative framework, noting that the LSVD connects career development with related fields such as human resources and industrial-organisational psychology and to other disciplines that apply a living systems model (see Chapter 9).

The systems theory framework

Within this broad theoretical background, the systems theory framework (STF; McMahon & Patton, 1995; Patton & McMahon, 1999, 2006, 2014, 2015, 2017, 2018) has been developed and subsequently refined. It was originally a response to the repeatedly pressing calls for convergence and integration in career theory in the early 1990s (Savickas & Lent, 1994), and echoes the suggestions made a decade earlier by Osipow (1983) and Collin (1985). A full description of the STF and its sustained and growing contribution to career theory and practice can be found in Patton and McMahon (2014).

In essence, the STF is a systemic map composed of several key interrelated systems, including the intrapersonal system of the individual, the social system, and the environmental-societal system all set within the context of time (see Figure 8.1). Depicted in the STF's systems is a broad range of content and process influences. The individual system is composed of several intrapersonal content influences which include gender, age, self-concept, health, ability, disability, physical attributes, beliefs, personality, interests, values, aptitudes, skills, world of work knowledge, sexual orientation, and ethnicity. Influences representing the content of the social system include peers, family, media, community groups, workplace, and education institutions. Environmental-societal system content influences include political decisions, historical trends, globalisation, socioeconomic status, employment market, and geographical location. The processes of these systems are explained via the recursive interaction within and between them, change over time, and chance. Recursiveness, a central construct of the STF, emphasises the inseparability of parts from the whole and the interaction within and between parts and the whole, and demonstrates that it is "essential to think of content and process as a dynamic, integrated package" (Vondracek et al., 2014, p. 15). Change over time acknowledges how nothing remains the same; change over time may be incremental or rapid. Chance, perhaps because of its intangible nature, has been omitted from most career theories. Chance, however, plays an important role in the careers of many people through unanticipated

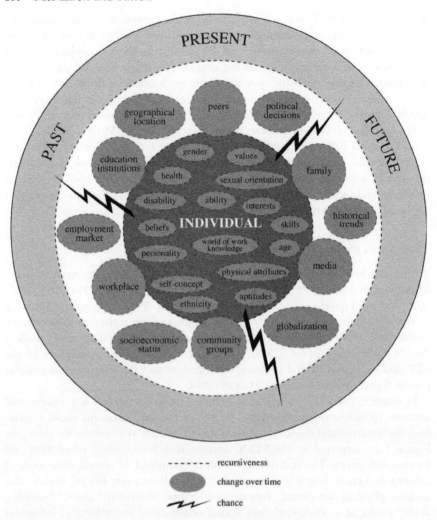

Figure 8.1 The systems theory framework of career development.
Source: Copyright © Patton and McMahon, 1999

personal, social, and natural events which bring about change, and is therefore recognised and depicted in the STF as a process influence.

Theoretical contribution of the STF

The systems theory framework (McMahon & Patton, 1995; Patton & McMahon, 1999, 2006, 2014, 2015, 2017, 2018) remains the first attempt to present a comprehensive metatheoretical framework of career development constructed using systems theory. It has been described as an "excellent synthesis of the systems perspective of career development" (Blustein, 2006, p. 94). Although other theoretical perspectives (e.g., chaos theory [Pryor & Bright, 2011] and contextual action theory [Young et al., 2011]) incorporate systems perspectives, the living systems theory of vocational behaviour and development (Vondracek et al., 2014) and the STF are the only contemporary developments based solely on systems theory. However, the STF is not a theory of career development and is not designed to be so; rather it employs systems theory as the basis for an overarching, or metatheoretical, framework within which all concepts of career development described in the plethora of career theories can be usefully positioned and utilised in theory and practice. With the individual in context as the central focus, constructing his or her own meaning of career, practitioners determine the relevance of career theories according to how they apply to each individual.

Key theoretical principles

The underpinning theoretical principles of the STF also inform its application to practice, primarily through systemic thinking. First and foremost, the interplay of *wholes and parts* is a critical construct of systems theory and of systemic thinking. From a systems theory perspective, individuals cannot be separated from their environments and parts (e.g., personality, interests) cannot be separated from the whole system. Thus, the STF assumes an *"individual in context* view . . . that avoids oversimplification of career decision-making and career development" (McMahon, Watson, & Patton, 2014, p. 30). The second underpinning construct is the notion that within dynamic, recursive systems, *patterns* are constructed that influence individuals. For example, attitudes toward learning and work and gender roles may become established as patterns within families and communities. The third construct, *acausality*, proposes that because of a multiplicity of recursively interacting influences, cause and effect cannot be determined and that linear explanations are insufficient and provide only partial explanations of phenomena. The fourth construct is the process influence of *recursiveness*. Systems are dynamic and change is occurring all the time as a result of the recursive interaction of influences. Recursiveness does not suggest reciprocal interaction or a constant level of influence. Rather, the degree and nature of influence may change over time. The fifth construct, *discontinuous change* in a system, may be sudden and results in a new set of patterns or a different form of organisation or functioning. For example, a family system may experience a discontinuous change when a marriage breaks down or a child leaves home, yet the family system remains but is reconfigured and interacts differently. The sixth construct is the notion of *open and closed systems*. Open systems, such as the STF and its subsystems, have permeable boundaries that are subject to influence from outside and may also exert influence beyond their boundaries. Closed systems have impermeable boundaries and, therefore, do not interact with or receive stimulation from outside. The seventh construct, *abduction*, is a form of reasoning in systems based on the patterns and relationships in the system. Abductive reasoning can be creative or intuitive and poses possible explanations on the basis of observations or information about a system; abductive reasoning does not draw definitive conclusions. Last of all is the construct of *story*, which is fundamental to how individuals make sense of their experiences (i.e., they tell stories to themselves and others about their experiences).

Practical applications of the STF

Story underpins practical applications of the STF in career counselling and qualitative career assessment by positioning clients as storytellers (McMahon, 2017); clients are expected to take an active role in career counselling and career assessment so that their stories are told and heard, patterns within and between stories are identified, and new stories are constructed. In applications of the STF – such as the story-telling approach to narrative career counselling (e.g., McMahon, 2017; McMahon & Watson, 2012) and the qualitative career assessment reflection activity, My System of Career Influences (MSCI; McMahon, Patton, & Watson, 2017; McMahon, Watson, & Patton, 2013) – key features of the STF, including story, systemic thinking, recursiveness, and the individual, are fundamental. Through the telling of stories, individual clients reveal the "complex web of relationships . . . the complex interactions that take place and so highlighting crucial influences and tensions" (Collin, 2006, p. 300).

Cultural validity of the theory

Culture is not directly depicted in the STF. Rather, culture is present in the spaces and recursiveness of the STF as a process constructed discursively (Misra & Gergen, 1993) through interaction and interrelationships in context with others; "relationships construct cultures and recursively cultures construct relationships" (Stead, 2004, p. 391). Culture is not static (Stead, 2004) and is "not merely a set of features" (Arulmani, 2017, p. 81) such as ethnicity, race, or language. Culture is also not only a one-way transmission between generations passed on by elders (Arthur & McMahon, 2005). Rather, it is invented and reinvented by successive generations through the dynamic interactions of people (Stead & Watson, 2017). Additionally, culture is not homogenous; "culture is what the individual perceives it to be . . . the influence of culture is variable as individuals engage with their cultural contexts, order their cultural experiences into meaningful patterns and relate to these in an ongoing developmental process" (Watson, 2017, p. 46). Thus, culture is theoretically embedded throughout the STF through the process influences of recursiveness and change over time, and must necessarily be central to practices based on the STF.

From an STF perspective, career practices such as career counselling and career assessment are inherently cultural encounters. The STF's "individual in context" (McMahon et al., 2014, p. 30) perspective and its emphasis on connectedness resonate with the Black African value of Ubuntu (I am who I am through others) (McMahon, Watson, Chetty, & Hoelson, 2012), with the relationalism of Chinese Confucian cultures, and also accommodate Western individualism and autonomy. The cultural validity of the STF is attested to by its practical applications such as the story telling approach and the qualitative career assessment instrument, *My System of Career Influences* (MSCI; McMahon et al., 2017), both of which have been utilised in diverse contexts. Career practitioners are urged to reflect on their own cultures and to work from a position of personal cultural awareness and to encourage clients to engage reflectively with their own cultures (Arthur, 2017).

Research in brief

Research example 1: researching the story-telling approach

An exploratory case study was used to investigate the story-telling approach to narrative career counselling with a 22-year-old female Black South African university student. In particular, the research investigated how the process constructs of reflection, connectedness, meaning making, learning, and agency manifested in the interview. The client was able to engage in a rich story-telling process, and her stories progressed from thin stories early in the interview to richer stories later in the interview. The researchers concluded that this approach may be appropriate in African cultures which have a history of story telling (see McMahon et al., 2012).

Research in brief: reflective questions

1   Who are the people who are influential in your life and how does your connectedness with them influence your career decision-making?
2   Think back to your childhood and identify something told to you by another person that has remained influential in your attitude to learning and work. How do you explain the lasting effect of this influence?
3   Consider your relationship with a significant person in your life. How are you influential in his or her career decision-making?

Research example 2: researching the MSCI in the context of Hong Kong

The MSCI has been translated into Chinese and its usefulness to Hong Kong Chinese students was investigated in a small study. Six secondary school leavers completed the MSCI in a two-hour session and participated in a 30-minute follow-up interview. Completing the MSCI involves a guided reflection process in which participants identify influences from each of their systems of influence and then represent them in a personal system of influences drawing (i.e., My System of Career Influences diagram). Most participants were positive about their experience of completing the MSCI and all found it useful by discovering "underlying themes of their life narrative", helping them to commit to "put their thoughts and words into actions", or becoming even more committed to a career choice (Yim, Wong, & Yuen, 2015, p. 243). They also found the follow-up session during which they discussed their MSCI with the career practitioner to be of great value because they consolidated their thoughts about career planning and decision-making (see Yim et al., 2015).

Research in brief: reflective questions

1   Consider the last career decision you made. What were the factors you considered and how would you prioritise them?
2   In your previous career decision-making, whose opinions were important to you in making your decision and why?
3   In your previous career decision-making, how did you balance your own wishes and preferences with the wishes and preferences of others such as family or peers?

Case study

The application of the STF is considered in the fictional case of Marnie, a 55-year-old female teacher. Marnie has been divorced for five years and rents an apartment in an Australian city where she lives alone. She has three adult children who work in other cities. Marnie taught in schools in rural Australia and also in England where she met her future husband who was also Australian. After they returned to Australia they married, both continued to work, and they bought a house. Periods of pregnancy and ill health with three children meant that Marnie took periods of unpaid leave. She ultimately resigned her full-time position and undertook supply teaching until her children completed secondary school.

When returning to full-time work, Marnie found that there were few permanent positions available unless she was prepared to move to the country. Her husband's job, however, was in the city. Marnie undertook contract positions until a full-time position became available. Shortly after obtaining permanent work, she and her husband divorced and sold their family home as part of the divorce settlement.

Now, at age 55, Marnie is finding teaching less satisfying and more physically demanding; the workload is increasingly difficult to manage, and her stress levels are rising. She can't see herself teaching until her retirement but she does not know what else to do. Because of her broken employment pattern, she has insufficient superannuation (a pension fund in Australia) to be able to live comfortably if she retired at age 60, the eligible age to retire, and envisages that she will need to work for at least another 10 years to feel financially secure. Marnie feels trapped. While she badly wants a change of employment, she needs the security of her permanent teaching position to increase her super- annuation and maintain her financial security. She wonders whether she should move out to the country where rent and house prices could be cheaper, but she imagines that she would have to continue teaching and is concerned about leaving her support network behind, including her parents, who increasingly need more help. Marnie consults a career counsellor.

Analysis of Marnie's case from the STF perspective

The STF's "individual in context view" (McMahon et al., 2014, p. 30) of Mar- nie's situation reveals the complexity of her career decision. On the surface, Marnie's decision is about changing employment, but that decision is recur- sively related to her intrapersonal system of influences (e.g., her age, gender, abilities, world of work knowledge), her social system (i.e., her aging parents and social network), and her environmental-societal system (i.e., the Australian industrial and political systems, her geographic location, her socioeconomic circumstances, and historical trends). Her present situation is inextricably recursively related to her past and to her future. Marnie, like many other Aus- tralian women, is realising the penalty of motherhood. Currently in Australia, older women are more likely than men to live in poverty after retirement, pri- marily because of broken career paths, more responsibility for unpaid care work, and greater levels of employment in casual and part-time work (Workplace Gender Equality Agency, 2015).

In terms of the key theoretical principles of the STF, Marnie's career decision needs to be considered holistically. For example, a partial view that focused only on her financial situation could disregard her care responsibilities for her parents. Thus, working with Marnie from an STF perspective would necessarily take a *wholes and parts* view by trying to gather as much information as pos- sible about potential influences on her decision. By encouraging Marnie to tell rich *stories* about her influences, *patterns* within and between stories may be elicited. For example, Marnie has spent her life caring for others (e.g., in her family, in her work as a teacher) because it is something she values and has generally enjoyed. This pattern may be useful in considering her possible future pathways. The complexity of Marnie's system of influences suggests that there is neither a simple nor a cause-and-effect explanation for her present situation (e.g., if Marnie had gone back to work sooner after the birth of her children, she would be in a better financial situation). Rather, *acausality*, that is, the *recursiveness* of the multiplicity of influences in Marnie's life, implies that such an oversimplified and narrow view provides only a partial account of her situation. Marnie's family has been a constant influence in her career decisions, although her family situation has experienced *discontinuous change* as a result of her divorce, resulting in the nature of family influence changing. As with the STF, Marnie's system of influences is an *open system* with permeable boundaries that is open to influence from outside. She is seeking support from an external influence, a career counsellor. Thus, the career counsellor will enter Marnie's system of influences and together, Marnie and the career counsellor will form a new system: in STF terms, a therapeutic system (see Figure 8.2). Together with Marnie, the career counsellor will consider themes and patterns in Marnie's system of influences through a process of reasoning called *abduction* in which they consider her circumstances and possible options.

As depicted in Figure 8.2, Marnie's system of influences meets with the career counsellor's system of influences to form a new system, the therapeutic system (the STF term for what is sometimes called the working alliance in other theories). The boundary of this new system must be permeable enough for a fruitful relationship to develop yet impermeable enough for both parties to maintain their individuality. Career counselling from the STF perspective is

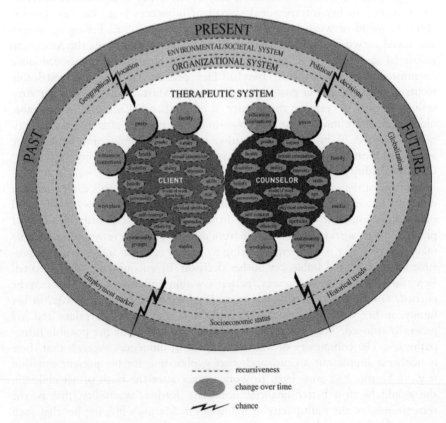

Figure 8.2 The therapeutic system.
Source: Copyright © Patton and McMahon, 1999

founded on "mattering" relationships (Schlossberg, Lynch & Chickering, 1989) that are reflective of Rogers (1951) three necessary conditions for counselling: genuineness, unconditional positive regard, and empathetic understanding.

Career counselling that is based on the STF employs the story-telling approach to narrative career counselling which is guided by six strategies, specifically:

1 providing a space for reflection;
2 listening deeply for clues in client stories;
3 using the clues to construct brief responses or invitations to tell further stories;
4 assisting clients to identify and make explicit themes and patterns in their stories; connecting previously disconnected stories through the identification of themes and patterns; and
5 incorporating themes and patterns as "ingredients" of future stories (McMahon et al., 2012, p. 138).

The story-telling approach does not rule out the possibility of using career assessment instruments and concerns itself with how career assessment is integrated into the narrative process. At the outset, whether a career assessment could be used should emerge out of the client's stories and be negotiated with the client. From an STF perspective, this means that the assessment results need to be invested in meaning in the context of Marnie's system of influences. For example, the qualitative *My System of Career Influences* (MSCI, Adult Version; McMahon et al., 2013) may assist Marnie to consider her career, identify her influences, prioritise them, and map the relationships between them in an MSCI drawing that she subsequently stories. Alternatively, a narrative systemic structured interview could be used to contextualise quantitative career assessment results, for example, the Integrative Structured Interviews (ISIs) for Holland's (1985) *Self-Directed Search* (SDS) (McMahon & Watson, 2012) and the ISI for Zytowski's (2006) *Super's Work Values Inventory–Revised* (SWVI-R) (Watson & McMahon, 2014). Essentially, combining quantitative career assessment into narrative career counselling necessitates using a qualitative, narrative approach to explore the personal meaning of the client's assessment results. By participating in such narrative processes, Marnie will be afforded an opportunity to *reflect* on her influences and identify *connectedness* within and between stories in the form of themes and patterns from which she can *make meaning*. In turn, she will come to *learn* about what is important to her and act as an *agent* in the construction of her future.

Case study: reflective questions:

1 How might it help Marnie to consider her situation from the perspective of the STF?
2 Identify people in your community who may be disenfranchised (e.g., women such as Marnie, people who are unemployed, people from immigrant and refugee backgrounds) and consider their career

development from the perspective of the STF. List influences from all parts of the STF that may affect their employment prospects. These influences could either help or hinder their employment prospects.

3   Consider your position as a career practitioner working with Marnie from the perspective of the STF. What values or beliefs do you hold or experiences have you had or are aware of that could in any way influence your work with Marnie?

Chapter summary

The systems theory framework (STF) of career development (McMahon & Patton, 1995; Patton & McMahon, 1999, 2006, 2014, 2017, in press) portrays the complexity and dynamic nature of career development. One strength of the STF is its connectedness between theory, research, and practice. The key theoretical principles of the STF guide its practice applications in career counselling, career assessment, and career education. In its application, a further strength is that the STF provides a conceptual and practical systemic map to guide career practitioners in their work. Systemic thinking, systemic questioning, and systemic mapping help practitioners take account of the context, complexity, and cultures of their clients' career development. The STF and the application of its career counselling and career assessment approaches in diverse settings attest to its cultural validity. A limitation of the STF is that as a metatheory, it does not provide detailed explanations of any particular phenomenon. Such explanations are provided by individual clients themselves or by career theories that are relevant to clients.

In its more than 20 year history, the STF has continued to prove useful for practitioners in diverse cultural contexts. Future directions for the STF could include expansion into more diverse settings and with more diverse client groups. Research into the STF applications will continue to build its evidence base and confirm its cultural validity. In addition, the STF's theoretical connectedness with other new and emerging theories will extend its capacity to be part of expanding integrative theoretical frameworks.

As reflected in the case study of Marnie, the STF provides a useful tool through which to conceptualise career development. Moreover, its core principles guide the STF's practice applications. The STF may be viewed metaphorically as a map through which to conceptualise career practices. Story is fundamental to the STF's application; a narrative career counselling approach, the story-telling approach, has been developed that applies the key theoretical principles of the STF. The STF has also influenced the development of qualitative career assessment instruments and structured interviews for integrating quantitative career assessment into narrative career counselling. The STF has fulfilled its original intention of addressing the convergence debate through its metatheoretical properties that have also been influential in career practice.

Learning activities

Learning activity 1: career decision-making

1   Reflect on the career decision you made when you left school and make a list of the influences that were affecting you at that time (e.g., values, abilities, family, peers, geographic location, socioeconomic circumstances).
2   Reflect on the last career decision you made and make a list of the influences that were affecting you at that time.
3   Compare and contrast your two lists of influences and identify any that were the same.
4   Even though these influences appeared in both lists, consider how they were similar or different at these different times.
5   Think about what you know about the STF and its theoretical principles, and tell a colleague or friend how the STF might explain these differences.

Learning activity 2: drawing my own system of influences

1   Consider the possibility of having to make a career decision within the next few months (e.g., beginning a program of study, receiving a promotion that would mean moving to another city, applying for a job in another organisation, reducing your work from full time to part time, deciding whether to begin a family).

   a   Using the subsystems of the STF as a guide, identify influences that you may need to factor into your decision.
   b   Illustrate these influences in a drawing that represents your own systems of influences.
   c   Consider the interrelationships of influences and their positioning in your drawing relative to other influences.
   d   Using your drawing, explain to a colleague or friend how you understand systemic thinking and why it matters in career decision-making and career development.

Learning activity: reflective questions

1   How would you explain career development to a colleague on the basis of what you have learned about the STF?
2   As a career practitioner, how could you envision using the systemic map of the STF in your practice?
3   What are the implications for your career development practice of employing systemic thinking?

References

Arthur, N. (2017). Constructivist approaches to career counselling: A culture-infused perspective. In M. McMahon (Ed.), *Career counselling: Constructivist approaches* (pp. 54–64). London: Routledge.

Arthur, N., & McMahon, M. (2005). A systems theory framework for multicultural career counseling. *The Career Development Quarterly*, 53(3), 208–222.

Arulmani, G. (2017). Contexts and circumstances: The cultural preparation process approach to career development. In M. McMahon (Ed.), *Career counselling: Constructivist approaches* (pp. 79–90). London: Routledge.

Bateson, G. (1979). *Mind and nature: A necessary unity*. New York: Dutton.

Berger, P., & Luckmann, T. (1967). *The social construction of reality. A treatise in the sociology of knowledge*. Garden City: Doubleday Anchor.

Blustein, D. L. (2006). *The psychology of working: A new perspective for career development, counseling, and public policy*. Mahwah, NJ: Erlbaum.

Capra, F. (1975). *The Tao of physics*. Berkeley, CA: Shambhala.

Collin, A. (1985). The learning circle of a research project on "mid-career change": Through stages to systems thinking. *Journal of Applied Systems Analysis*, 12, 35–53.

Collin, A. (2006). Conceptualising the family friendly career: The contribution of career theories and a systems approach. *British Journal of Guidance and Counselling*, 34, 295–307.

Collin, A., & Young, R. A. (1986). New directions for theories of career. *Human Relations*, 39, 837–853.

Ford, D. (1987). *Humans as self-constructing living systems*. Hillsdale, NJ: Lawrence Erlbaum.

Ford, D., & Lerner, R. (1992). *Developmental systems theory: An integrative approach*. Newbury Park, CA: SAGE.

Ford, M. (1992). *Motivating humans: Goals, emotions, and personal agency beliefs*. Newbury Park, CA: SAGE.

Ford, M., & Ford, D. (Eds.). (1987). *Humans as self-constructing living systems: Putting the framework to work*. Hillsdale, NJ: Lawrence Erlbaum.

Holland, J. L. (1985). *The Self-Directed Search: A guide to educational and vocational planning*. Odessa, FL: Psychological Assessment Resources.

Lewin, K. (1951). *Field theory in social science*. New York: Harper.

McMahon, M. (2017). Working with storytellers: A metaphor for career counselling. In M. McMahon (Ed.), *Career counselling: Constructivist approaches* (pp. 17–28). London: Routledge.

McMahon, M., & Patton, W. (1995). Development of a systems theory of career development. *Australian Journal of Career Development*, 4, 15–20.

McMahon, M., & Patton, W. (2017). The Systems Theory Framework: A conceptual and practical map for career counselling. In M. McMahon (Ed.), *Career counselling: Constructivist approaches* (pp. 123–126). London: Routledge.

McMahon, M., & Patton, W. (2018). Systemic thinking in career development theory: Contributions of the systems theory framework. *British Journal of Guidance and Counselling*, 46(2), 229–240.

McMahon, M., Patton, W., & Watson, M. (2017). *The My System of Career Influences (MSCI – Adolescent): Reflecting on my career decisions*. Brisbane: Australian Academic Press.

McMahon, M., & Watson, M. (2012). Telling stories of career assessment. *Journal of Career Assessment*, 20, 440–451.

McMahon, M., Watson, M., Chetty, C., & Hoelson, C. (2012). Examining process constructs of narrative career counselling: An exploratory case study. *British Journal of Guidance and Counselling, 40*, 127–141.

McMahon, M., Watson, M., & Patton, W. (2014). Context-resonant systems perspectives in career theory. In G. Arulmani, A. Bakshi, F. Leong & T. Watts (Eds.), *Handbook of career development: International Perspectives* (pp. 29–42). New York: Springer.

McMahon, M., Watson, M., & Patton, W. (2013). *The My System of Career Influences Adult Version (MSCI – Adult): A reflection process.* Brisbane: Australian Academic Press.

McMahon, M., & Watson, M. (2012). Story crafting: Strategies for facilitating narrative career counselling. *International Journal for Educational and Vocational Guidance, 12*(3), 211–224.

Misra, G., & Gergen, K. J. (1993). On the place of culture in the psychological sciences. *International Journal of Psychology, 28*, 225–243.

Osipow, S. H. (1983). *Theories of career development* (2nd ed.). Englewood Cliffs, NJ: Prentice-Hall.

Patton, W., & McMahon, M. (1999). *Career development and systems theory: A new relationship.* Pacific Grove, CA: Brooks/Cole.

Patton, W., & McMahon, M. (2006). *Career development and systems theory: Connecting theory and practice* (2nd ed.). Rotterdam, The Netherlands: Sense.

Patton, W., & McMahon, M. (2014). *Career development and systems theory: Connecting theory and practice* (3rd ed.). Rotterdam, The Netherlands: Sense.

Patton, W., & McMahon, M. (2015). The systems theory framework of career development: 20 years of contribution to theory and practice. *Australian Journal of Career Development, 24*, 141–147.

Patton, W., & McMahon, M. (2017). The systems theory framework of career development. In J. P. Sampson Jr., E. Bullock-Yowell, V. C. Dozier, D. S. Osborn, & J. G. Lenz (Eds.), *Integrating theory, research and practice in vocational psychology: Current status and future directions* (pp. 50–61). Tallahassee: Florida State University.

Pryor, R., & Bright, J. (2011). *The chaos theory of careers: A new perspective on working in the 21st century.* Hoboken, NJ: Taylor & Francis.

Rogers, C. R. (1951). *Client-centered therapy.* Boston, MA: Houghton-Mifflin.

Savickas, M. L., & Lent, R. W. (Eds.). (1994). *Convergence in career development theories.* Palo Alto, CA: CPP Books.

Schlossberg, N. K, Lynch, A. Q., & Chickering, A. W. (1989). *Improving higher education environments for adults.* San Francisco, CA: Jossey-Bass.

Stead, G. B. (2004). Culture and career psychology: A social constructionist perspective. *Journal of Vocational Behavior, 64*, 389–406.

Stead, G. B., & Watson, M. B. (2017). Indigenisation of career psychology in South Africa. In G. B. Stead & M. B. Watson (Eds.), *Career psychology in the South African context*, pp. 209-220. Pretoria, South Africa: Van Schaik.

Von Bertalanffy, L. (1950a). The theory of open systems in physics and biology. *Science, 111*, 23–29.

Von Bertalanffy, L. (1950b). An outline of general system theory. *British Journal of Philosophy of Science, 1*, 139–164.

Von Bertalanffy, L. (1968). *General systems theory.* New York: George Braziller.

Vondracek, F. W., Ford, D. H., & Porfeli, E. J. (2014). *A living systems theory of vocational behavior and development.* Rotterdam, The Netherlands: Sense.

Vondracek, F. W., & Kawasaki, T. (1995). Toward a comprehensive framework for adult career development theory and intervention. In W. B. Walsh & S. H. Osipow (Eds.), *Handbook of vocational psychology* (2nd ed., pp. 111–141). Mahwah, NJ: Erlbaum.

Vondracek, F. W., Lerner, R. M., & Schulenberg, J. E. (1986). *Career development: A life-span developmental approach*. Hillsdale, NJ: Erlbaum.

Watson, M. (2017). Career constructivism and culture: Deconstructing and reconstructing career counselling. In M. McMahon (Ed.), *Career counselling: Constructivist approaches* (pp. 43–53). London: Routledge.

Watson, M., & McMahon, M. (2014). Making meaning of quantitative assessment in career counseling through a story-telling approach. In G. Arulmani, A. Bakshi, F. Leong, & T. Watts (Eds.), *Handbook of career development: International perspectives* (pp. 631–644). New York: Springer.

Whitehead, A. N. (1925). *Science and the modern world*. New York: Macmillan.

Workplace Gender Equality Agency. (2015). *Women's economic security in retirement*. Retrieved from www.wgea.gov.au/sites/default/files/PP_womens_economic_security_in_retirement.pdf

Yim, A., Wong, S-W., & Yuen, M. (2015). Qualitative career assessment approaches in Hong Kong. In M. McMahon & M. Watson (Eds.), *Career assessment: Qualitative approaches* (pp. 239–246). Rotterdam, The Netherlands: Sense.

Young, R. A., Marshall, S. K., Valach, L., Domene, J. F., Graham, M. D., & Zaidman-Zait, A. (2011). *Transition to adulthood: Action, projects and counseling*. New York: Springer Science.

Zytowski, D. G. (2006). *Super's Work Values Inventory – Revised*. Technical manual. Adel, IA: Kuder.

9 Living systems theory of vocational behaviour and development

Fred W. Vondracek and Donald H. Ford

Learning objectives

The purpose of this chapter is to:

- introduce a comprehensive living systems framework,
- describe a process model of career development, and
- facilitate application of the model in counselling and research.

A brief history of the LSVD

Both senior authors of the LSVD (Vondracek & Ford) have been involved in the field of career counselling and development for more than half a century, as professionals and as scientists. Ford's search for a sound theory for understanding the development and dynamics of a self-constructing, self-directing, self-regulating and self-controlling person led him to discover von Bertalanffy's general systems theory (GST; 1950, 1968). After 25 years of comprehensive evaluation of GST and related ideas and scientific evidence concerning developmental processes in humans, Ford published an extensively documented, integrative theory: *Humans as Self-Constructing Living Systems: A Developmental Theory of Behaviour and Personality* (Ford, 1987). At about the same time, Vondracek collaborated with Richard Lerner (and graduate student John Schulenberg) in articulating a meta-theory of career development: *Career Development: A Life-Span Developmental Approach* (Vondracek, Lerner, & Schulenberg, 1986).

Thirty years later, having witnessed the impact of systems thinking in the human sciences (including biology and medicine), Vondracek proposed to Ford to collaborate in applying his living systems framework in the formulation of a new theory of career development, and invited his former graduate student Erik Porfeli to participate. The result was *A Living Systems Theory of Vocational Behaviour and Development* (Vondracek, Ford, & Porfeli, 2014).

Use of Ford's living systems framework offered an opportunity to create the LSVD as a career theory that fully integrates individual and context, not only conceptually but also methodologically, in counselling and in research. Equally important, it provided a means, through the constructs of behaviour episodes (BEs) and behaviour episode schema (BES), to explain how the person-in-context sets goals, plans actions to pursue them, and engages with the context to implement those plans. Moreover, because it is a dynamic process model, the LSVD also incorporates and describes functions that continuously monitor the effects of the person's goal-directed activities and, through feedback and feedforward, makes necessary adjustments to optimise goal attainment. In the following pages, we endeavor to more fully describe the components and principles of the LSVD, and by means of a case study, we demonstrate how counsellors can assist their clients in constructing successful and satisfying career pathways.

Key theoretical principles

The focus of LSVD is on understanding vocational behaviour and development across the life span. The concept "vocational behaviour and development" is broader than "career development" because career development has roots in childhood and adolescent experiences, well before people start thinking about careers (e.g., Hartung, Porfeli, & Vondracek, 2005; Watson & MacMahon, 2005). Consistent with Ford's (1987) theory of humans as self-constructing living systems, the LSVD posits that the basic human development processes are the same for all kinds of human development (e.g., interpersonal relationships, family, health, career). It is thus essential that any theory aiming to explain career development explain the meaning, not only of career but also of development (e.g., see Vondracek, Lerner, & Schulenberg, 1983). Moreover, because the living system of interest is the human being (i.e., the person), we need to address how it is conceptualised in the LSVD.

What is a person?

Humans evolved so they could function as integrated dynamic units, organised to behave in specific ways for specific purposes through patterns of interactions with specific contexts. Each person is made up of a great diversity of attributes, which are always *"organised into complex, integrative adaptive patterns that function as a unit to serve the person's purposes"* (Vondracek et al., 2014, p. 34). The person attributes are represented by the *biological, psychological,* and *transactional* subsystems.

The biological subsystem is an organisation of inborn, self-constructed biological parts and biochemical processes that collaborate to function as an integrated team. It has received little attention in theories of career development, but it is self-evident that one's physical capabilities, body structure, energy level, and the biological components of emotional functioning play important roles in deciding which career pathways are chosen and pursued.

The psychological subsystem has inborn capabilities for information collection, processing, and application. To deal with the massive amount of information generated in dealing with ever-changing dynamic contexts and circumstances, humans developed the capability for entering varying states of consciousness and attention that selectively control the kinds of information to be ignored, used, or attended to. Cognitive processes enable envisioning of potential future conditions (e. g., goals, aspirations), engagement in problem solving, planning, decision-making, and regulatory and evaluative thoughts designed to anticipate how one might achieve a particular goal and whether and to what extent one's efforts are producing the desired results. Emotions, pain, and other affective states are non-cognitive evaluative/regulatory aspects of the psychological subsystem. They have evolved to serve different functions and are activated by different conditions. Most concepts described in contemporary theories of career development (e.g., aspirations, interests, preferences, self-efficacy beliefs, cognitive capabilities/skills, emotions) represent aspects of a person's psychological functioning.

The transactional subsystem represents those processes in human functioning that influence the relationship between persons and contexts. For example, physical transactions could involve moving to a new, more supportive context, while various kinds of communication can be used to influence relationships with people.

The principle of unitary functioning

A person always functions as an integrated unit, combining a *biological person* and a *psychological-behavioural-social person* organised to behave in specific ways for specific purposes in specific contexts (D. H. Ford, 1987). Breaking this principle down to its components means that (a) a person always functions as a holistic, integrated unit (e.g., emotions, cognition, instrumental behaviours, and biological processes cannot be understood in isolation from each other); (b) a person is always pursuing some purpose or goal (although the person may not always be consciously aware of it); (c) every behaviour takes place in a specific, unique context, thus making the *person-in-context* the only unit of analysis that captures what a specific person actually does and why that person behaves in a specific way in a real-life situation. The challenge presented by this insight was to capture this dynamic person-in-context unit in such a way that it could be usefully employed by professionals as well as by researchers.

The behaviour episode (BE)

Ford's solution to this challenge was the identification of *behaviour episodes* (BEs) as context specific, goal-directed patterns, which unfold over time until the goal directing the episode is (a) achieved, (b) revised and then achieved, or (c) it is postponed or abandoned. Figure 9.1 is a graphic representation of a typical BE. It demonstrates why a person's behaviour on a particular occasion

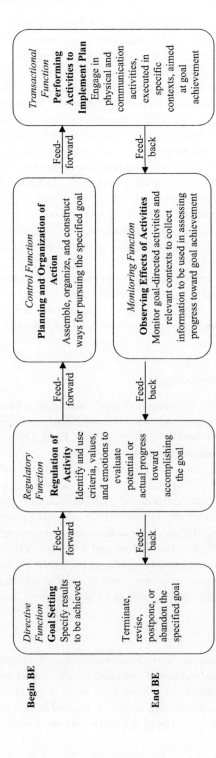

Figure 9.1 A typical behaviour episode (BE); the basic unit of analysis in living systems.

Note: The schematic representation of a typical BE is provided for clarity of exposition and does not fully convey its dynamic nature. In fact, during the course of any BE, individuals can choose to rapidly cycle back and forth between any of the five major functions and make adjustments accordingly.

cannot be understood unless one understands the context and the underlying processes. These processes include identifying potential goals, mobilising the person-in-context system to be organised in the evaluation and pursuit of selected goals, and remaining committed and engaged until the goals are achieved.

This can be understood best with reference to the basic system functions that are shown in the figure: (1) through the *directive function*, goals are set (i.e., the results to be achieved are identified); (2) then, the *regulatory/evaluative functions* (which are both cognitive and affective/emotional) examine the properties, priorities, and potential consequences of implementing potential ways of pursuing each goal, which is then used to possibly alter the goal and the method of pursuing the goal; (3) *control functions*, then guide the implementation of a selected approach, which involves planning how to selectively assemble, organise, reorganise, integrate, and construct ways of pursuing the specified goals in specified contexts; (4) *feedforward processes* (which are future-oriented processes) are then used to forward this information to mobilise *transactional functions*, which are designed to perform the physical and communications activities that have been selected to achieve the desired goals in specific contexts; (5) in the *monitoring function*, selective attention is focused on collecting relevant information about the progress of the implementation activity; (6) *feedback processes* (which provide information about current system conditions) then enter new *regulatory/evaluative* information into the *directive* (goal setting) and *control functions*, which use it to advance or revise the ongoing implementation activity.

Although a person may be pursuing several goals simultaneously, a person cannot attend to everything that may be going on at any given time all at once. Consequently, every BE is focused specifically on the pursuit of its guiding goal. The person and context attributes that contribute to achieving the goal form a large integrated dynamic pattern. A person's activities in any given day can be conceptualised and analysed as a series of BEs, sub-BEs, and patterns of each. BEs may be directed by specific short-term goals (e.g., getting to an appointment on time), or they may be hierarchically organised long-term goals (e.g., graduating from high school, getting admitted to college, choosing a major, graduating from college, getting a job). Failure to achieve any sub- or sub-sub-goals of a BE will disrupt that pathway and lead to changes in it.

Behaviour episode schemas (BESs)

Behaviour episodes serve as the basic building blocks for a person's developmental pathways because formulating, pursuing, and achieving personal goals through behaviour episodes provides the experiential basis for all human learning. Given that we propose to explain how people develop personal vocational goals and career pathways, we must describe the role BEs play in these developmental processes. The key to human learning is represented by similarities and differences among BEs in terms of their contents and contexts. Because many BEs are similar in content and context, they lead to the development of generalised versions of BEs, which are called behaviour episode schemas (BESs). "BES are subject to continual modification and elaboration through their use in constructing, and incorporating the consequences of, new behaviour episodes; hence, behaviour episodes serve as the fodder for BES, which in turn serve to guide future behaviour episodes" (Vondracek et al., 2014, p. 62). The construction of BESs in this manner leads to the assemblage of a complex repertoire of enduring behaviour patterns, which are unique to each individual. Collectively, they represent a person's past experiences.

Because these processes are so fundamental in the functioning of the living human system, some elaboration may be useful. When people begin a new BE they do not start 'from scratch.' Instead, the evolving BE's goal and context activate reconstruction of a relevant BES, which provides guidance about what one should pay attention to and how one should feel and act. It should thus be clear that BESs are flexible frameworks that can be shaped and adapted to fit current circumstances, quite unlike presumably stable values, traits, or habits. The operation of BEs and the attendant construction of flexible BESs constitute a dynamic model of continuous learning and adaptation, which always represents specific individuals in their unique contexts. This model is thus "tailor made" for career counsellors who are engaged in person-focused interventions. In contrast, prominent models in vocational psychology and career counselling have been of limited utility in person-focused interventions because of their focus on presumably stable and enduring patterns of functioning, such as vocational interests and personality, while largely ignoring the context specificity and functional variability of behaviour patterns.

BESs may be developed based on three distinct kinds of BEs. *Instrumental* BEs are particularly important for acquiring competencies and skills because they involve actually carrying out tasks in specific contexts. This largely explains why internships and apprenticeships (hands-on, instrumental BEs) are especially effective in helping individuals decide what vocational pathway they may (or may not) want to follow. BESs may also be developed through *observational* BEs, which are primarily involved in acquiring information about person and context activity by tuning in to what is going on and through observing how things work. Finally, BESs may be developed based on *thinking* BEs, which are important for imaginative cognitive activities that deal with preparation for and selection of future possibilities through the activation, analysis, and creation of new combinations of information/meaning patterns. BESs that are based on a combination of these three types of BEs tend to be most powerful as starting points for personal development and for the creation of career pathways.

Career pathways

Conceptualising and understanding the person-in-context as an integrated, indivisible whole; operationalising this conceptualisation as the BE process model (represented by Figure 9.1); and explaining how learning and development take place through the formation of a BES based on three types of BEs provides the theoretical foundation for explaining the development of vocational behaviour and career pathways. The actual behavioural repertoire for developing career pathways is produced through sequences of relevant goal-directed activities (BEs) and the learned generalised activity patterns (BESs) that are constructed from similar BEs. To better understand the formation of career pathways, we have found M. Ford's (M. Ford, 1992) motivational systems theory (MST) particularly useful (e.g., Vondracek et al., 2014; Vondracek & Kawasaki, 1995) because of its focus on behavioural patterns that are *effective* in achieving one's goals.

According to MST (which, like the LSVD, is also based on Ford's living systems framework), there are four critical requirements for the effective pursuit of one's goals. The person must have the following: (1) sufficient motivation to persist in working toward the goal directing any particular BE until the goal is achieved; (2) the skills necessary for achieving the desired goal; (3) the biological/physical system capable of supporting the motivation and skills components of the BE; and (4) a responsive environment/context that permits the successful conclusion of the BE. Some elaboration of this framework may be helpful. When motivation is persistent and strong, chances of achieving one's career goals are high. Just thinking about or wishing for desired consequences to occur is not a sufficient condition for strong motivation. Strong motivation is based on clear (not vague) goals as well as a commitment (an intention) to produce the desired conditions represented by the goal. An additional component of motivation is represented by what M. Ford calls *personal agency beliefs*, consisting of *capability beliefs* (commonly referred to as "self-efficacy beliefs") and *context beliefs*. The former are beliefs about whether one has the skills and abilities to achieve the desired goal, while the latter refers to whether one believes that the context is supportive of one's efforts to achieve the goal. The explicit joint consideration of capability and context beliefs is a critical distinction between M. Ford's MST and other efforts to utilise the construct of self-efficacy beliefs in career theory (e.g., Lent, Brown, & Hackett, 1994). When clear goals and a strong commitment to engage in the behaviours required to achieve them are accompanied by robust capability and context beliefs and by positive emotions (which can energise behaviours), all ingredients are in place for being strongly motivated.

Strong motivation, however, is not sufficient for optimal effectiveness in achieving one's goals. Having the requisite skills to achieve the goals is also important. M. Ford conceptualises the skills component in MST as an integrated pattern of psychological and behavioural processes focused on planning, decision-making, and activity patterns designed to achieve the goal. The last two requirements for effective functioning are self-explanatory: one must possess the biological/physical capabilities for achieving one's goals and the context must, at least in principle, contain the opportunity for achieving the goals.

Research in brief

Research consistent with the LSVD theoretical framework must be focused on the intraindividual variability of the person-in-context instead of studying large groups of individuals and then reaching conclusions about individuals on the basis of group data. One example of this approach is represented by a P-technique factor analysis of self-reported work values (Schulenberg, Vondracek, & Nesselroade, 1988). After intensively studying seven individuals' pattern of responses to *Super's Work Values Inventory* over a span of 100 days, it was found that intraindividual variability was coherently structured across individuals. The authors concluded that "the findings call into question the overarching assumption in the vocational literature that work values behave exclusively as trait-like dimensions" (Schulenberg et al., 1988, p. 377). Since publication of that study, the study of intra-individual variability (and system processes) has benefitted from methodological advances such as time series analysis, dynamic factor analysis, and the use of combined qualitative and quantitative methods (see Vondracek et al., 2014, pp. 115–124).

Research in brief: reflective questions

1   Using the previous brief description, would you classify work values as traits or are they states?
2   In traditional factor analysis, data are collected across many individuals. Across what dimension are data collected in P-technique factor analysis?
3   What is the difference between intraindividual variability and interindividual variability?

Cultural validity

The LSVD's basic unit of analysis is the person-in-context. Thus, it accounts for the fact that every moment of a person's life is lived in some context, whether it is one's living room, workplace, family, or coworkers. We have distinguished between context and environment by suggesting that the former refers only to that part of one's current environment with which one can directly interact, while the latter refers to both proximal and distal phenomena surrounding a particular reference point (Vondracek et al., 2014). The cultural environment would be considered context if the person directly interacts with some aspect of it by, for example, participating in an "equal pay for women" protest. Conversely, it would be considered the person's broader environment if such a protest occurred without her direct participation. Neither the context nor the environment can *cause* a person's behaviour as suggested, for example, by a "stimulus–response" framework. Contexts and the environment they are embedded in represent, however, a fundamentally important influence on behaviour (and thus on career pathways) "by providing possibilities (affordances) for and limitations (barriers) on how a person might behave" (Vondracek et al., 2014, pp. 39–40).

It is important to recall that the processes involved in every BE and those involved in the formation and utilisation of a BES are the same for all human beings regardless of whether they are men, women, or children, and they are the same for people of all racial backgrounds, cultures, and nationalities. Differences in BEs and BES, which make them unique for each and every person, are their content and context. For example, cultural factors in a person's context and environment often play a critical role in whether certain career opportunities are readily available or difficult or nearly impossible to reach. In the LSVD, the person-in-context is the basic unit of analysis; therefore, the context can never be ignored in the analysis of human behaviour. Moreover, the theory emphasises the analysis of intra-individual change and development. Generalisations across multiple individuals are made only when significant similarities are found in patterns of intraindividual change and development, making superficial conclusions (prejudices) about cultural (or any other) sub-groups of individuals unlikely (see Vondracek et al., 2014).

Case study

In the interest of brevity, we present here a shortened and modified version of a case study that was originally presented in Vondracek et al. (2014, pp. 82–97). "Ted" is a young man who is nearing high school graduation and who is thinking about attending college without, however, having clear ideas about what to study, how much it would cost, and how long it would take. He came to see a counsellor to help him "sort things out." In all likelihood, Ted had previously developed a characteristic way (a BES) of relating to authority figures (e.g., teachers, doctors). Consequently, the counsellor's initial task was to establish a comfortable relationship with Ted and to ensure that Ted viewed him as a caring, knowledgeable consultant and not as an authority figure. This involved using multiple strategies to help Ted to modify his "dealing with authority figures BES" and ranged from how the counsellor introduced himself to how he arranged his office furniture. One strategy used by the counsellor was to describe how he ended up being a counsellor (i.e., his developmental pathway). Such self-disclosure was designed to reduce what Ted might consider their status difference and to put him at ease in sharing his own pathway that led him to seek help.

Having achieved a positive beginning in their relationship, the next step was to encourage Ted to discuss openly the ideas, concerns, and doubts that often accompany a young person's early efforts to formulate goals and plans for their occupational future. As Ted began to share his ideas as to what he hoped to get out of his counselling sessions, the counsellor paid close attention to ensure that they formed an effective partnership in which both of them worked toward the same shared goals. Did Ted expect the counsellor to help him to choose an occupation or did he want help in evaluating the feasibility of pursuing an occupation he was already considering, or did he want help with both? Was Ted hoping for the counsellor's support in pursuing a career path that did not have his father's approval? Once Ted and the counsellor agreed on their shared goals for their counselling sessions they began to explore his history of activities he had liked (and disliked) in the past, or in other words, his *activity pathways*, because *change and development always starts with what exists*.

The LSVD is a person-focused theory, meaning that standardised vocational measures would have been of very limited use in assessing what Ted needed, wanted, or hoped for, and they would have offered very limited guidance to the counsellor on how to best assist Ted: "Knowledge about individual persons must start with a 'real' person and not with an abstraction of a real person created from data about large groups of individuals" (Vondracek et al., 2014, p. 112). To ensure that a valid assessment of Ted's unique situation would be accomplished, the counsellor focused on exploring with Ted his history of activity pathways (and their guiding goals) that were satisfying in the past and that resulted in well-developed BESs that could potentially serve as starting points for the emergence of vocational (career) pathways.

For Ted, one such activity pattern was that of being a volunteer firefighter. As a child, Ted had observed and admired his father, who was a firefighter (*observational BE*). He often dreamed of becoming a firefighter (*thinking BE*) and he actually became involved in firefighting when his father started to take him along so that he could experience first-hand what it was like (*instrumental BE*). BESs developed from all three types of BEs tend to be most complex and elaborate and therefore prime candidates for further development. In further exploring this promising activity pattern with Ted, the counsellor assessed whether the pattern met the four critical requirements for *effective* goal pursuit described previously. First, did he have sufficient motivation, consisting of positive emotions and a strong pattern of capability and context beliefs, to persist in pursuing the potential goal of becoming a firefighter? Second, did he have the requisite skills to be a firefighter? Third, was he physically capable of doing the work of a firefighter, and fourth, was his environment/context responsive (i.e., did opportunities exist for becoming a firefighter)?

In talking with Ted it was apparent that he had shown persistent interest in firefighting as an unpaid volunteer, strongly suggesting that he experienced positive *emotions* related to this potential occupational role. His involvement with the role in many different BEs over time resulted in his feeling confident in his ability to perform in the role (i.e., he experienced robust *capability beliefs*). Moreover, his father and other firefighters provided a positive and supportive context for learning about firefighting, thereby strengthening Ted's positive *context beliefs* regarding that activity pathway. This led to the conclusion that his motivation was adequate for pursuing this potential career pathway. During his frequent participation in firefighting activities over a two-year period, Ted was often praised for being able to pick up the requisite skills quite easily, and he demonstrated excellent endurance and physical stamina, thus meeting further requirements for *effective* goal pursuit. Exploration of the final requirement for effective goal pursuit, a responsive environment/context, was put off pending the exploration of additional activity pathways and the clarification of Ted's ultimate choice of a career goal.

Ted and his counsellor continued their exploration of other activity pathways in Ted's past, focusing on any that had resulted in fairly elaborate BESs because the activities were accompanied by positive emotions and self-evaluations. For example, at an early age Ted started to draw pictures and portraits, enjoyed the activity, became quite accomplished, and (through positive feedback processes) was supported and encouraged by his parents, teachers, and friends in those activities. As was the case regarding firefighting, Ted's activity pathway in art had all the ingredients necessary for becoming a potential vocational pathway.

Counsellors often recognise potential educational or vocational pathways that may not be readily apparent to their clients and they may choose to suggest that such pathways deserve to be evaluated. After identifying a number of such activity pathways, Ted and his counsellor explored whether any of them could serve as a starting point for a tentative vocational pathway. Most importantly, Ted was encouraged and supported in examining and clarifying the goals he would be pursuing and the implementation issues he might be facing by choosing a pathway or a combination of pathways. The counsellor suggested that Ted could start by investigating educational and training opportunities for the most promising potential vocational pathways, talk with people who had pursued careers in those areas, and think of creative ways to perhaps combine several of his interests.

Vocational guidance and career counselling are not "once and done" activities because career development is a life-span process (Vondracek et al., 1986). With the help of his counsellor, Ted progressed toward making and implementing career decisions, only to be forced to revise them repeatedly over the years as his life circumstances changed. In each subsequent encounter, their initial efforts were designed to ensure that their goals in the counselling situation were aligned. Importantly, the counsellor encouraged Ted to always speak openly about past experiences, thoughts, feelings, and contexts. After identifying and exploring several activity pathways, Ted and his counsellor usually worked toward identifying those pathways that would be best suited to become potential vocational or career pathways. Invariably, this would involve careful exploration and determination of the clarity of Ted's goal(s), determination of his motivation to pursue the goal, and assessment of his relevant capabilities and skills. The final step always involved assisting Ted, as needed, in investigating whether the occupational and economic environment was conducive to the pursuit of Ted's chosen career pathway.

Case study: reflective questions

1   How do you see the *beliefs* and *contexts* influencing Ted's career pathways?
2   What role do BESs play in the formation of career pathways?
3   How can one determine whether motivation is adequate for pursuit of a particular pathway?

Chapter summary

The LSVD stresses the complexity of whole person-in-context functioning by insisting that vocational behaviour and development cannot be understood by examining selected person parts like vocational interests or self-efficacy and at the same time ignoring the unique and varied contexts in which each person operates, as well as the biological affordances and limitations that are unique to every individual. Using the BE as the basic unit of analysis, the theory offers a means for assessing and explaining the integrated functioning of the person-in-context. Moreover, the theory explains how learning continually takes place through the formation and modification of BESs, which, in turn, represent the raw material for the development of vocational and career pathways. The principal limitation of the LSVD is that it is a complex model that requires more than a superficial reading because it resists reductionism, oversimplification, and the reification of constructs.

Vocational behaviour and development (including career development) should be recognised as a core topic in the field of human health and development, reflecting the fact that work occupies more time and effort in people's lives than any other activity. Moreover, work has been linked to the health and happiness of individuals and families across the life span (e.g., Vondracek & Crouter, 2013). Because of these linkages, the LSVD could serve to better connect the study of all aspects of vocational behaviour and development to related scientific and professional specialties in fields such as medicine, psychology, sociology, and management, which are already relatively advanced in their use of systems models.

The focus of the LSVD on the individual person as the unit of analysis (and the emergence of systems models in the human sciences) has promoted the study of intraindividual variability. Nesselroade and Molenaar (2010, p. 38) have observed that differential psychology focused on identifying differences among individuals, while intraindividual variability allows for "seeking similarities in patterns of individuals' behavior, thereby describing a functional individual of some generality rather than trying to synthesise an individual from the ways people differ from one another." Differential psychology and the study of individual differences have been the dominant approaches in vocational psychology and in studies of career development. We believe that these fields would be enhanced if those approaches were to be complemented by an emphasis on dynamic, living systems approaches and the attendant focus on patterns of intraindividual variability. The result would be a better understanding of individual functioning that would benefit researchers and practitioners alike.

Conclusion

Every person is a dynamic, living system made up of numerous interrelated subsystems. This view, now widely accepted in the physical and biological sciences and in medicine and supported by persuasive scientific evidence, has struggled to be adopted by vocational psychologists and career counsellors. Barriers to adopting a living systems framework have included a reluctance to address the complexity of the human living system, as well as a perceived lack of tools for using such a framework in research and practice. The LSVD demonstrates how to overcome these barriers by presenting a comprehensive conceptual and propositional theoretical framework based on Ford's (1987) conceptualisation of humans as self-constructing living systems.

Learning activities

Learning activity 1

Examine your pattern of activities during the course of one entire day. Specifically, identify *thinking BEs, observational BEs, and instrumental BEs.* List all goals you were pursuing in these BEs and examine which of them were long-term, intermediate term, or short-term goals, and how (and whether) they were interrelated.

Learning activity 2

Think about the role of motivation in the emergence of your career pathway. Identify the specific components (e.g., capability and context beliefs, supportive context, emotions, skills) that were particularly important in how your career pathway unfolded over time.

Learning activities: reflective questions

1   Why is the identification and analysis of system processes of central importance in living systems?
2   If career counselling focuses on facilitating intraindividual change, should career theory and research also focus on intraindividual change processes? Why?
3   What are the main arguments for comprehensive theories of career development as opposed to what Super called "segmental theories"?

References

Ford, D. H. (1987). *Humans as self-constructing living systems: A developmental perspective on behaviour and personality.* Hillsdale, NJ: Lawrence Erlbaum.

Ford, M. E. (1992). *Motivating humans: Goals, emotions, and personal agency beliefs.* Newbury Park, CA: SAGE.

Hartung, P. J., Porfeli, E. J., & Vondracek, F. W. (2005). Child vocational development: A review and reconsideration. *Journal of Vocational Behaviour, 66,* 385–419.

Lent, R. W., Brown, S. D., & Hackett, G. (1994). Toward a unifying social cognitive theory of career and academic interest, choice, and performance. *Journal of Vocational Behaviour, 45*(1), 79–122.

Nesselroade, J. R., & Molenaar, P. C. M. (2010). Emphasizing intraindividual variability in the study of development over the life-span. In W. F. Overton (Ed.), *Cognition, biology, and methods across the lifespan: Vol. 1. Handbook of lifespan development* (pp. 30–54). New York: Wiley.

Schulenberg, J. E., Vondracek, F. W., & Nesselroade, J. R. (1988). Patterns of short-term changes in individuals' work values: P-technique factor analysis of intraindividual variability. *Multivariate Behavioral Research, 23,* 377–395.

von Bertalanffy, L. (1950). The theory of open systems in physics and biology. *Science, 111,* 23–29.

von Bertalanffy, L. (1968). General system theory. New York: George Braziller.

Vondracek, F. W., & Crouter, A. C. (2013). Health and human development. In I. B. Weiner (Editor-in-Chief), R. M. Lerner, M. A. Easterbrooks, & J. Mistry (Vol. Eds.), *Handbook of psychology: Vol. 6. Developmental psychology* (2nd. ed., pp. 595–614). New York: Wiley.

Vondracek, F. W., Ford, D. H., & Porfeli, E. J. (2014). *A living systems theory of vocational behaviour and development.* Amsterdam, The Netherlands: Sense.

Vondracek, F. W., & Kawasaki, T. (1995). Toward a comprehensive framework for adult career development theory and intervention. In W. B. Walsh & S. H. Osipow (Eds.), *Handbook of vocational psychology* (2nd ed., pp. 111–141). Hillsdale, NJ: Lawrence Erlbaum.

Vondracek, F. W., Lerner, R. M., & Schulenberg, J. E. (1983). The concept of development in vocational theory and intervention. *Journal of Vocational Behaviour, 23,* 179–202.

Vondracek, F. W., Lerner, R. M., & Schulenberg, J. E. (1986). *Career development: A life-span developmental approach.* Hillsdale, NJ: Erlbaum.

Watson, M. B., & McMahon, M. (2005). Children's career development: A research review from a learning perspective. *Journal of Vocational Behaviour, 67,* 119–132.

10 Careers as fractal patterns
The chaos theory of careers perspective

Robert Pryor and Jim Bright

Learning objectives

The purpose of this chapter is to:

- describe career counselling and key theories in terms of the application of different forms of pattern,
- identify the key features of the chaos theory of careers concept of fractal patterns in careers, and
- explain the benefits of career counselling interventions based on the chaos theory of careers' identification of fractal patterns.

Introduction to the chapter

Within the world of career counselling, the central importance of patterns is reflected in the mantra that first we must understand ourselves and then we must understand the labour market in order to make an informed career decision (e.g. Parsons, 1909). Pattern identification is important in all forms of counselling as part of the process of seeking to create new patterns that are deemed to be solutions or corrections to the client's absent or dysfunctional extant patterns. The chaos theory of careers identifies patterns as characteristic ways in which complex dynamical systems function. Major patterns or attractors will be outlined and illustrated in their application with a case study.

Patterns enable us to see how aspects of the world in which we live fit together, interact, change, develop, and disappear. When we make plans, as in career development, we are constructing patterns that we hope to impose on the world. Success or failure rests on the correspondence between the world and those plans, and the capacity of both to accommodate and to adapt to unforeseen changes that will inevitably arise.

Career counselling and development theories can be characterised by the nature of the patterns that they privilege or that form the basic unit of analysis. For instance, in John Holland's (1959) theory of vocational choice, measured vocational interests from the central organising pattern composed of three-letter client interest codes matched to corresponding occupations also organised into the same three-letter codes. Criticisms of Holland's theory frequently point to the oversimplification of the process, the difficulties in reducing a person to a three-letter code, the static view of individuals and their environments, and the failure to account for the subtlety of individual differences.

Constructivist theorists that embrace narrative as their unit of analysis claim to address these shortcomings (e.g. Patton & McMahon, 2014; Savickas, 1997). They argue that narratives reflect the basic structures of interpretation of human experience. In particular, narrative provides a framework for understanding personal experience. Savickas (1997) explicitly links story to patterns: "Career counsellors who care for the spirit possess the ability to see patterns. Events that cannot be patterned are useless to the client" (p. 10), and "stories are modes of knowing that capture the richness, uniqueness, complexity of what life means to a client" (p. 11). Savickas (2004) asserted the linearity of the plots of stories and their ability to account for change.

From a systems perspective, the development of career theory from matching paradigms to constructivist narrative approaches can be seen as an increase in the complexity of the patterns that are considered. However, in identifying patterns we come to see that our world comprises systems within systems within systems. The complex realities of both human characteristics and the reality they experience cannot be reduced to a three-letter code without gross oversimplification nor can it be "captured" within the confines of a linear story. This is not to deny the usefulness of techniques such as psychological measurement and constructed stories in the process of career development counselling. However, it is to assert that overreliance on any one or even a combination of these and other techniques or tools cannot and will not ever be sufficient to capture the complexity of either our clients or the contexts in which they live and act.

In complex systems such as humans, the whole is greater than the sum of the parts (Morin, 1992). Thus, attempting to reduce human interests, preferences, personality, or values to component parts can at best provide only limited insights. Conversely, the whole is less than the sum of the parts (Morin, 1992). Some of the individual properties of the parts are suppressed under the "influence or constraints resulting from the organization as a whole" (Morin, 1992, p. 4). Thus "holistic" approaches that attempt to understand the "whole person" are equally limited. Finally, the whole is greater than the whole because the whole affects the parts retroactively and the parts in turn then affect the whole. In a complex system, the whole has dynamic organisation and cannot be completely isolated from the other systems to which and within which it is connected. There is inherent uncertainty at the heart of complex dynamical systems. The implication of this is that the nonlinear, dynamical, and complex patterns that emerge from these systems must be considered as one unit of analysis. However, it also follows that the parts of the system must also be simultaneously considered. Thus, under certain circumstances a test score may be more valuable than a story, and under others, a story may be the most valuable basis for analysis. Accordingly, in career counselling, it is unnecessarily limiting and in career development theory it constitutes another form of reductionism, to only consider singular units of either method or analysis.

The chaos theory of careers (CTC)

The chaos theory of careers (CTC) (e.g. Pryor and Bright, 2003, 2011) was formulated in an attempt to provide a framework that better captured the changeable, complex, and uncertain nature of careers as experienced by individuals. The patterns in human career development have to be understood in terms of the patterns in the rest of reality since careers development occurs in that very context. To consider careers and career counselling as somehow functioning in a way distinct and different from the rest of how the world works and needs to be understood is both a contradiction and another form of theoretical fragmentation. When applied to career development, the CTC posits that the description of systems' functioning provided by chaos theory may ultimately provide the most effective way to comprehend and negotiate career development in a world that comprises system patterns that are complex and nonlinearly dynamical.

The term "chaos" can be misleading for many bringing with it connotations of randomness and disorder. The term "chaos theory" was coined by James York (Li & Yorke, 1975) to describe systems that demonstrated nonlinear sensitivity to initial conditions. That is, small incremental changes in the initial conditions of systems can lead to disproportionately large and unpredictable outcomes and vice versa. However, it is important to note that while these systems can give the appearance of being "chaotic," they produce emergent, self-similar patterns. For instance, we cannot predict the personality of a newborn baby, but as that baby matures into adulthood, emergent, self-similar patterns of behaviour, or trait-like themes, become increasingly evident.

The self-similar but dynamical patterns that emerge from complex dynamical (chaotic) systems are called "fractals" (Mandelbrot, 1982). Briggs (1992) describes fractals as the "tracks and marks left by the passage of dynamical activity" (p. 22). The recursive process of the parts influencing the whole that influences the parts leads to a repeating pattern in fractals that, due to the nature of the system, never exactly repeats but is typically self-similar. For instance, an individual's motor vehicle route to work may appear to be identical from day to day or week to week, but close inspection will reveal that, at the very least, small daily changes always occur in the time of departure, the position of car on the road, the condition of the road, the amount and flow of traffic, the weather conditions, and the person's state of mind, to name just a few possibilities.

Fractal patterns are evident throughout nature attributable to the functioning of the complex dynamical systems that underpin everything – living or not. Human bodies, clouds, trees, coastlines, lions, planets, and galaxies – are all examples of fractal patterns formed through the processes of complex dynamical systems. When we talk about family resemblance we are talking about the fractal pattern of self-similarity within a family or within communities or the human race as a whole.

Fractal patterns in more complex dynamical systems demonstrate "roughness" or random variation. In nature, trees are not composed of a series of straight lines; they exhibit variations from the straight and linear. Closer inspection reveals the surface of the trunk and bark to be rough and variable. Fractal patterns also demonstrate similarity across scale. Thus, at every level of magnification similar patterns emerge as in, for example, the pattern of DNA found in every living cell.

As career counsellors, we must be constantly vigilant when working with clients to appreciate that these individuals are themselves complex dynamical patterns nested in systems that, in turn, reveal complex dynamical patterns. The complexity and the continually changing nature of these patterns means that we can never fully describe or capture them irrespective of the nature or number of techniques we might employ. This does not mean that we are unable make any statements about the operation of the system but rather that our insights are always going to be limited, partial, and potentially out of date. Consequently, this serves as a potent warning to eschew overly neat and complete descriptions – either self-descriptions offered by a client or case conceptualisations constructed by a counsellor. Human experience, including career development, does not yield to simple explanations and clear causes. This in turn points to the sterility of the some of the debates in the career development field, such as that of the primacy of scores or stories. Fractals, as the traces of dynamical activity of systems, delineate the limits of such activity and such limits can be used to identify characteristic system patterns of functioning, called "attractors."

Attractors as patterns

One way of understanding the characteristics of a complex dynamical system is by considering the limits on the system, or the motivational forces applied to the system. In chaos theory, these are called attractors. There are four different types of attractor. In order of complexity they are the: point attractor, pendulum (or periodic) attractor, torus attractor, and strange attractor (Pryor & Bright, 2007). The first three of these attractors are characterised by closed systems thinking identified by the belief that individuals can have sufficient knowledge and achieve sufficient control over their interactions with their environment, to be able to disregard contingency by limiting the range and number of inputs into the system that are considered. Conversely, open systems thinking is characterised by an acknowledgement of the limitations of human knowledge and control in negotiating a reality that is complex and, at times, unpredictable.

Point attractor

The *point attractor* limits a system to evolve to a fixed point. The classical example is a damped pendulum that eventually will come to rest at the bottom of its swing. The system operates in a manner in which it appears to be drawn or directed toward the fixed point. Goal-directed behaviour is an example of a point attractor. It involves placing intentional limitations on one's system to influence it toward a desired point. For instance, we set a career goal to become a carpenter and as a consequence, then limit our option search to training opportunities, apprenticeships, and jobs related to the construction industry.

A point attractor operates as a closed system because all alternative possibilities within the system or external to the system are excluded. One of the advantages of goal setting is that it provides a person with a clear focus and discourages distraction. Understanding that goal setting is a form of point attractor is helpful because it highlights an often neglected concern with goal setting: that it comes at the expense of a drastic simplification of complexity. Further, it explains why goal setting tends to work best over the very short term or in laboratories, because the closed system conditions required for goal setting rarely can be constrained in a naturally complex open system world (Bright & Pryor, 2013).

Pendulum attractor

The *pendulum attractor* is said to operate when a system is constrained to move backward and forward between two fixed points, much like a friction-free perpetual pendulum. A client who presents with the career dilemma of being unable to choose between becoming a cook or a clarinettist is said to be stuck in a pendulum attractor. Dichotomous or black-and-white thinking such as "I must pass this examination or it will be the end of the world" is another example of a person captured in the pendulum attractor.

The pendulum attractor is also a closed system attractor, as it permits only one of two competing outcomes to obtain at any one time. As with the point attractor, pendulum attractor behaviour can be effective and helpful in the short term. However in the longer term, the natural open systems complexity of the world will inevitably intrude and undermine the attractor. The career counsellor confronted with such clients may wish to encourage them to consider that their career choices are not necessarily limited only to cook or clarinettist. There may be ways to creatively combine such options, vocationally and avocationally, as well as canvas many other options that may also be available. In so doing, more complexity is being introduced into an oversimplified career dilemma, which may help the client escape from his or her self-limiting predicament.

Torus attractor

The third form of attractor is another closed system called the *torus attractor*. This attractor is observed to be operating when the system is limited to cycling through a series of predetermined fixed points but ultimately returning to its starting point before the next predictable cycle begins. People intentionally seek to impose torus attractors when they enforce routines and develop codes of conduct and regulations. Of course routinised behaviour has many advantages.

Routines can be quickly learned and their repetition can be achieved with less mental effort. Having a set menu of dinner meals every week removes the bothersome task for busy people of staring hungrily at supermarket shelves while awaiting culinary inspiration. It also means recipes can be cooked without the need to consult the cookbook every few minutes. Road rules, another form of torus attractor, are essential to modern city transportation and are generally effective.

However, like the point and pendulum attractors, the torus attractor ultimately breaks down in the face of complexity. People and situations may change over time. Thus, in the dinner menu routine, there may be exceptions to the setup pattern: the ingredients are not available for Thursday's meal; the stove goes on the blink; one's family gets fed up eating sausages and becomes vegan.

In counselling, recognising the patterns of behaviour that are described by the attractors is extremely useful because it provides insights into the constraints and limitations that either clients by their own volition have imposed on their systems or the limitations within which they are obliged to operate. The goal of CTC-based counselling is to move a client from the closed systems' limited reality that they are operating in to the open systems' reality of the strange attractor.

Strange attractor

The *strange attractor* is the only open systems attractor and it is also the attractor associated with the natural state of complex dynamical (chaotic) systems. It is from the functioning of this attractor that fractal patterns emerge. The strange attractor operates to limit the system to a self-similar but not identical cycle. Each iteration of the system contains at the least subtle differences in which the potential for change is present. Negative feedback within the system seeks to maintain or bring the functioning of the system into equilibrium and continue its existing structure. Positive feedback within the system amplifies change, which portends, or actually initiates, change in the system's functioning and structure.

As an open system, the strange attractor is both an influence interacting with other systems and is itself subject to other systems' influences. Another way of saying this is to indicate that the defining limits of the system are permeable and that the nature of the influences which a strange attractor may both exert and be subject to are nonlinear, acausal, mutual, multidirectional, and ahistorical (Patton & McMahon, 2014).

The strange attractor as the "natural" state of complex dynamical systems functions to produce emergent dynamical order, a self-similarity over time and scale; however, also produced is unpredictable variation, sometimes of a minor nature and sometimes more dramatic. Career counselling within the strange attractor, therefore, takes into account the constant interplay between structure and surprise, both within the counselling process itself and in its outcomes in terms of career development. The importance of agentic action is considered along with the real possibilities of unforeseeable change and failure. Complexity is both acknowledged and utilised to encourage individuals to constructively and creatively explore new patterns of understanding and action strategies.

The cultural validity of the CTC

The cultural validity of the chaos theory of careers can be considered in terms of theories of culture and more pragmatically with reference to the successful application and practice of CTC-based counselling in different cultures. From a theoretical perspective, chaos theory has its foundations in the functioning of physical systems, such as weather patterns, water flows, predator/prey balances, or beating hearts and the mathematics used to describe such functioning. Therefore, in a fundamental sense, it is culture-free to the extent that such systems occur in all parts of the physical world across all cultural contexts. The only general cultural belief underlying such scientific endeavour is the assumption that the world is ordered and can be understood deterministically.

In systemic terms, culture is a macrosystem subsuming a wide range of other systems, including, among other things, historical tradition, social mores, religious expression, labour market structures, gender role expectations, and legal and political constraints, and subsuming less general systems (or for the purpose of the context, subsystems), including, but not limited to, social groups, families, and individuals. The specific content of these systems at varying levels of generality and inclusiveness is not the particular focus of chaos theory. Varying kinds of cultural content can be inserted into such systems. Chaos theory focuses attention on how such systems function as complex dynamical systems which manifest a wide range of characteristics in their functioning, including nonlinearity, emergence, recursion, aperiodicity, phase shift, self-organisation, boundedness, self-similarity at different levels of focus, causality, and unpredictability.

The influential work of Hofstede (2011) identified six dimensions of national cultures: power distance, uncertainty avoidance, individualism/collectivism, masculinity/femininity, long-/short-term orientation, and indulgence/restraint. Considering just one of these dimensions, the CTC has most relevance to uncertainty avoidance. "Uncertainty avoidance" varies across cultures and can be defined as a society's tolerance for ambiguity and the extent to which their members are acculturated to be comfortable or uncomfortable with unstructured situations. The CTC actually can account for these different reactions in terms of the application of different characteristic attractors, with high uncertainty avoidant cultures being more likely to embrace the closed system torus, pendulum, or point attractors compared to their counterparts.

In practical terms, the CTC has been adopted and deployed in a wide variety of different cultures. The CTC is being used in practice and research in many countries around the world that represent a diversity of cultures, including predominantly "Western" cultures such as Australia, Canada, Netherlands, New Zealand, the United States, and the United Kingdom, and predominantly "Eastern" cultures such as China, Taiwan, and Japan, as well as in Africa.

Space does not permit citing all of the country examples individually but the work of Lui et al. (2014) in Taiwan is particularly relevant, as it describes explicitly linking the principles of CTC to the concept of yin-yang derived from the I-Ching to develop successful career interventions entitled "touching the sky yet grounded."

Research in brief

The role of chance events in career decision-making

One of the most neglected areas in career development research and theory turns out to be one of the most common experiences in people's careers. Rojewski (1999) defined "chance events" as "unplanned, accidental, or otherwise situational, unpredictable, or unintentional events or encounters that have an impact on career development and behaviour" (p. 269). In this paper (Bright, Pryor, & Harpham, 2005), we reported on two studies that investigated just how common chance events were in people's careers. We were also interested in the idea that people may differ in their tendency to attribute events to chance depending on their locus of control. "Locus of control" is a term to describe people's tendency to attribute the causes of events to things either within their personal control or outside their control. Thus people are termed "internal" or "external" types. The idea was that people who tend to be more external in their explanatory style may over-report chance events and vice versa.

We found in a sample of 772 high school and university students that 69.1 per cent reported chance events having influenced their career decisions. We also found that external types reported more chance events than internal types. However, the effect was quite small, and not sufficient to conclude that the very large proportion of the sample reporting chance events was simply an artefact of explanatory style. In other words, it seems that the majority of people experience significant chance events that affect their career decision-making. Consequently, given the ubiquity of these experiences, accounts of career development can be considered inadequate if they do not have a coherent account of the role of chance events. The CTC is an example of a theory that has both a coherent account of chance events and also places them centrally in the career development process.

Research in brief: reflective questions

1   Have you ever experienced an unplanned, accidental, or otherwise situational, unpredictable, or unintentional event or encounter that has had an impact on your career development and behaviour?

2 If you have, what were the circumstances? Was it a positive or negative event? How did you react? What was the outcome? What did you learn about yourself and the world? How could you use or even seek out chance events to develop your career in the future? Or if you have not, think of a friend or someone you know who has, and answer these questions.

3 How do you feel about uncertainty? How could you feel (even) more positive about uncertainty? What are the benefits of uncertainty in career development? Do you think it is important that you are certain about where you will be in five years? Is this realistic? Do you have to make up your mind about your future?

Case study

The fractal patterns that we observe and construct about the nature of reality and ourselves have a determinative effect on how we understand our world, ourselves, our options, and our future and how we take action to develop our careers. Since 2003, the current authors have outlined CTC career counselling paradigms and strategies as they have developed and changed over time and in light of our own counselling experience. An alternative career counselling approach based on the CTC can be found in Schlesinger and Pasquarella Daley (2016). However, for the current purposes, the most recent career counselling paradigm outline (Pryor & Bright, 2017) is followed for this case study.

From recognition of the nature of complexity, the CTC has come to place significant importance on the humble realisation for both counsellor and counselee, of the human limitations of knowledge and control in all our interactions, and specifically with respect to career development. As a consequence, CTC counselling practice is distinguished from traditional matching models by the following characteristics (Pryor & Bright, 2017):

a   Exploring a mystery – acknowledging the limitations of all human knowledge;
b   Trying a strategy – appreciating human limitations and so forming an open action plan;
c   Investigating several options – complexity means that actions may fail and that more than one possibility may need to be considered;
d   Influencing systems – proactively changing oneself and the environment;
e   Fuzzy goals – developing aims that are flexible and responsive to change;
f   Embracing uncertainty – using adaptability and resilience in response to unexpected and nonlinear change.

Pryor and Bright (2017) detailed an eleven-step career counselling paradigm, which we flexibly follow in the presentation of the case study of Jack (pseudonym).

1 What help is sought?

Jack narrated his story that as a teenager, he had decided to set his sights on a career in professional golf. However, he was so ambitious and confident that he did not want to follow the path of a traineeship at a local golf club. Instead, he aspired to build an outstanding amateur record, which would allow him to transfer directly into the professional ranks following the example of several predecessors. With intense coaching, practice, and competition, Jack became increasingly aware that he was sustaining repetitive strain injuries in his right shoulder and lower back. Now, age 21, Jack felt exasperated that despite all his commitment, sacrifice, pain, and effort, he was faced with the prospect that he could not fulfil his dream of a career in professional golf. Sometimes life does not seem fair. Some chance events present opportunities to develop our careers and some are roadblocks that disappoint our expectations and undermine our efforts. We can all do our best to maximise the probabilities of recognising and utilising opportunities and to minimise the possibilities of encountering obstacles (Pryor & Bright, 2011). However, ultimately it is simply an ineluctable reality of human experience that even our most assiduous and informed efforts will not prevent us, on occasions, from missing those opportunities and crashing into those roadblocks. Jack sought counselling help because he felt frustrated, angry, and aimless.

2 What are the expectations?

Jack was then asked to consider what kind of story he was telling himself. To help him answer this question, he was presented with the seven archetypal story categories as outlined in Pryor and Bright (2008). Jack chose "the quest" (setting out on a journey, going through ordeals, and achieving a better life). He explained that he saw his career as a "journey" that he was destined to travel, given the talent that he was given and that he had worked hard, overcome "obstacles," and had been in sight of his goal and now was facing "frustration." In chaos theory terms, Jack's pattern of functioning was centred in the point attractor. From an early age, he had been encouraged to believe he could achieve virtually anything he wanted to, exclusively by his own efforts. He now felt stuck because his single-minded focus and all his abilities and efforts were no longer sufficient for him to achieve his perceived single goal.

Pryor and Bright (2017) outlined a twin-perspective approach that is needed to come to terms with complexity: the emergent (asking questions, generating possibilities, taking risks) and the convergent (deciding what is relevant, focusing on the most apposite for action). This approach provides an orientation for case conceptualisation in counselling.

What is apparent is that Jack is exhibiting a high-convergent/low-emergent perspective (see Table 17.4, Pryor & Bright, 2017). Relevant aspects of this high-convergent/low-emergent perspective for Jack include:

Needs: *Conflicted: Frustrated: Fear of failure: Plateaued: Lacking direction.*
    Goals: *Accept uncertainty: Explore meaning: Recognise the possibility and value of failure: Brainstorm possibilities.*
    Career Challenge: *To reflect.*

Implementing these counselling goals set the course for the rest of the interactions with Jack. He was asked to complete the Reality Checklist Exercise (Pryor & Bright, 2006) through which he came to appreciate reflection on the importance of chance, change, limitation, and failure. Had time permitted, Jack would have also been returned to the archetypal stories categories to see if he now wanted to change the story he sought to tell himself to maybe "rebirth" (triumph through travail and trial) or "voyage and return" (learning through challenges).

3 Work out what really matters and how work fits into that.

Jack was invited to explore what matters to him further through the use of journaling cards (Weston, 2003). He was presented with thirty-two cards and asked to choose which ones he would like to use. Each focused on a topic (e.g. fear, hope, patterns, shadow) with a paragraph for reflection and an invitation to respond in writing. He wrote up his journal in between counselling sessions and then was invited to share at the next meeting what he felt comfortable disclosing. It emerged that personal achievement, self-development, and the desire to contribute to the community were fundamental to what Jack wanted to accomplish through his work.

4 Keep the mind open to opportunities.

At the same time Jack was encouraged to use his contacts in the "golfing community" to network as a way to investigate other options in the sport.

5 Generate and try several possibilities.

Jack completed a Creative Thinking Strategies (Bright & Pryor, 2009) exercise to assist in generating possible career options. In addition, Jack was introduced to strategies such as work trials, work shadowing, work volunteering, and short-term contract employment. As a result he explored four possibilities: (1) golf club designer, (2) golf club personal fitter and sales representative, (3) professional golf caddy, and (4) golf tournament administration officer.

    Jack has continued to explore these options. An iconic golf club in his city of residence offers professional caddy training and he has been accepted for entry into the programme. Golf club designing is his most preferred option but to undertake such training and employment will probably require him to travel and work in the home countries of the golf manufacturers, and so he is saving for such an option and making representations to various overseas companies. He has been working part time as well at an indoor golf training facility learning about personalised golf club fitting and he has volunteered at several major golf tournaments as an event organiser.

6 *Expect that some possibilities will fail.*

Jack will continue to explore and probably end up rejecting one or more of these options. He recognises now that there is nothing wrong with not being good at everything, or even that he has to put all his effort into only one career option.

7 *Make failure survivable.*

Jack has come to understand that it would not be advisable just to rush off overseas in search of a club design position and in the process running up debts that he may struggle subsequently to repay. He hopes he will be able in the future to uncover some realistic employment possibilities in the golf club design field. He also has a better appreciation of the likely sacrifices he would need to make including undertaking a form of apprenticeship which he previously eschewed.

8 *Seek and examine feedback to learn what works and what does not.*

Jack is still considering an apprenticeship as a future option. He now has a better understanding of the risks involved and has come to recognise the possibility that he may need a backup option, such as caddying, in case a more preferred aspiration either fails to materialise or he fails in its execution.

9 *Utilise what works and examine what has emerged.*

Jack has been encouraged to continue to evaluate his ongoing training and work experience to gain a further understanding of what matters to him and what he is now capable of doing.

10 *Combine and add as seems likely to improve career prospects.*

Jack has been introduced to work options other than one job for life including the protean career, boundaryless career, psychological contract, customised career, and intermittent career. Thus, he is now considering ways to combine some of the options he has identified rather than think in terms of a single career for life.

11 *Iterate the process.*

Jack is now aware that career development and decision-making are lifelong processes and that the experience of career counselling in which he has engaged can be a model or prototype for future career development. In addition he has been given an open invitation to resume career counselling in the future as he deems appropriate and helpful.

Jack still has many important decisions to make: he is continuing to come to terms with his need to compromise his aspirations; he continues to explore new options with a new perspective on change, opportunity, and uncertainty; and he remains unsure which of the options that have opened up now for him he would like and would be able to pursue, in light of what he now understands to be his highest personal priorities. However, he has moved from the frustration of disappointment to a place where positive action is being taken and where hope has been restored. Truth be told, he would still prefer to be pursuing a career playing professional golf. However, the chances of achieving at elite levels of professional sport are always low and very few succeed, but that does not mean that life and work cannot still be purposeful, productive, and satisfying, even if we fail to achieve our most desired goal. Often dealing with failure can help us to better understand ourselves and the limits of our control over our lives and circumstances.

Case study: reflective questions

1   In what ways did the identification of Jack's career fractal as a point attractor elucidate his career situation and suggest possible interventions?
2   Identify the different ways that Jack was encouraged to develop his career thinking through the use of narrative techniques. What different contributions did these make to the counselling process and outcome?
3   The CTC emphasises a balance between the structure of systems and their inherent unpredictability. What contribution did this insight make to Jack's career development thinking?

Summary and conclusions

There are several strengths evident in the CTC. First, the CTC links career development to all other fields of scientific endeavour since chaos theory itself has applications anywhere in which prediction and control become problematic. Second, as a systems theory, the CTC incorporates a wide range of conceptualisations and techniques from other parts of career development theory and practice and links with the external environmental systems in which individuals develop their careers. Third, it is a theory "whose time has come" – in general science now, there is an appreciation that both disorder as well as order has to be investigated; in counselling, when outlined to clients, the CTC strikes an immediate chord of recognition, understanding, and, at times, relief and enlightenment. Fourth, there is an increasing body of evidence supporting the applicability and utility of the CTC for the career development of students, adults, intervention programmes, and organisations.

In turn, there are some limitations of the CTC at present. First, some chaos terms (such as "torus attractor"), having been derived from other fields of science, can be unfamiliar and off-putting for counselling clients. Second, concepts in chaos theory such as resonance, bifurcation, recursion, emergence, self-organising, phase shift, nonlinearity, and synchronicity remain relatively unexplored or applied to career development. Third, there remains an ongoing challenge to develop research strategies that can focus on the operation of open systems, as further ways to explore and validate CTC theoretical propositions.

As an increasing number of career development experts show interest in the CTC, there are likely a variety of directions in which the future development of chaos theory will go. For the current authors, the future directions for the CTC will focus on the three areas of its ongoing development. First, in the domain of theory, attractors and fractals remain major conceptualisations that require further explication. For example, what accounts for some individuals becoming "stuck" in one attractor? Second, in the domain of research, empirical investigation of the efficacy of programmes based on the CTC for the career development of high school students continues. Third, in the domain of counselling, the development of a counselling tool to identify individuals' combination of convergent and emergent thinking styles as a basis for career counselling processes is proceeding.

In summary, the chaos theory of careers places considerable emphasis on systems' self-organising processes and outcomes. Individuals, like Jack, can be very successful in career development terms following closed system attractors such as the point attractor. However, almost inevitably at some point, the reality that the world is an open system will intrude in some way, either or both, positively and/or negatively. If positively, then individuals who are only thinking and acting in closed systems terms may miss important opportunities. If negatively, then their dreams may be shattered and they may end up feeling angry, disoriented, frustrated, depressed, and despairing. In this chapter, the CTC has been presented in terms of fractal patterns as attractor paradigms for career development in a complex, connected, and changing work environment. Three attractors (point, pendulum, and torus) all focus on career development as a closed system endeavour. The strange attractor was seen as the fractal paradigm for open systems thinking and one that allows individuals to understand and respond to the contemporary world in the most responsive way. The applicability of chaos theory across cultures was addressed and an illustrative case was presented. Finally, this chapter has attempted to demonstrate the importance of chaos theory's concepts relating to fractals for career development theory and practice since understanding reality in terms of fractal patterns of complexity enables all of us to live on the edge of chaos where "the processes of self-organisation and stability coalesce with the contingency of human experience and the creativity of human potential" (Pryor & Bright, 2011, p. 46).

Learning activities

Learning activity 1: the triangles and trees exercise

Aim: To explore your career using simple and fractal patterns.

Step 1: Simple and complex patterns: look around you and identify a circle, a square, and a triangle. How could these shapes be used to describe your career? For instance, you may think you are going around in circles, or that you are travelling inevitably towards the point at the apex (or bottom) of the triangle, or that your career involves moving in a regular routine through four different quadrants.

Step 2: Now have a look outside at a tree or other plant. Observe the branches or stems. Notice how each one resembles the others in the plant, but at the same time is unique. Notice how more smaller branches emerge from each branch. How could this shape describe your career? Take a closer look at one of the branches, and notice the stems growing off those. Do you see a sort-of-old-but-not-exactly repeating pattern? What repeating patterns like these can you identify in your career? How are they facilitating your career? How are they limiting your career?

Learning activity: reflective questions:

1   How do different places on the tree or plant provide opportunities for growth? How about in your career?
2   Think about what cannot be seen, the root system beneath the earth. What is supporting your career and its growth?
3   Which patterns do you prefer? The ones you considered in step 1 or step 2? Which patterns provide the most certainty? Which provide the most opportunities for growth? What do your answers tell you about the relationship between uncertainty and growth in your career?

Learning activity 2: the fractal limits exercise – what will you let change?

Aim: To explore your fractal's limits and openness to change (see Figure 10.1).

Where would you place the following concepts:

Gender, Health, Values,

Abilities, Interest in Using Tools or Machines, Interest in Nature, Interest in Science, Interest in Culture, Interest in the Arts, Interest in Helping, Interest in Persuading, Interest in Organising, Skills,

Beliefs, Openness to Experience, Conscientiousness, Extroversion, Agreeableness, Emotionality, Mental Health, Sexuality, Knowledge,

Labour Market Knowledge,

Physical State, Relationship, Family, Friends, Finances,

Work Reward Expectations,

Political Persuasion,

Home, Future, Current Circumstances, Future Circumstances.

Thinking about the quadrants you have placed each of these in. What circumstances can you imagine that might cause these items to move between the quadrants? Circle the items that you would like to see move and place an arrow on the circle indicating the direction you'd like to see it move (to which quadrant). Thinking about these desired moves, can you see a pattern emerging? How could you take small steps to move these labels in your preferred direction?

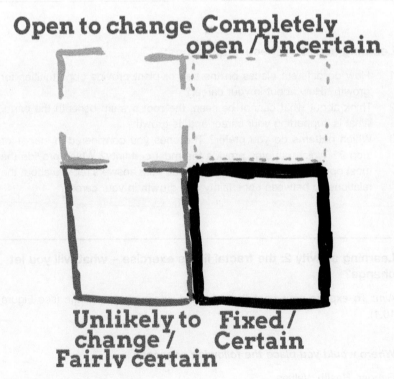

Figure 10.1 Openness to change.

Learning activity: reflective questions

1   Thinking about emergent fractal patterns, how could you use this concept with your clients to help them appreciate the relationship between certainty and uncertainty, stability and change, order and disorder, closed and open systems?
2   How could fractals assist in trying a strategy and appreciating human limitations in forming an open action plan?
3   How could you experiment with fractals in career counselling?

References

Briggs, J. (1992). *Fractals the patterns of chaos: Discovering a new aesthetic of art, science and nature*. New York: Simon & Schuster.

Bright, J. & Pryor, R. (2013). Goal setting: A chaos theory of careers approach. In S. David, D. Clutterbuck, & David Megginson (Eds.), *Beyond goals* (pp. 185–210). Farnham, UK: Gower.

Bright, J. E. H. & Pryor, R. G. L. (2009). *Creative thinking strategies*. Sydney: Congruence.

Bright, J. E. H., Pryor, R. G. L. & Harpham, L. (2005). The role of chance events in career decision making. *Journal of Vocational Behavior*, 66(3), 561–576.

Hofstede, G. (2011). Dimensionalizing cultures: The Hofstede model in context. *Online Readings in Psychology and Culture*, 2(1). doi:10.9707/2307-0919.1014

Holland, J. L. (1959). A theory of vocational choice. *Journal of Counseling Psychology*, 6, 35–45.

LiT-Y., & Yorke, J. A. (1975). Period three implies chaos. *American Mathematical Monthly*, 82, 985–992.

Liu, S., Wang, C., Deng, C., Keh, F., Lu, Y., & Tsai, Y. (2014). Action research using a Chinese career model based on the Wisdom of Classic of Changes and its applications. *Journal of Pacific Rim Psychology*, 8(2), 83–94. doi:10.1017/prp.2014.11

Mandelbrot, B. (1982). *The fractal nature of geometry*. San Francisco, CA: WH Freeman.

Morin, E. (1992). From the concept of system to the paradigm of complexity. *Journal of Social and Evolutionary Systems*, 15, 371–385.

Parsons, F. (1909). *Choosing a vocation*. Boston, MA: Houghton Mifflin.

Patton, W. & McMahon, M. (2014). *Career development and systems theory: Connecting theory and practice* (2nd ed.). Rotterdam, The Netherlands: Sense.

Pryor, R. G. L., & Bright, J. E. H. (2003). Order and chaos: A twenty-first century formulation of careers. *Australian Journal of Psychology*, 55(2), 121–128.

Pryor, R. G. L., & Bright, J. E. H. (2006). Counselling chaos: Techniques for counsellors. *Journal of Employment Counselling*, 43(1), 2–17.

Pryor, R. G. L., & Bright, J. E. H. (2007). Applying chaos theory to careers: Attraction and attractors. *Journal of Vocational Behavior*, 71, 375–400.

Pryor, R. G. L., & Bright, J. E. H. (2008). Archetypal narratives in career counselling: A chaos theory application. *International Journal for Educational and Vocational Guidance*, 8(2), 71–82.

Pryor, R. G. L., & Bright, J. E. H. (2011). *Chaos theory of careers*. New York: Routledge.

Pryor, R. G. L., & Bright, J. E. H. (2017). Chaos and constructivism: Counselling for career development in a complex and changing world. In M. McMahon (Ed.), *Career counselling: Constructivist approaches* (2nd ed., pp. 196–209). London: Routledge.

Rojewski, J. W. (1999). The role of chance in the career development of individuals with learning disabilities. *Learning Disability Quarterly, 22*(4), 267–278.

Savickas, M. L. (1997). The spirit in career counseling: Fostering self-completion through work. In D. Bloch & L. Richmond (Eds.), *Connections between spirit and work in career development: New approaches and practical perspectives* (pp. 3–26). Palo Alto, CA: Davies-Black.

Savickas, M. L. (2004). Career as story: Using life themes in counseling. [Power Point slides] 13th AACC National Conference, Coolangatta, Australia.

Schelsinger, J., & Pasquarella Daley, L. (2016). Applying the chaos theory of careers as a framework for college career centers. *Journal of Employment Counseling, 53*, 86–96.

Weston, D. (2003). *Inside out: A journaling kit*. Bendigo, Victoria, Australia: Innovative Resources.

11 The psychology of working theory

A transformative perspective for a challenging era

David L. Blustein, Ryan D. Duffy, Maureen E. Kenny, Ellen Gutowski, and AJ Diamonti

Learning objectives

The purpose of this chapter is to:

- instruct readers on the major tenets of the psychology of working framework and psychology of working theory,
- apply the perspectives and assumptions of psychology of working framework and psychology of working theory to counselling practice, and
- inspire readers to consider the importance of new and transformative theories given the radical changes taking place in the world of work.

Introduction to the chapter

The challenges in preparing for and adjusting to the radically shifting occupational landscape have been well-documented in career development (e.g., Arulmani, Bakshi, Leong, & Watts, 2014; Blustein, 2006, 2013; Savickas, 2013) and in many other relevant bodies of knowledge (e.g., International Labour Organization, 2017; Organization for Economic Co-operation and Development, 2015). Work is no longer as accessible or stable as it was half a century ago, particularly for individuals without high levels of skills. Indeed, the 21st century has witnessed growing rates of unemployment, underemployment, and precarious work across the globe (Kalleberg, 2009). In this chapter, we review the psychology of working framework (PWF) and the psychology of working theory (PWT), which collectively offer a uniquely informative lens that is well suited for addressing the challenges that confront people as they seek to find their way to a life of survival, social connection, and self-determination.

Overview of the psychology of working framework/theory

The PWF and PWT are presented in a historical context to furnish a sense of how the goals of this work evolved. As we propose in this chapter, the PWF and PWT reflect a broad and ambitious agenda that seeks a fundamental transformation of the discourse in vocational psychology and career development.

Origins of the psychology of working framework/theory

The PWF emerged out of various critical perspectives of traditional career development theory, research, and practice that evolved during the middle and later parts of the 20th century. Harkening back to the seminal work of Frank Parsons, scholars and activists within vocational psychology have raised concerns about the privileging of the interests of middle-class and affluent students and clients, which resulted in the growing marginalization of poor and working class individuals and communities (Blustein, 2017). Some of the earliest critiques came in the 1970s from progressive thinkers (i.e., Warnath, 1975), who realized during the first major recessions since the Great Depression that many clients had limited access to the American Dream. At around the same time, feminist scholars were critiquing the male hegemony both in the leadership of career development and in its major theories (e.g., Betz & Fitzgerald, 1987). A third stream of critique emerged from scholars and activists who were leading the nascent multicultural and race studies movements, which had powerfully decried the pervasive impact of racism and other forms of oppression in the world of education, training, counselling, and the labor market (e.g., Gordon, 1974; Smith, 1983).

Integrating and advancing these critiques was fueled in part by scholars who identified the need for more relativistic and justice-based perspectives. Leading this charge was Mary Sue Richardson (1993), who argued that a focus on work, including caregiving, as opposed to the traditional emphasis on hierarchical and volitional careers in the marketplace, would create a more inclusive and less privileged body of knowledge to inform our field. Richardson also advocated for the active consideration of social constructionist and post-modern perspectives, which she proposed would help to unpack the deterministic features of existing theories and practices in traditional career development theory and practice.

By the turn of the 21st century, the critique of career development began to gain momentum as the various streams of pushback against the middle-class and male bias began to take shape in a movement that Blustein (2006) called the psychology of working. Identifying the limitations of the major assumptions and practices within career development, Blustein argued that the field needed a radical shift that would encompass both a revitalized moral compass and an expanded intellectual framework. The moral perspective that Blustein proposed clearly challenged existing systems that had privileged some communities and marginalized others. The inclusive intellectual perspective encompassed a movement inspired by the need to expand the impact of our work to include the full gamut of relevant social sciences and an equally broad scope of epistemologies and methods.

The psychology of working framework: an overview

By 2006, Blustein's views were fully articulated in the publication of *The Psychology of Working: A New Perspective for Career Development, counselling, and Public Policy*, which provided a comprehensive critique as well as the framework for a new direction for our field. Central to this book were the following features: First, a core feature of this new framework was the notion that our field should focus on work as well as traditional, hierarchical careers. According to Blustein (2006), work "includes effort, activity, and human energy in given tasks that contribute to the overall social and economic welfare of a given culture. This includes paid employment as well as work that one does in caring for others within one's family and community" (p. 3). Blustein did not propose that we should abandon the traditional notion of career or career development; rather, he advocated that a broader focus on work would promote positions and policies that would encompass all those who work and who want to work. Second, Blustein integrated existing taxonomies of the needs that working optimally could fulfill, and identified the central role of the need for survival and power, need for social connection, and the need for self-determination. Third, macro-level forces were highlighted, including marginalization due to oppressed social identities, poverty, classism, disability status, and other factors. Fourth, Blustein proposed a new model of integrative counselling, known as inclusive psychological practice, which sought to enhance existing practice models to embrace people who did not have as much choice in their work lives. This perspective also provided a framework for integrating work-based and non-work-based interventions into a coherent perspective that seeks to validate any experiences that clients bring to counselling.

The PWF has generated considerable research, theory, program development, and new counselling models, many of which were summarized in *The Oxford Handbook of the Psychology of Working* (Blustein, 2013). Two particularly prominent outcomes of the PWF include two new theories—the relational theory of working (Blustein, 2011) and the newly developed psychology of working theory (Duffy, Blustein, Diemer, & Autin, 2016), which we review next.

The psychology of working theory: an overview

In 2016, several scholars immersed in research stemming from the PWF collaborated to develop an integrated psychology of working theory (PWT; Duffy, Blustein, et al., 2016). The authors sought to combine key principles from the PWF and associated research to develop an empirically testable model that would be useful to scholars and practitioners alike. The centerpiece of the model, decent work, is a construct developed by the International Labour Organization (ILO, 2008), which proposes that stable and dignified work is a fundamental right of all human beings. As defined by the ILO, decent work is a job with physically and interpersonally safe working conditions, hours allowing free time and adequate rest, organizational values that complement family and social values, adequate compensation, and access to adequate health care (Duffy, Blustein et al., 2016). Decent work is conceptualized as a threshold that, once achieved, can provide the foundation for individuals to meet their survival, social connection, and self-determination needs and in turn experience fulfillment in work and life. While decent work has become a hallmark of an aspirational foundational baseline for working people across the globe, it does not encompass some of the psychological aspects of working (such as meaningful work) and it does not include work in the personal care context. Nevertheless, this ILO initiative has established a clear social justice framework for the consideration of work that is dignified and stable, an ideal that is becoming less possible for increasing numbers of working people across the globe.

Contextual and psychological variables are proposed to conjointly predict an individual's ability to secure decent work. In the PWT, economic constraints and experiences with marginalization (e.g., on the basis of race, gender, disability, etc.) are placed as the primary, contextual predictor variables, with individuals who have greater constraints and experiences of marginalization being less likely to secure decent work. Work volition, or the perception of choice in one's career decision-making (Duffy, Diemer et al., 2012), and career adaptability, or the ability to cope with and complete tasks associated with developing and implementing one's career plans (Savickas, 2013), are the primary psychological predictors. Specifically, those with greater work volition and adaptability are hypothesized to be more likely to secure decent work, and these constructs are positioned to also, in part, explain why higher levels of economic constraints and marginalization link with a lower likelihood of securing decent work. Namely, individuals who are constrained and/or marginalized are less likely to have choice in their career decision-making and less likely to have developed adaptability in the workplace.

This grouping of contextual and psychological predictors is theorized to explain differences in access to decent work for individuals around the globe. In addition to these predictors, Duffy, Blustein et al., (2016) proposed one structural factor (economic conditions) and three malleable factors (critical consciousness, social support, and proactive personality) that may attenuate the effects of economic constraints and experiences of marginalization on decent work. According to the PWT, when overall economic conditions are strong, economic constraints and experiences of marginalization will be less robustly linked with decent work. Analogously, when individuals can boost their critical consciousness (which refers to the capacity to discern and act on social and political forces affecting one's life), proactivity, and support networks—constructs that represent ideal targets for counselling interventions—the deleterious effects of economic constraints and marginalization on access to decent work can be attenuated. In the subsequent sections of the chapter, we highlight these variables in greater depth regarding practitioner strategies.

Research in brief

Douglass, Velez, Conlin, Duffy, and England 2017) examined predictors of decent work among a sample of 218 sexual minority employed adults, finding support for the majority of propositions within the PWT. Specifically, social class, marginalization experiences, and work volition were each found to predict decent work and the relation of social class and marginalization to decent work was mediated by work volition.

Duffy, Velez, England, Autin, Douglass, Allan, and Blustein (2018) conducted a similar study focusing on racial and ethnic minority employed adults. Here, marginalization and work volition were each found to significantly predict decent work and work volition was found to—analogously—mediate the relation between marginalization and economic resources to decent work.

Overall, the results of these two research exemplars provide preliminary support for many of the theory's propositions—in particular the role of work volition as a direct predictor and mediator variable—but also raise questions about the place of career adaptability in the model. Specifically, both articles discuss how alternative conceptualizations and assessments of adaptability may be needed in future studies to better capture this construct.

Research in brief: reflective questions

1   To what extent is it possible to assess such complex constructs and relationships that are summarized in this textbox in quantitative studies?
2   How can the concept of marginalization be defined in a way that is both relevant to diverse individuals, yet also useful in model-building research?
3   What does career adaptability mean to you? How does your definition of this construct relate to the definitions provided in this chapter?

Cultural validity

The PWF (Blustein, 2006, 2013) and the PWT (Duffy, Blustein et al., 2016) are rooted in Western society and were developed to offer a critique of existing discourses that had long neglected people who have been marginalized because of constrained access to the options available to the privileged. Although the development of PWF/T drew from empirical work that included North American samples that were inclusive with regard to gender, race, ethnicity, social class, and sexual orientation (see Blustein, 2006, 2013, for reviews), the cultural validity of the model beyond the North American context needs to be explored in further research. We expect that the model will be relevant, at least in part, in many societies across the globe. Indeed, some components of the model, such as self-determination needs (e.g., Deci & Ryan, 2008), career adaptability (e.g., Buyukgoze-Kavas, Duffy, & Douglass, 2015), and work volition (e.g., Cheung, Wu, & Yeung, 2016), have evidenced utility in non-Western cultures. Moreover, PWF/T is framed around a social constructionist perspective, such that the model should be considered relativistic, with new constructs and relationships likely to emerge as the research base expands.

Applications to counselling practice

Counselling models informed by the PWF perspective and the newly developed theories have served as the foundation for individual, group, and programmatic interventions with a wide range of client populations (e.g., Blustein, 2006; Kenny, 2013). PWF-informed practice encourages the critical examination of contextual factors in clients' lives as a central pillar of counselling. This position—also known as an emancipatory communitarian (EC) approach (Prilletensky, 1997)—encourages a movement away from the historical tendency for psychologists to "blame the victim" when working with clients who face systemic barriers (Blustein, Kozan, Connors-Kellgren & Rand, 2015). Blaming-the-victim approaches often occur inadvertently when counsellors focus too much on individual factors to the exclusion of contextual and systemic factors. Moreover, inclusive psychological practice promotes a thorough integration of work and mental health–based interventions (Blustein, 2006) when such a synthesis is indicated and agreed upon by the client. Although each individual is unique and many individuals enter counselling demonstrating a high level of resilience and adjustment, it is important for counsellors to be mindful, particularly when working with clients who live in poverty, that such individuals may be facing multiple, simultaneous stressors (Goodman, Smyth, & Banyard,, 2010) and could therefore benefit most from a synthesis of mental health and vocational interventions (Blustein et al., 2015). In the case that is presented next, we integrate PWT- and PWF-informed concepts to discuss how a practitioner would approach a client who is presenting with multiple challenges related to external barriers and internal psychological factors.

Case study

Lia is a 28-year-old White woman with a high school diploma and most of the credits needed to receive an associate's degree at a local community college[1]. Lia works in quality control at a U.S.-based call center. She begins counselling with concerns about her distressing work life, which seems to be central in her overall sense of dysphoria and anxiety about the future. Lia started off at the company as a customer service agent 4 years ago, and was later promoted to quality control. She describes herself as "a pretty boring person"; she likes to keep to herself, and does not have very many friends, other than her boyfriend. She claims not to drink or go out much and says she is often in bed by 7 p.m. She currently lives with her boyfriend and young son, from a previous relationship.

Lia says her current job, which involves listening to customer support calls and supervising call center employees, is not what she thought she would be doing. In her early 20s, she left community college a few credits shy of completing her associate's degree, after becoming involved in a 4-year relationship with a man she describes as extremely controlling and jealous. She talked about having had bigger dreams when she was in high school, but once she left college, started working, and her son was born, she found it difficult to return to school for financial reasons.

Although she does not like working at the call center, and fantasizes about returning to school to study law, she fears that she is going to be stuck forever in a dead-end job. She calls herself complacent and lazy, and says she is just not motivated to go back to school. Lia feels that work is important for practical reasons (to pay the bills), but she also always imagined that her work life would be something she enjoyed, where she made a contribution and was valued, rather than a place she dreads the thought of going back to from the moment she leaves.

At one time, Lia did apply for a managerial position in the company, but was turned down. She feels that the person who was hired was underqualified, and that the reason she was passed over was because she is "too nice" and because she is a woman. Lia says she used to be excited when postings came up that would lead to the opportunity to advance within the company, but now she just does not care and believes she will be stuck doing quality control forever. She reports feeling humiliated when people ask her what she does and dreads having to answer that question. Despite these feelings, she blames herself for her work struggles and indicates that her failure to finish college and to find a fruitful career direction are due to her own internal deficits and that these are the primary reasons for her stagnation and misery at work.

Lia describes her father instilling in her a strong work ethic, and a feeling that people should love and be proud of what they do. She began working at age 15; her earnings provided her with some spending money in high school, but mostly contributed to family expenses. Although Lia identified dissatisfaction with work as her primary concern, she described feelings of increasing alienation and depression, concluding that if it was not for work and for the need to take care of her son, she feels that she might not get out of bed in the morning.

Summary and case analysis

The PWF (Blustein, 2006, 2013) and PWT (Duffy, Blustein et al., 2016) are based on the core assumptions that work is an essential part of life and mental health. Issues of power, survival and material need, social disconnection, and self-determination are evident throughout the case of Lia. Lia's narrative describes dissatisfaction with her work life and a conspicuous lack of hope or confidence that she possesses the capacity to move beyond her current context. As she narrates the years that have passed since she dropped out of community college and began at the call center, Lia describes initial feelings of self-determination, work volition, and motivation for advancement. However, this experience soon diffused into hopelessness, "laziness," and apathy in the face of promotions that she has not been granted and for which she has been passed up in favor of younger, less qualified, single men. Currently, Lia's life is framed by the interplay of social marginalization, economic constraints, her own financial instability, the needs of her child, and the sense that she has failed and strayed from the values by which she was raised.

Turning toward a consideration of how an intervention might be designed, perhaps the most noteworthy aspect of Lia's case from a PWT perspective is how the psychology underlying Lia's experience irreducibly intertwines the various aspects of her relationship to work, her sense of identity, and her relationship to others, necessitating a holistic approach to counselling. For example, Lia repeatedly identified aspects of systemic oppression that influenced her position, insecurity, and some of the choices she made; yet she remains thoroughly self-blaming, leading to the question: What would it mean for her to view systemic forces as playing a greater role in her life?

According to PWT, the contextual factors affecting Lia's ability to secure decent work—marginalization and economic constraints—are considered in the context of the unique experiences, restrictions, and affordances provided by her social identities and their intersections. From this perspective, Lia's social identities are products of social constructions and structured inequality, such that identity is not an individual characteristic, but a socially embedded location (cf. intersectionality theory; Cole, 2009). Therapeutic work with Lia requires multiple layers of examination, working through issues, and skill building. It is important for the work to include a discussion of how her experience of work is fueled by the broader societal/cultural context in which Lia and the rest of us (i.e., the therapist, her coworkers and employers, her past partners, her child, her family of origin) are situated (Comstock et al., 2008). While Lia is clearly struggling with intrapsychic concerns related to self-worth and motivation, she is also dealing with contextual challenges that frame her understanding of her own suffering.

Intervention strategies

Developing the working alliance

A crucial first step in working with Lia is to cultivate the working alliance (Blustein, 2006; Blustein et al., 2015). In doing so, the counsellor must maintain a critical awareness of the contextual factors that shape Lia's presenting concerns and identity, as well as the psychological factors that contribute to her experience of work and her overall psychosocial functioning. For example, a counsellor working with Lia may consider the gender role expectations to which she has been exposed in her past and present relational contexts, and how such expectations have limited and continue to limit her access to decent work (Blustein, 2006). A careful recognition of contextual factors involves self-examination on the part of the counsellor. Specifically, the counsellor must critically examine any biases so as to be aware of how her or his own experiences and identities may shape the work with Lia. For example, given Lia's history with controlling relationships with others who are in relative positions of power, the counsellor may focus on reducing inherent power differentials within the counselling relationship. One way this may be achieved is through sharing power with Lia when co-constructing goals for counselling. In this context, the counsellor also needs to take an empathic and reflexive stance that affirms Lia's experience (Blustein et al., 2015). This may be done, for example, by validating the very real stress that results from Lia's experiencing limited opportunities to advance in her current work environment.

Assessment considerations

The PWF and PWT advocate for an inclusive psychological practice, which necessitates a thorough assessment of Lia's potential mental health, vocational, and contextual needs (Blustein, 2006; Blustein et al., 2015). The counsellor is advised to assess the extent to which Lia may benefit from psychological support that targets mental health in an integrated format with the work-based intervention. In inclusive psychological practice, clients and counsellors are encouraged to intentionally clarify the nature of the counselling process, which in the case of Lia would be manifested by the counsellor discussing the utility of an integrative mental health– and work-based approach. Early in the counselling relationship, the counsellor should also ask Lia about her resources and barriers, so as to get a sense of what vocational choices are available to her.

In relation to traditional vocational assessments, PWF and PWT have generally focused on tools that are developmentally and culturally relevant to a given client's needs. In Lia's case, tools that may help to increase her sense of having options in the world might be useful. One particularly compelling instrument that the counsellor may use is *My Career Story* (Savickas & Hartung, 2012), which helps explore new vistas and options and is fairly relevant to a broad array of clients.

Skills development

Lia is presenting with dissatisfaction with her work, limited work volition, and ambivalence about pursuing further education and training. Although a full assessment of resources and barriers that are available to Lia would assist her with this decision, skills development also may be a viable option for expanding Lia's opportunities in the current labor market. For example, finishing her education may not only increase her volition, and ultimately lead Lia to secure decent work, but also be an empowering experience for her (Blustein, 2006). Skills development is an integral aspect of inclusive psychological practice; as Lia develops more options that are meaningful to her, specific directions for further skills development options might be suggested and explored in the counselling process.

Critical consciousness

Inclusive psychological practice identifies critical consciousness development as a useful form of intervention (Blustein et al., 2015; Duffy et al., 2016), as it has the capacity to reduce self-blame, buffer against declines in self-esteem, and enhance agency (Blustein, 2006). During the initial phases, the counsellor may facilitate an open discussion about identity during which Lia would be invited to recall any experiences with prejudice. Such a conversation could provide the counsellor with crucial insight into the nature of systemic barriers that Lia encounters. Helping Lia become increasingly knowledgeable about the socio-political structures that influence her life may be a productive intervention. However, promoting critical consciousness in clinical settings is complex, and direct confrontation is not advised, as such an intervention assumes the counsellor's perspective as truth, rather than maintaining that the counsellor and client are collaboratively exploring Lia's trajectory (Blustein, 2006).

Case study: reflective questions

1   How does your own personal identity and context influence how you would approach working with Lia?
2   What external factors may contribute to the extent to which Lia dreams of a better future?
3   How would you consider promoting Lia's critical consciousness?

Summary and conclusion

Taken together, PWF/T provides a rich framework that has shaped scholarship and practice in career development and vocational psychology. Specifically, PWF has inspired the development of counselling models that promote inclusion, attend to the fundamental needs that are fulfilled through work (i.e., survival and power, social connection, and self-determination), and advocate for inclusive psychological practice (Blustein et al., 2015). As with any theory, there remain limitations in our current understanding that need to be addressed in future research. At present, it is not clear that the theory will be generalizable outside of individualistic cultures, as are found in North America. Work also remains to be done to increase understanding of the relations between each of the primary PWT variables across diverse backgrounds and cultures. In addition, research is needed to support the use of inclusive psychological practice, which is based on an amalgam of evidence-based approaches; however, the full synthesis of these strands of practices has not been validated empirically.

In closing, we believe that these new frameworks are ideally suited for a working context that is increasingly characterized by instability, change, and uncertainty. Moreover, we view these contributions as enacting the core commitment to inclusiveness that first inspired Frank Parsons over a century ago in his noble project of developing a conceptual and practice system to help people navigate their work lives with meaning, purpose, and dignity.

Learning activities

Learning activity 1: exploring the good life

This exercise is based on the PWF's notion that values strongly influence the perceptions and experiences of counsellors. As described in the Lara, Pope, and Minor (2011) anthology of career development exercises, participants are asked to reflect on the attributes of a good life. The question about what constitutes a good life and a good society is a core element of Prilleltensky's (1997) discussion of an emancipatory communitarian approach, which was adapted to the psychology of working by Blustein (2006). First, the Good Life Worksheet is completed, which asks for a listing of values along with the context for that value and an opposing value. After the list is completed, students and clients then discuss their values and their antithetical values, which provide a powerful way of delineating how we construct meaning about a good life and good society. The role of these values in shaping one's experiences and hopes for a meaningful work life are then discussed either in individual counselling sessions or in career development workshops and classes.

Learning activity 2: what is work?

An exercise that has been developed by Blustein and his colleagues that is useful for counsellors in training is "What is Work?". It requires the students and clients to define work, career, and then indicate how their families and communities would define these terms. By writing out these definitions without using resources, the participants are able to examine their own internal constructions of these constructs and are able to identify how their socialization has influenced how they view work and career. The definitions of work, career, and family/community influences are discussed extensively in counselling sessions and in psychoeducational interventions.

Learning activities: reflective questions

1   What are the most prominent influences in how you develop your ideas about work and a good society?
2   To what extent have your ideas about work and career been shaped by expectations from your families and communities?
3   As you worked on these exercises, were you able to consider ways that you have experienced both privilege and barriers in your life? Please elaborate.

Note

1   This case is fictional, based on an amalgam of interviews that some of the authors and their colleagues conducted for the Boston College Working Project.

References

Arulmani, G., Bakshi, A. J., Leong, T. L., & Watts, A. G. (Eds.). (2014). *Handbook of career development: International perspectives*. New York: Springer.

Betz, N. E., & Fitzgerald, L. (1987). *The career psychology of women*. Orlando, FL: Academic Press.

Blustein, D. L. (2006). *The psychology of working: A new perspective for counselling, career development, and public policy*. New York: Routledge.

Blustein, D. L. (2011). A relational theory of working. *Journal of Vocational Behavior*, 79, 1–17.

Blustein, D. L. (Ed.). (2013). *The Oxford handbook of the psychology of working*. New York: Oxford University Press.

Blustein, D. L. (2017). Integrating theory, research, and practice: Lessons learned from the evolution of vocational psychology. In J. P. Sampson, E. Bullock-Yowell, V. C. Dozier, D. S. Osborn, & J. G. Lenz (Eds.), *Integrating theory, research, and practice in vocational psychology: Current status and future directions* (pp. 179–187). Tallahassee: Florida State University.

Blustein, D. L., Kozan, S., Connors-Kellgren, A., & Rand, B. (2015). Social class and career intervention. In P. Hartung, M. L. Savickas, & W. B. Walsh (Eds.), *The APA handbook of career intervention* (pp. 242–257). Washington, DC: APA.

Buyukgoze-Kavas, A., Duffy, R. D., & Douglass, R. P. (2015). Exploring links between career adaptability, work volition, and well-being among Turkish students. *Journal of Vocational Behavior*, 90, 122–131.

Cheung, F., Wu, A. M., & Yeung, D. Y. (2016). Factors associated with work volition among aging workers in Hong Kong. *Journal of Career Development*, 43, 160–176.

Cole, E. R. (2009). Intersectionality and research in psychology. *American Psychologist*, 64, 170–180.

Comstock, D. L., Hammer, T. R., Strentzsch, J., Cannon, K., Parsons, J., & Salazar II, G. (2008). Relational–cultural theory: A framework for bridging relational, multicultural, and social justice competencies. *Journal of Counseling & Development*, 86, 279–287.

Deci, E. L., & Ryan, R. M. (2008). Self-determination theory: A macrotheory of human motivation, development, and health. *Canadian psychology/Psychologie Canadienne, 49*, 182.

Douglass, R. P., Velez, B. L., Conlin, S. E., Duffy, R. D., & England, J. W. (2017). Examining the psychology of working theory: Decent work among sexual minorities. *Journal of Counseling Psychology, 64*(5), 550–559.

Duffy, R. D., Blustein, D. L., Diemer, M. A., & Autin, K. L. (2016). The psychology of working theory. *Journal of Counseling Psychology, 63*, 127–148.

Duffy, R. D., Diemer, M. A., Perry, J. C., Laurenzi, C., & Torrey, C. L. (2012). The construction and initial validation of the Work Volition Scale. *Journal of Vocational Behavior, 80*, 400–411.

Duffy, R. D., Velez, B. L., England, J. W., Autin, K. L., Douglass, R. P., Allan, B. A., & Blustein, D. L. (2018). An examination of the psychology of working theory with racially and ethnically diverse employed adults. *Journal of Counseling Psychology, 65*(3), 280–293.

Goodman, L. A., Smyth, K. F., & Banyard, V. (2010). Beyond the 50-minute hour: Increasing control, choice, and connections in the lives of low-income women. *American Journal of Orthopsychiatry, 80*, 3–11.

Gordon, E. W. (1974). Vocational guidance: Disadvantaged and minority populations. In E. L. Herr (Ed.), *Vocational guidance and human development* (pp. 452–477). Boston, MA: Houghton Mifflin.

International Labour Organization. (2008). ILO declaration on social justice for a fair globalization. Retrieved from www.ilo.org/wcmsp5/groups/public/—dgreports/—cabinet/documents/genericdocument/wcms_371208.pdf

International Labour Organization. (2017). *World employment social outlook: Trends 2016*. Geneva, Switzerland: International Labour Office.

Kalleberg, A. (2009). Precarious work, insecure workers: Employment relations in transition. *American Sociological Review, 74*, 1–22.

Kenny, M. E. (2013). The promise of work as a component of educational reform. In D. Blustein (Ed.), *Oxford handbook of the psychology of working: An inclusive psychology for the 21st Century* (pp. 273–291). New York: Oxford University Press.

Lara, T. M., Pope, M., & Minor, C. A. (Eds.). (2011). *Experiential activities for teaching career counseling classes and for facilitating career groups, Volume III*. Broken Arrow, OK: National Career Development Association.

Organization for Economic Co-operation and Development. (2015). *Securing livelihoods for all: Foresight for action (Development Centre Studies)*. Paris: OECD.

Prilleltensky, I. (1997). Values, assumptions, and practices: Assessing the moral implications of psychological discourse and action. *American Psychologist, 52*, 517–535.

Richardson, M. S. (1993). Work in people's lives: A location for counseling psychologists. *Journal of Counseling Psychology, 40*, 425–433.

Savickas, M. L. (2013). Career construction theory and practice. In S. D. Brown & R. W. Lent (Eds.), *Career development and counselling: Putting theory and research to work* (2nd ed., pp. 42–70). Hoboken, NJ: Wiley.

Savickas, M. L., & Hartung, P. (2012). *My career story: An autobiographical workbook for life-career success*. Retrieved from www.vocopher.com/CSI/CCI_workbook.pdf

Smith, E. J. (1983). Issues in racial minorities' career behavior. In W. B. Walsh & S. H. Osipow (Eds.), *Handbook of vocational psychology: Vol. 1, Foundations* (pp. 161–222). Hillsdale, NJ: Erlbaum Associates.

Warnath, C. (1975). Vocational theories: Direction to nowhere. *Personnel & Guidance Journal, 53*, 422–428.

12 Choice or constraint?

Sociological career theory

Jenny Bimrose

Learning objectives

The purpose of this chapter is to:

- consider the academic discipline of sociology as a major contributor to the development of career theory, together with one notable example;
- highlight broader theoretical issues relevant to sociological approaches; and
- examine some implications of sociological perspectives for career practice.

Introduction to the chapter

Many academic disciplines have contributed to career theory (Arthur, Hall, & Lawrence, 1989; Brown, 2002). Scrutiny of its origins reveals richness in philosophical and intellectual influences, perhaps helping explain why career theory and the occupational identity of some career practitioners remain somewhat ambiguous. In the United States, for example, career practitioners tend to identify themselves as vocational psychologists, while in some European countries, there is closer alignment with pedagogy. Whilst the dominant contributor to career theory continues to be the academic discipline of psychology, contributions from other disciplines should not be overlooked, nor their impact underestimated. This chapter examines how sociology contributes an important social equity and cultural dimension by focusing on the contextual influences on careers rather than the primacy of individual choice. A sociological lens is used to frame a case study on gender inequality. In so doing, implications for career practice are examined.

Overview of theory

During the second half of the last century, critiques of the traditional psychological career theories that had dominated careers practice began to emerge. Because of its neglect of the social structures in which occupational choice occurred, one such critique came from a sociologist (Roberts, 1968). By end of this century, the number of critiques of career theory was growing, mainly from US vocational psychologists targeting their own discipline. These voices grew more forceful, criticising the lack of attention that had been paid to the constraining influences exerted by social structures on some groups of individuals who were socially disadvantaged, thereby echoing established sociological concerns. For example, Fitzgerald and Betz (1994) highlighted the "general lack of utility of major career theories to large segments of the population" (p. 103), calling for career development to take account of cultural context, taking cognisance of gender, race, class and sexual orientation. Around the same time, Savickas (1995) argued for theoretical convergence to address weaknesses, but within the discipline of psychology.

Summaries of sociological and economic theories that have relevance to career choice and development, but do not have career as their primary focus, have been presented as having a sociological perspective (e.g., Kirkpatrick Johnson & Mortimer, 2002). Others have produced career theory that is specifically aligned with the academic discipline of sociology, like Hodkinson and Sparkes' (1997) *Careership*, which is a book about the sociological theory of career decision-making. Yet others borrow heavily from sociology, like the community interaction theory developed by Law (1981). An interesting fusion of psychological and sociological approaches is evident in Gottfredson's (1981) theory of circumscription and compromise, which represents an attempt to reconcile the two academic perspectives. Gottfredson set out to explain "how the well-documented differences in aspirations by social group (e.g., race, sex, social class) develop" (1983, p. 204). As a student of psychological theorist John Holland and a sociologist by professional training, Gottfredson was concerned with career aspirations and how they develop. Although acknowledging the influence of the theories of both Holland and Super on her own thinking, she argued that her theory was different from psychological theories (Gottfredson, 1996) since it proposes that career development is an attempt to implement, first, a social self and, second, a psychological self. Gottfredson's theory pays attention to the ways in which beliefs about the self and an occupation develop, treating vocational choice largely as a process of eliminating options and narrowing choices. It also considers how individuals compromise their goals in coming to terms with reality as they try to implement their aspirations (Gottfredson, 2005).

One unequivocal sociological theoretical contribution, the opportunity structure theory (Roberts, 1968), which has been refined over seven decades, will now be explored.

Origins of the opportunity structure theory

The opportunity structure theory was proposed by Roberts (1968) as an alternative to developmental theories of career advanced by Ginsberg, Ginsburg, Axelrad, and Herma (1951) and Super (1957, 1969, 1990). In contrast to the theories he criticised, Roberts (1968) never claimed universality for his theory

(p. 179). Rather, he argued that entry of different groups of individuals to employment, in different social contexts, required different explanatory frameworks and, therefore, different intervention responses. The primary determinants of occupational allocation for young people were, he argued, the home, the environment, the school, peer groups and job opportunities (Roberts, 1968). His original research sample, like that of the original research sample on which Super's theory was based (1969), the theory he was criticising, was based on a sample of young men. Roberts (1968) found that the "momentum and direction of school leavers' careers were derived from the way in which their job opportunities become cumulatively structured . . . with different ease of access to different types of employment" (p. 179). He challenged the utility of the concept of choice for most individuals, emphasising rather the structures of constraints: "'An adequate theory for understanding school-leavers' transition to employment in Britain needs to be based around the concept not of 'occupational choice', but of 'opportunity structure'" (Roberts, 1977, p. 183).

This critique of psychological, particularly developmental, theory and the new theory of opportunity structure were, unsurprisingly, received with caution and scepticism by the career theorists, and wider academic community. One critic of Roberts' early ideas was Peter Daws. He criticised both Roberts' (1977) opportunity structure model and his views about the limited effects of careers interventions as both conservative (Daws, 1981) and fatalistic (Daws, 1992). In contrast, Daws (1992) promoted the value of careers education programmes as being capable of encouraging social change by supporting and educating the individual. Far from changing his ideas as a result of these criticisms, Roberts expanded his determinants of occupational allocation on the basis of the empirical results of the second and third phases of his research into comparative labour markets in the UK and Germany (Bynner & Roberts, 1991; Roberts, 1984). Findings from this cross-cultural research continued to emphasise the importance of local labour markets for the job-seeking behaviour of young people, finding that their average journey to work was limited on average to just three miles, because of the costs of travel. Even low-grade exam achievements were also found to make a difference between finding work and becoming (or remaining) unemployed, with both factors linking back to family background and related socio-cultural capital. The extent to which large firms operated as internal labour markets, especially for young people, was considerable, highlighting the importance of informal networks and, again, social capital. Results from the second phase of his research also focused attention on the importance of ethnicity, operating as a multidimensional disadvantage because of the strong interconnection between housing and education, and education and employment. Together with ethnicity, gender was confirmed as a significant barrier to entry into, and progression through, employment. Even though the proportion of working women in economies throughout the world was steadily increasing, and despite an upward social trend for marriages to end in divorce, Roberts (1984) found that women's career aspirations remained low and short term.

A particular strength of the empirical research underpinning Roberts' theory is the comparative nature of his research across country and cultural contexts. "Only through comparative study can investigators become aware of the ways particular features of contexts determine the timing, character, and outcomes of vocational development" (Kirkpatrick Johnson & Mortimer, 2002, p. 43). This comparative approach was unusual for career research, especially in the 1980s. The third phase of his research continued with cross-country comparison, revealing striking similarities in labour market constraints operating across the two countries. Despite very different education and training systems in the UK and Germany, broadly similar routes to employment in the two countries were found to exist, referred to as career trajectories (Bynner & Roberts, 1991). For each career trajectory, dominant influences could, once more, be traced to education systems, family and social background (Roberts, 1993). Roberts' research interest into the transferability of his key concepts across developing (Kovacheva, Kabaivanov, & Roberts, 2018) and developed countries has continued, with his conclusion the same: "The power of social origins is due to their cumulative impact at successive career junctures" (p. 40, 2012).

Like other career theorists, Roberts (1995) modified his views over a 70-year period. By 1995, he conceded that the debate about "choice versus opportunity" (p. 111) was never won decisively by either side. Roberts noted various reasons, including a wider acknowledgement that the opportunities for choice have always been different, and unequal, among different groups of individuals. The transition period between leaving education and training and entering employment had become extended, so that all young people were able to exercise choices at some stage of this process, even if this was limited to the type of subject or qualification taken in education or training. The debate had been replaced by a new set of debates because of changes occurring in labour markets across the world, including economic restructuring and higher unemployment. New concepts were needed in order to understand the process of transitions into employment (Roberts, 1995, 1997). These included individualisation, referring to the notion that life patterns have become more unique than ever before because of shrinking social networks and changed social behaviour. Uncertain destinations were another feature of transition because of economic, social and educational change, with career transitions likely to involve risk.

> It is as if people nowadays embarked on their life journeys without reliable maps, all in private motor cars rather than the trains and buses in which entire classes once travelled together. . . . These 'cars' in which individuals now travel don't all have equally powerful engines. Some young people have already accumulated advantages in terms of economic assets and socio-cultural capital. Some have to travel by bicycle or on foot. But everyone has to take risks.
>
> (Roberts, 1995, p. 118)

Roberts continued to discuss and highlight the importance of career support (2012, 2015), with the implications of continuous, individualised support for young people throughout their transitions emphasised: "The macro-role of guidance, as ever, will be to assist young people in handling their own transition problems without, in most cases, affecting the eventual outcomes" (Roberts, 1997, p. 352).

Key theoretical principles

Key theoretical principles characterising sociological theory of career relate to structure versus agency. That is, this theory questions the extent to which an individual has, in reality, the ability to exercise choice and autonomy over his or her career development. It focuses attention on the importance of structures within society that may operate as barriers to individual career progression, as well as enhancers, to individuals achieving their aspirations and following their career dreams. Political conflicts (like civil wars), natural disasters (like earthquakes and hurricanes) and economic crises (like the financial crash of 2007/2008) create circumstances that can be beyond the control of individuals living in those societies. For example, refugee status is not chosen, but imposed by political conflict and turmoil. While individual agency prevails for some, others feel overwhelmed by circumstances, at least in the short term. This is an extreme example, though social variables like social class, gender, ethnic origin, age and/or disability exist in every society and are strongly associated with different levels and types of disadvantage (for example, economic, educational and employment), especially where they intersect. Indeed, because of the varying nature of opportunity arising from the contrasting and changing fortunes of different country contexts and cultures around the world, some sociologists have argued that "at the extreme, there may be no such thing as occupational choice as we know it" (Kirkpatrick Johnson & Mortimer, 2002, p. 43).

Sociological theories are regarded by some as deterministic and negative, yet they have always acknowledged the agency of privileged individuals. These theories accept that those with access to resources, both economic and human, are more likely to succeed in their career development than those who do not have such access. Further, sociological theories have never denied that disadvantaged individuals can also progress their careers, but for some it is more difficult than for others. Many of these disadvantaged individuals need careers support that recognises and accommodates their particular situations and needs. Recently, the divergent theoretical concepts that have distinguished sociological theory from psychological theory have begun to merge. Psychologists have become more aware and interested in the social contexts and systems that affect individual behaviour, with sociologists acknowledging the mediating influence of factors like occupational values and identities (Kirkpatrick Johnson & Mortimer, 2002). However, in an assessment of the current relevance of the opportunity structure theory, Roberts (2009) remains adamant that "there is a wealth of talent and a wealth of ambition, and an overall shortage of jobs, not least good jobs" (p. 365). He concludes that choice is not irrelevant, but fails to explain enough. It cannot account for the contexts, including the labour market contexts, in which young people make their choices, and it cannot identify the different limits within which different groups of young people choose.

(Roberts, 2009, p. 362)

Sociological theory has always focused the attention of career practitioners on the particular career development and counseling needs of individuals who may not always feel in control of their destinies. It also alerts practitioners to the types and levels of support required by such individuals to help them to develop or regain a sense of agency and control over their career development.

Cultural validity

The need for cultural responsiveness in careers practice is now well established. It came with the recognition that mainstream counseling and psychotherapy approaches, to which career theory is closely aligned, were predominantly White, middle-class male activities that operated with many distinctive values and assumptions. The approaches were further critiqued for being ethnocentric, or culturally encapsulated, holding at their centre a notion of normality that is different from and irrelevant to many clients (Wrenn, 1962). As a consequence, a multicultural approach to practice evolved, the origins of which have been traced back to the civil rights movement in the United States in the 1950s, 1960s and 1970s (Bimrose, 1998). Its effect on counseling and psychotherapy was considerable, and by 1991 it was being proposed that "we are moving toward a generic theory of multiculturalism as a 'fourth force' position, complementary to the other three forces of psychodynamic, behavioural and humanistic explanations of human behaviour" (Pederson, 1991, p. 6). The definition of culture was gradually expanded beyond ethnic diversity to include gender, sexual orientation, disability, social class, age, and other dimensions of identity. (Bimrose, 2006). By so doing, its importance is emphasised generically for career counseling practice (Arthur & McMahon, 2005; Bimrose, 1993; Bimrose, 1996; Collins & Arthur, 2010). The need for career practitioners to deal effectively with the complex interaction of cultural diversity and social context simply becomes unavoidable for ethical and effective practice.

So in what way is sociological career theory culturally valid? Society and culture are at its very heart. Ethnicity, gender and social class (Roberts, 1968), together with other factors like education and labour markets, compose the "web of determinants" (Roberts, 2009, p. 355) that many individuals must navigate. Social hierarchies, characterised by social and cultural capital, are recognisable in all societies, with economic wealth and opportunities inexorably linked. Cultural validity is the very essence, and at the core, of sociological career theory. An international research study into the career development of women across the life span, in nine countries, emphasises the impact of sociological variables on the career development of women, who comprise approximately half of the world's population (e.g. Bimrose, 2015).

The ways in which sociological theory can be integrated into career practice will now be considered.

Case study

Patti, age 46, completed her degree in Mechanical Engineering before securing a job with a large engineering company. Patti was attracted to engineering because, as she said, "I had always been the person in my house who had fixed things, or taken things apart, or whatever, so I had always had a sort of interest in mechanical things, how things worked, and those sorts of things".

One of seven children, Patti had been educated in a girls' school, which had not been able to provide her with adequate preparation for her career aspiration. Nor had the careers teacher been encouraging:

> I had no technical drawing, or anything like that. And I think it was partly the fact that the careers' master . . . didn't really want anybody to go and do an engineering degree, from [my school], because nobody ever had. And so that probably stirred me on.

Sociological career theory recognises the strong influence exerted on young people's career pathways, or trajectories, by family. Patti's family determined the choice of the school she attended, preferring her to attend a same-sex school. The geographical location of the family also determined the school attended, because it permitted daily travel. The school offered careers support, but from a careers master who demonstrated a strong gender bias in preferring girls from the school did not go into nontraditional occupational areas like engineering. This attitudinal mechanism operates effectively to maintain gendered occupational segregation in the labour force (Bimrose, in press), where women predominately work in a narrow range of jobs. When an individual's career ambitions go beyond gendered stereotypes, barriers often have to be overcome.

Case study: reflective questions 1

Patti overcame these initial barriers and gained entry to her engineering course at university. From a sociological perspective, what careers support might have helped in supporting her with first selecting, then completing, her engineering course successfully, given that the majority of the other students were male, as were the lecturers?

Having completed her degree, Patti's first job was in a large engineering company, working in a team on engine testing and planning of the manufacture of aeroplanes. It did not take her long to work out that career progression was going to be difficult: " [after 5 years] I felt as though I didn't really get that far, and I was a bit frustrated by what I would say was a bit of a glass ceiling in the organisation, frankly". She wanted something more challenging: "I was motivated to find something else" and recognised that the skills developed in her first job were transferrable to other contexts: "It wasn't exactly running away, but it was like, 'Oh, for goodness sake, if I'm not going to make an improvement here, I shall have to go and look somewhere else'".

According to sociological career theory, Patti's experience reflects that of the majority of women who try to establish careers in male-dominated sectors like engineering. As the only woman in the work team, and after five years of trying, she felt her voice was consistently being 'drowned out'. She realised that if she stayed in that part of the company, she would become increasingly frustrated by the lack of any opportunity to progress. Despite gender equality legislation, barriers to women's career progression largely prevail (Bimrose, in press; Blustein, 2015). Sociological career theory argues that careers support cannot improve the reality of work for employees, so should support clients to adjust to realities they confront. Practitioners can do this by helping clients to develop strategies for coping with sometimes hostile employment environments, for example, by supporting them in developing assertiveness skills so that they encouraged to confront inappropriate behaviour directly. If relevant, practitioners should also advocate on their clients' behalf; for example, where practitioners have direct contact with employers, perhaps through visits to increase their occupational knowledge, they could speak directly with them to draw their attention to the negative impact of allowing posters or pictures of attractive young women in revealing attire and sexually provocative poses to be hung in factory workshops or offices, which are likely to endorse a culture of sexual exploitation. Or where practitioners are submitting a client about whom they have particular concerns, a practitioner may speak directly on that client's behalf (e.g., where a female client who has experienced bullying or harassment is being submitted for a vacancy to a male-dominated environment, and with her explicit permission, a request could be made for a female mentor to be initially allocated).

Case study: reflective questions 2

What workplace barriers do you think Patti confronted? What does sociological career theory tell us about the type of careers support that could have helped her with these gendered constraints? What other course of action would sociological career theory indicate that she might she have taken?

In fact, Patti's line manager recognised the transferability of her skills and moved her to a project management role. This job she found interesting and challenging. After a few years, another opportunity arose when a different male colleague put Patti forward for the job role in technology he was about to leave: "The guy who was the team leader on this IT systems development thing was leaving, and he basically, sort of put me forward, as somebody to be considered to go and work in that area, which I subsequently did".

However, this job role involved considerable travel. She wanted to move to a particular part of country to marry: "I'd made a personal decision that I was going to try and find a job in the [location] area. And this business manager job came up and it fitted what I thought I could do". Unfortunately, this decision coincided with economic recession in the manufacturing sector. Her employer introduced 'massive redundancies' which precipitated an unplanned career change for Patti: "I took the voluntary redundancy, and I took some time out. I wasn't actually intending to take a year out, but that's just the way it worked out, really". She recalled how: "I was getting less and less comfortable with being in the [engineering company]... I think that political, and frankly, testosterone-fuelled environment that was the [engineering] business was quite objectionable to me". Her discomfort with her employment situation was fundamental: "I actually felt it was a horrendously backbiting, you know, one-upmanship, empire building, nightmare of an organisation". Her employment experiences, being virtually the only female in what was a nontraditional occupation sector had made an impact on her: "there were none [women] actually of my age, but there were a couple who were younger ....it certainly, it taught me personally an amount of toughness, which has perhaps made me feel hard....". She then took employment in the public sector, in health care.

Sociological career theory foregrounds gender inequality in educational achievement, the labour market and other social domains. It acknowledges the realities for women who have secured jobs in industries that employ a minority of women. Patti talks about the hostile, often toxic, male orientated environment of engineering. Her job changes within her employing organisation only came about because of the sponsorship and favour of individual male line managers. Sociological theory highlights the importance of informal networks in companies, which operate to preserve the dominance of the White male workforce, marginalising women and nondominant ethnic groups from positions of authority and influence. Women's deeply embedded gendered role, culturally determined by marriage, is also reflected in Patti's story. When she wanted to marry, she was obliged to make a personal sacrifice to leave her current job since it involved much travel. This ultimately led to her redundancy. Trailing spouses, in nearly all cases wives, are expected to undertake residential moves in support of the husband (usually the primary wage earner), with gendered localisation (that is, when women are restricted geographically to employment opportunities available within the general location of their husband's employment) further restricting occupational options (Green, 2015). Sociological career theory acknowledges the importance of ethical career practice by supporting, appropriately, women who aspire to nontraditional jobs. The concept of intersectionality is useful in reminding us how gendered inequality is often multidimensional, intersecting as it does with other structural dimensions of disadvantage, like ethnicity, age, and social class. (Bimrose, McMahon, & Watson, 2015). Sexual harassment is one challenge with which women in these environments may be confronted (Bimrose, 2004). These women need labour market information from career practitioners about exactly what they might encounter in particular occupational sectors and need to be equipped with strategies and techniques for coping with inappropriate behaviour when and if it arises.

Case study: reflective questions 3

What would sociological career theorists say about how careers support can be made relevant for girls and women considering careers in science, technology, engineering or mathematics? Should practitioners attempt to encourage girls and women into nontraditional sectors of employment? If so, how might they prepare them for these challenging occupational environments?

From the perspective of opportunity structure theory, Roberts (2000) noted that effective career practice demands a combination of what he refers to as universalistic and particularistic knowledge (Roberts, 2013). The universal knowledge required by practitioners is defined as the theory underpinning practice that can be applied anywhere, anytime and is acquired through formal education and training courses. In contrast, the particularistic knowledge relates to the specialist understanding of labour markets within reach of the individual client.

Summary

The relevance of sociological theory to practice has been questioned: "Perhaps because sociologists have not taken the time to extrapolate from theory and research to practice" (Brown, 2002, p. 10), though conceding that they "do have implications for certain aspects of practice" (p. 6). Roberts (2009) has, however, always argued that opportunity structure theory is indeed a theory, spelling out implications for practice. Because the practice of careers guidance cannot make jobs more rewarding or less alienating for individuals, nor provide opportunities for personal growth and development, its scope remains somewhat restricted. Psychological theories, he argues, are based on false premises since they imply that career practitioners are able to support the development of an individual's self-concept, assist individuals into jobs that fit their abilities and attributes, control their own destinies and/or teach individuals to manage their futures more efficiently (Roberts, 1977). The alternative conception of careers practice was that it became, rather, a matter of adjusting most individuals to opportunities to which they would have been reconciled. Practice should be centred on an individual's immediate problems, with careers support services concentrating on providing a good labour market information service, with more emphasis on advocacy, placement and follow-up. The role of the career practitioner, according to this sociological career theory, is of labour market expert with specialist knowledge, and advocate rather than educator, facilitator, or indeed anything else implicated by psychological theories (Roberts, 1977). As explained previously, these somewhat deterministic views were modified considerably over time, as Roberts refined his theory. In his latest versions, he becomes a strong proponent of career development and counseling support for individuals undergoing multiple transitions.

The main contribution of sociological career theory is the manner in which it increases our understanding of the complex, volatile labour markets and social contexts in which individuals develop their careers, creating unequal opportunities and pathways. It acts as a reminder that wider factors beyond the control of individuals may be in play, challenging the view that lack of success is attributable entirely to the individual. Career practitioners can no longer offer services and support to their clients that do not acknowledge and accommodate the profoundly variable life chances that are a feature of human society. Sociological career theory offers practitioners strategies and techniques for working with structures that may constrain, as well as facilitate, individual career development.

Learning activities

Learning activity 1

Use a search engine (e.g., Google Chrome) to find out the 10 highest paid jobs in your country. Chose one of these and then find out how many men compared with women are employed in this job sector. If the information is available, how many people are represented from non-dominant ethnic groups? How many age 55 or over? How do you explain this/these trends?

Learning activity 2

What is the role of labour market information (LMI) in your career counseling practice? For example, do you provide it directly to clients as part of an intervention to inform them about employment and training/education opportunities? Or perhaps you facilitate the development of their own research skills so that they can find the information they need for themselves? How would sociological career theory indicate the use of this resource?

Learning activities: reflective questions

1   Think about a member of your family, or a friend, who is currently employed. How do you think their career path might have been different if they were a different social class, a different ethnic group, or suffered a type of disability?
2   How do you imagine your own career have been different if you had been a different gender?
3   Have you ever considered a course and/or job that you have not pursued? What were the reasons you did not pursue it? Did you perceive any of these to be acting as barriers to pursuing these opportunities?

References

Arthur, M. B., Hall, D. T., & Lawrence, B. S. (Eds.). (1989). *Handbook of career theory*. Cambridge, UK: Cambridge University Press.

Arthur, N., & McMahon, M. (2005). Multicultural career counseling: Theoretical applications of the systems theory framework. *The Career Development Quarterly, 53*, 208–222.

Bimrose, J. (1993). Social context of counseling. In R. Bayne & P. Nicolson (Eds.), *Applied Psychology for Health Professionals* (pp. 149–165). London: Chapman Hall.

Bimrose, J. (1996). Multiculturalism. In R. Bayne, I. Horton & J. Bimrose (Eds.), *New directions in counseling* (pp. 237–247). London: Routledge.

Bimrose, J. (1998). Increasing multicultural competence. In R. Bayne, P. Nicolson, & I. Horton (Eds.), *Counseling and communication skills for medical and health practitioners* (pp. 88–102). Leicester, UK: BPS.

Bimrose, J. (2004). Sexual harassment in the workplace: An ethical dilemma for career guidance practice? *British Journal of Guidance and Counseling, 32*, 109–121.

Bimrose, J. (2006). Multicultural issues in support and supervision. In H. Reid & J. Westergaard (Eds.), *Support and supervision for personal advisers and youth support workers* (pp. 71–83). London: Routledge Falmer.

Bimrose, J. (in press). Guidance for girls and women. In J. A. Athanasou & H. Perera (Eds.), *International handbook of career guidance*. London: Springer.

Bimrose, J., McMahon, M., & Watson, M. (2015). Introduction. In J. Bimrose, M. McMahon, & M. Watson (Eds.), *Women's career development through the lifespan: An international perspective* (pp. 1–9). London: Routledge.

Bimrose, J. (2015). Voices of older women from England. In J. Bimrose, M. McMahon, & M. Watson (Eds.), *Women's career development through the lifespan: An international perspective* (pp. 139–151). London: Routledge.

Blustein, D. (2015). Implications for career theory. In J. Bimrose, M. McMahon, & M Watson (Eds.), *Women's career development through the lifespan: An international perspective* (pp. 221–230). London: Routledge.

Brown, D. (2002). Introduction to theories of career development and choice: Origins, evolution, and current efforts. In D. Brown & Associates (Eds.), *Career choice & development* (4th ed., pp. 3–24). San Francisco, CA: Jossey-Bass.

Bynner, J., & Roberts, K. (Eds.). (1991). *Youth and work: transition to employment in England and Germany*. London, UK: Anglo-German Foundation.

Collins, S., & Arthur, N. (2010). Culture-infused counseling: A fresh look at a classic framework of multicultural counseling competencies. *Counseling Psychology Quarterly, 23,* 203–216.

Daws, P. P. (1981). The socialisation/opportunity-structure theory of the occupational location of school leavers: A critical appraisal. In A. G. Watts, D. E. Super, & J. M. Kidd (Eds.), *Career development in Britain: some contributions to theory and practice* (pp. 246–278). Cambridge, UK: Hobsons.

Daws, P. (1992). Are careers education programmes in secondary schools a waste of time? – A reply to Roberts. In W. Dryden & A. G. Watts (Eds.), *Guidance and counseling in Britain: A 20-year perspective* (pp. 197–210). Cambridge, UK: Hobsons.

Fitzgerald, L. F., & Betz, N. (1994). Career development in cultural context. The role of gender, race, class and sexual orientation. In M. L. Savickas & R. W. Lent (Eds.), *Convergence in career development theories. Implications for science and practice* (pp. 103–117). Palo Alto, CA: CPP Books.

Ginsberg, E., Ginsburg, S. W., Axelrad, S., & Herma, J. L. (1951). *Occupational choice: An approach to a general theory.* New York: Columbia University Press.

Gottfredson, L. S. (1981). Circumscription and compromise: A development theory of occupational aspirations. *Journal of counseling Psychology Monograph, 28,* 545–579.

Gottfredson, L. S. (1983). Creating and criticizing theory. *Journal of Vocational Behavior, 23,* 203–212.

Gottfredson, L. S. (1996). Gottfredson's theory of circumscription and compromise. In D. Brown, L. Brooks, & Associates (Eds.), *Career, choice and development* (3rd ed., pp. 179–232). San Francisco, CA: Jossey Bass.

Gottfredson, L. S. (2005). Using Gottfredson's theory of circumscription and compromise in career guidance and counseling. In S. D. Brown & R. W. Lent (Eds.), *Career development and counseling: Putting theory and research to work* (pp. 71–100). New York: Wiley.

Green, A. (2015). Geographical perspective on women's careers: Why and how space matters. In J. Bimrose, M. McMahon, & M. Watson (Eds.), *Women's career development through the lifespan: An international perspective* (pp. 9–11). London: Routledge.

Hodkinson, P., & Sparkes, A. C. (1997). Careership: A sociological theory of career decision making. *British Journal of Sociology of Education, 18,* 29–44.

Kirkpatrick Johnson, M. K., & Mortimer, J. T. (2002). Career choice and development from a sociological perspective. In D. Brown & Associates (Eds.), *Career choice and development* (4th ed., pp. 37–85). San Francisco, CA: Jossey-Bass.

Kovacheva, S., Kabaivanov, S., & Roberts, K. (2018). Interrogating waithood: Family and housing life stage transitions among young adults in North-West Africa countries. *International Journal of Adolescence and Youth.* doi:10.1080/02673843.2018.1430595

Law, B. (1981). Community interaction: A 'mid-range' focus for theories of career development in young adults. *British Journal of Guidance & Counseling, 9,* 142–158.

Pedersen, P. B. (1991). Multiculturalism as a generic approach to counseling. *Journal of Counseling & Development, 70,* 6–12.

Roberts, K. (1968). The entry into employment: An approach towards a general theory. *Sociological Review, 16,* 165–184.

Roberts, K. (1977). The social conditions, consequences and limitations of career guidance. *British Journal of Guidance & Counseling, 5,* 1–9.

Roberts, K. (1984). *School leavers and their prospects,* Buckingham, UK: Open University Press.

Roberts, K. (1993). Career trajectories and the mirage of increased social mobility. In I. Bates & G. Riseborough (Eds.), *Youth and inequality* (pp. 229–245). Buckingham, UK: Open University Press.

Roberts, K. (1995). *Youth employment in modern Britain*. Oxford, UK: Oxford University Press.

Roberts, K. (1997). Prolonged transitions to uncertain destinations: The implications for careers guidance. *British Journal of Guidance and Counseling, 25,* 345–360.

Roberts, K. (2000). Cause for optimism: Current reforms can work. *Careers Guidance Today, 8,* 25–27.

Roberts, K. (2009). Opportunity structures then and now. *Journal of Education and Work, 22,* 355–368.

Roberts, K. (2012). Career development among the lower socioeconomic strata in developed countries. In M. Watson & M. McMahon (Eds.), *Career development: Global issues and challenges* (pp. 29–43). New York: Nova Science.

Roberts, K. (2013). Career guidance in England today: Reform, accidental injury or attempted murder? *British Journal of Guidance & Counseling, 41,* 240–253.

Roberts, K. (2015). Implications for career policy. In J. Bimrose, M. McMahon, & M. Watson (Eds.), *Women's career development through the lifespan: An international perspective* (pp. 243–252). London: Routledge.

Savickas, M. L. (1995). Current theoretical issues in vocational psychology: Convergence, divergence, and schism. In W. B. Walsh & S. H. Osipow (Eds.), *Handbook of vocational psychology: Theory, research and practice* (2nd ed., pp. 1–34). Mahwah, NJ: Lawrence Erlbaum.

Super, D. E. (1957). *The psychology of careers*. New York: Harper and Row.

Super, D. E. (1980). A life-span, life-space approach to career development. *Journal of Vocational Behavior, 16,* 282–298.

Super, D. E. (1969). Vocational development theory: persons, positions and processes. *The counseling Psychologist, 1,* 2–9.

Super, D. E. (1990). A life-span, life-space approach to career development. In D. Brown, L. Brooks, & Associates (Eds.), *Career choice and development* (2nd ed., pp. 197–261). San Francisco, CA: Jossey-Bass.

Wrenn, C. G. (1962). The culturally encapsulated counsellor. *Harvard Educational Review, 32,* 444–449.

13 Career development theory and practice
A culture-infused perspective

Nancy Arthur

Learning objectives

The purpose of this chapter is to:

- introduce the four domains of the culture-infused career counselling (CICC) model,
- describe guiding theoretical principles that underpin the CICC model,
- encourage active reflection about the influence of culture in career counselling with all clients, and
- advocate for moving beyond cultural sensitivity to adopting a social justice lens in case conceptualisation and intervention planning.

Introduction to the chapter

Cultural influences on people's career development have been addressed in a variety of ways, ranging from a notable absence of discussion about cultural context, highlighting specific cultural variables such as race and gender, focusing on specific populations deemed as "culturally diverse", to considering the complex interplay of cultural norms and beliefs for explaining career-related behaviour. The central premise of this chapter is that cultural contexts and people's cultural identities are inseparable for understanding their career-related behaviour. Rooted in social constructivism, the CICC model (Arthur, 2017, in press; Arthur & Collins, 2011) is premised on the position that people's cultural identities are formed through social interaction. Given that all people are cultural beings, culture influences the collaborative work between all career practitioners and all clients. Through the social construction of people's cultural identities, inequities emerge in opportunities for education and employment, connecting the work of career practitioners to social justice. The guiding theoretical principles of CICC are introduced. A case study illustrates reflexive practices for collaborating with clients, for understanding their career concerns, and for intervention planning.

Four domains of the CICC model

The culture-infused counselling (CIC) model (Collins & Arthur, 2010a, 2010b; 2018) was originally developed for application in general counselling practice. The four domains of the CICC model applied in the field of career development include active reflection about (a) personal cultural identities, (b) the cultural identities of other people, (c) cultural influences on the working alliance, and (d) socially just professional practices (Arthur, 2005, 2014, 2017; Arthur, in press; Arthur & Collins, 2011). The fourth domain was added to the original model to encourage career practitioners to reflect about how people are positioned in our society, attributable to the social construction of their identities, and how differential access to resources, privilege and power influences people's educational and occupational attainment. Incorporating a social justice lens in career counselling or in their other roles is fundamental for career practitioners to address social inequities directly with clients, advocate on their behalf, and/ or for leveraging professional roles to address broader systemic and social change. Although the four domains are described separately, interconnecting relationships between the domains guide the actions of career practitioners, in collaboration with their clients.

Guiding theoretical principles of culture-infused career counselling

Four central theoretical principles underpin the CICC model. These principles are discussed generally, in light of the variety of roles and functions performed by career practitioners, and with specific attention to career counselling.

Cultural influences are relevant for all career practitioners

The CICC model emphasises the importance of reflective practice by career practitioners. Consequently, career practitioners are invited to deeply reflect about their personal cultural identities and how their worldviews have been shaped through their personal socialisation. In doing so, career practitioners engage in a process of deconstructing the influences of culture in their own lives to better understand potential biases that they hold. For example, practitioners may reflect about the meaning and role of work across generations of their family and in their community contexts. Practitioners may also consider the messages from their formative years and how they were socialised about notions of work, career, employment success or unemployment. Internalised beliefs and values may surface in the ways that career practitioners view other people, including views about career issues, how they assign causality, and in preferences for intervention approaches. The risk of unconscious bias is that career practitioners avoid the tension of embracing ambiguity and sustaining curiosity about new or contrasting perspectives presented by their clients while collaborating with them to co-construct shared meaning.

Career practitioners are also encouraged to reflect about their professional socialisation and their adoption of theories and models that contain explicit and implicit cultural norms. Curriculum choices in professional education inevitably result in the foregrounding and marginalisation of particular perspectives in the field. More popular perspectives often become sanctioned without critical examination of the contexts in which they were developed, who is represented in the theory or model, and the positions espoused about career-related concerns and preferred interventions. For example, concerns have been raised that early theories of vocational and career development arose within particular eras, country, and cultural contexts (Watson, 2017). Concerns have also been raised about the lack of attention to contextual influences, including cultural diversity, and the interplay between individual and systemic and structural forces that impact people's educational and vocational options (Arthur & McMahon, 2005; Bimrose & McNair, 2011). The overfocus on psychological theories in career development has emphasised individualism and detached people and their career-related behaviour from the cultural contexts of their lives (Arulmani, 2017). Sociological theories (see Chapter 12), which have historically addressed workplace norms, the structure of opportunity, and emphasised the interactions of gender, race, and social class, have been marginalised in favour of theories that emphasise individual determinism. Career practitioners are encouraged to reflect about the embedded assumptions and the relevancy of theory for application across country and cultural contexts.

Cultural influences are relevant for all clients of career services

Career practitioners are invited to reflect about how they construct cultural similarity or difference, and whom they consider to be culturally diverse from themselves. People's cultural identities may include a myriad of dimensions such as gender, age, ethnicity, sexual/affectional orientation, ability, religion, and social class, or their intersections. Cautions are advised against equating dimensions of people's identities as variables and something to be controlled (Stead, 2004), or categorising people arbitrarily for the purpose of group comparisons. Although it is important to continue to highlight the inequities faced by members of nondominant groups in society, it is prudent to remember that such positioning occurs through social processes such as racialisation, sexism, classism, and other forms of oppression. It may not be a single dimension of people's cultural identities that is most salient or important; peoples' unique intersections of identity (e.g., gender, social class, situational contexts) combine for experiences along an axis of social privilege or disadvantage. Career interventions can be designed to surface and deconstruct internalised cultural understandings, while attending to aspects of people's experience that they deem as relevant for their presenting career concerns. Career practitioners are encouraged to take a stance of curiosity and naivety in exploring the salience, or importance, of people's cultural identities for presenting career issues and for designing relevant interventions with all clients.

The goals and processes of career counselling are collaboratively negotiated

As noted earlier, unique patterns of social interaction are relevant for understanding people's conceptualisation of their cultural identities Adopting a social constructivist perspective fundamentally means honouring the complexity of multiple realities and possibilities in people's experiences (Patton & McMahon, 2017). People construct meaning through a social process, formed through our interactions and experiences in specific cultural contexts. In turn, career counselling can be generally described as a cultural process of meaning making (Stead, 2004). Entering the life world of another person involves exploring personal beliefs and values and being open to the experiences of other people, which may be relatively similar or different, depending on people's social locations. Although this process seems relatively easy on the surface, it requires career practitioners, such as career counsellors, to break away from their personal notions of truth and a singular reality, to recognising the multiplicity of realities held by other people. Together, career counsellors and clients negotiate and construct meaning regarding past and present influences to create possibilities for future career goals and actions (Arthur, 2017).

Help seeking is culturally defined and many people may be reluctant to access services or simply not know they exist. Career counsellors can provide orientation to help individuals to make informed choices. As previously noted, career counselling is a social process in which the counsellor and client co-construct meaning and action. In order for a client to be engaged in a change process, it is essential to collaboratively negotiate counselling goals and processes. In recognition of interconnected family and community relationships, conflicting agendas may be the reason that individuals seek independent support or want to have family or significant others involved in intervention planning. Some clients will prioritise decisions in the context of their families and communities. Career counsellors are invited to reflect about their personal values and to avoid imposing personal preferences; their role is to support clients to explore the cultural contexts and relationships that are most relevant for career planning and decision-making.

Terminology commonly used in the field may have implied meanings, which may or may not resonate with the public. It is critical that career practitioners carefully consider which terminology to use, as language is symbolic of deeper cultural meanings. For example, people's notions about educational attainment and employment goals are constructed within their particular cultural contexts. Such views incorporate attitudes toward education and work as central, marginal, obtainable, or beyond their reach, depending on their life circumstances, and what they believe and have experienced in their life course, and over the life course of previous generations. The term *career* has been criticised for being elitist and overshadowing the realities of people whose lives are consumed with finding sustainable forms of employment income to support basic needs (Blustein, 2013). The emphasis on paid work is also problematic in light of the unpaid social and relational work required in society (Richardson, 2012) and the lack of recognition for the gendered nature of such work.

Overreliance on linear models may or may not resonate with clients' views of how decisions are made or align with the key influences on career goals in their lives. Presumptions of affluence, individualism, progression, and equal opportunity are common assumptions (Flores, 2009) that may not be either commonly understood or valued. Career counsellors need to be open to the life worlds of their clients and consider culturally learned perspectives on the role of fate, respect for family decision-making, and the roles of affect and intuition in people's cultural context. Through the unique relationship between career counsellors and clients, cultural understandings are constructed. The processes that underpin any change process need to be negotiated and enacted in ways that are meaningful to clients.

Cultural identities and social justice are inextricably connected in career practice

It is through exploring people's experiences that career practitioners gain perspective about the relevancy of people's cultural identities and social locations. Career practitioners are cautioned against assigning a cultural identity to their clients based on an arbitrary group membership; it is through the social process of interaction that clients reveal and co-construct the meanings of their lives. People's cultural identities are fluid and shift across situations and across social interactions. Some aspects of cultural identity may be strongly emphasised by other people in a social process of labelling that leads to relative advantages of privilege or disadvantages (Arthur, 2017). To recap, it is important to move beyond identity labels or arbitrary assignment of group affiliation to consider how people's intersections of identities, across situations, can be understood along an axis of privilege and oppression (Kang, Callaghan, & Anne, 2015)

Career practitioners are encouraged to reflect about how they define a client's presenting concerns and how they design interventions. As noted previously, career practitioners need to be cognisant of their own experience of power, privilege, or oppression, and how such experiences may come into play in professional roles. People's career concerns emerge amidst a myriad of interpersonal, organisational, and structural influences. When intrapersonal causes are overemphasised, there is a risk that the individual's experience is decontextualised from their environment. A further risk occurs when clients are blamed for their lack of success in educational or occupational attainment, without considering the social and political conditions that often create barriers for equitable access and mobility.

Research in brief

A study conducted in the Canadian context investigated how career practitioners conceptualised social justice, the barriers faced by clients, and their competencies for practice (Arthur, Collins, McMahon, & Marshall, 2009; 2013). Practitioners linked presenting career concerns to inequities faced by groups of clients (e.g., women, immigrants, people with a criminal record), and took into account the systemic forces that contributed to difficulties accessing resources such as upgrading educational qualifications and entry into the labour market. Some practitioners allocated resources within and between agencies to address complex client needs, whereas others reported seeking additional resources beyond their agency mandates and doing so on their own time. Additional structural barriers in their workplaces included funding mandates, time, lacking support from supervisors, fear of job loss, and the need for further education about social justice interventions. Despite the expression of a strong commitment to social justice advocacy in their career practitioner roles, many respondents in this study wanted additional training on competencies that would support their roles directly, better support their clients, and support organisational change.

How do career practitioners plan interventions connected to social justice? Career practitioners reported the majority of their interventions related to social justice were enacted with individual clients, as this was the primary modality through which practitioners were trained and how their models of practice were endorsed in their practice settings (Arthur, 2016). There was an inverse relationship in the frequency with which career practitioners engaged in interventions to address systems change on behalf of clients, and interventions directed at organisational change and influencing policy makers.

Research in brief: reflective questions

1   Imagine working with a client whose career issues seem to be related to barriers in a work context or in the larger environment, such as lack of resources to pursue education or employment goals. What kinds of interventions might be designed to address those barriers through career counselling, or in other advocacy roles that a career counsellor might pursue?

2   How could career practitioners use collective action versus individual action to address systemic and societal barriers that adversely affect their clients?

3   What key competencies could be incorporated into the education and training of career development practitioners to prepare them for interventions that have a social justice focus?

Beyond reflection, career practitioners are called upon to actively address forms of oppression that are related clients' career concerns, through consciousness-raising with clients, through intervening with or on behalf of clients, or through other forms of intervention that directly address the source of oppression. These forms of social justice interventions represents a stance against the drift to remedial services and working solely from a coping model, in which career practices are synonymous with helping clients to cope with noxious and oppressive conditions in their lives; it is a call for action for interventions that address the social inequities that impinge negatively on people's educational and occupational attainment (Arthur, 2005, 2016). For example, in working with a female client who is experiencing workplace difficulties, the counsellor may invite discussion about gender and power issues in the workplace to help the client resist self-blaming; with the client's permission, the counsellor might make an inquiry to the HR department of the company; and/or the counsellor might work with professionals from other disciplines to combine efforts to overcome gendered barriers and institutionalised discrimination in the workplace (e.g., Bimrose et al., 2014). Intervention options are negotiated carefully with clients in light of their needs for employment, issues of confidentiality and safety, and in light of expanding options for clients within their life contexts.

To further illustrate, many internationally educated professionals experience de-skilling after migration to another country, due to the lack of recognition for their education and employment credentials (Bimrose & McNair, 2011; Kennedy & Chen, 2012). Such experiences compound the challenges of migration and negotiating identities as a worker, as a provider, and fully as a citizen in a new cultural context. As noted earlier, people's identities are formed through social interaction, including interaction in the workplace. Workplaces are not gender neutral, and the dynamics associated with seeking employment and integrating into workplaces differentially affects women immigrants, due to their age, employment sector, family responsibilities, and other contextual influences on their lives (Arthur, 2015). The following case example introduces the first session with a professionally educated female engineer who was referred for career counselling.

Case study

Hanna (pseudonym) is a 32-year-old woman who migrated to Canada with her husband and three children from a country in the Middle East, to escape political strife, and with hopes of a better life for their family. Since arriving in the Canada, Hanna accepted employment as a technologist for an oil and gas company, with the idea that she would eventually be able to work as an engineer. While underemployed, Hanna deals with mundane work assignments. Hanna sees many inefficiencies in her employment setting, but she is reluctant to speak up, as she does not know how expressing her opinions may be perceived by managers and coworkers, even though they seem happy with her work. There are few women working in senior positions in the company and she notices that her direct manager spends a lot of time with the engineers talking about non-work related matters.

Hanna is now the main earner in the family because her husband has only been able to secure part-time employment as a cleaner. There has been conflict in the home about household tasks and time spent with the children. Her husband often comments that he wishes the family had never left their home country. Hanna feels quite isolated, as she has no extended family in the city where she now lives.

Hanna enjoyed her contact with the settlement worker who was assigned to the family from the local immigration agency. Sensing Hanna's dissatisfaction with her employment situation, the settlement worker encouraged Hanna to seek career counselling and set up a referral. At the first appointment, Hanna offered compliments about her life in Canada and how helpful everyone has been to her. When asked what she would like to talk about, Hanna stated that she would like to know how to become an engineer.

Case analysis

The first thing to note in this case is that a referral was made, due to a strong relationship that had been built between the career counsellor and the staff at a local immigration settlement agency. Building community resources for consultation and referral is important for practitioners to draw upon interdisciplinary resources to support career counsellors' roles and to provide options and resources for their clients. When the referral was made, the career counsellor asked the settlement worker about what information had been shared with Hanna and her expectations for career counselling. The counsellor listened for cues about what might be important for orienting Hanna to the career counselling process and for forming a strong working alliance.

After talking with the settlement worker, the career counsellor briefly reflected about other clients she had worked with from Hanna's country of origin and considered some assumptions. For example, through reflection, the career counsellor wondered if Hanna might be from a more patriarchal society with prescribed gender roles in both public and household settings. The career counsellor had worked with other highly skilled professionals from Hanna's country and knew the value placed on education and securing professional status. After reflecting about these assumptions, the counsellor noted that it would be important to be open to hearing Hanna's story and to learn more about how Hanna situated her career concerns amidst her family, community, and broader cultural contexts.

Hanna presented as polite but very nervous, noting that she came to the appointment because she really respected the opinion of the settlement worker. The career counsellor leveraged that point to compliment Hanna about reaching out to seek additional resources, taking a strength-based approach to build rapport. The terms of confidentiality were reviewed, noting that Hanna asked several questions about what information would be needed and who else the counsellor knew in the local community from her ethnocultural group. The career counsellor took the time to explain how the relationship with the settlement agency was formed and how she currently worked with individuals who were referred for career counselling. The career counsellor asked Hanna directly about her concerns for confidentiality and specifically noted that no information would be shared with the settlement worker. Hanna appeared to relax more with the reassurance about confidentiality and asked Hanna to explain what forms of help she had already explored or had used in the past. Through encouraging dialogue together about help seeking, the counsellor affirmed a strength-based approach, underscoring the choice that Hanna made to seek career counselling.

Hanna stated that the purpose of coming to the appointment was to find out how she could qualify as an engineer. The career counsellor took Hanna's lead and began exploring the presenting career goal to have international credentials and work experience recognised in the regulated profession of engineering. The counsellor aimed to provide concrete information to help Hanna access the provincial registry for professional engineers and went on the website with her to show her how to initiate contact and what resources she might use. The career counsellor also encouraged Hanna to connect with a local professional group that was organised for women engineers, so that Hanna could begin to build professional support outside of the workplace.

The career counsellor invited Hanna to explore some of the other influences on her presenting concern. For example, the counsellor learned that Hanna was originally from an affluent family and the family was able to bring some resources with them to provide for the first two years in Canada. The immigration choice might be considered as voluntary, yet the circumstances in her country had disrupted her extended family connections. Hanna's husband had difficulty securing meaningful employment and Hanna's children did not want to leave their friends behind. Two of the younger children were doing well in school, but the oldest child was struggling in school and did not seem to be making new friends. Hanna was experiencing the loss of professional status that both she and her husband had enjoyed, and there was major role disruption in her home with the shift in income sources. Hanna stated she felt exhausted from managing the strains of figuring out life in a new country. The career counsellor gently invited Hanna to tell her family story, listening for the cultural influences and reflecting meaning and affect to ensure accuracy of understanding and to offer possibilities for co-constructing new meaning.

The career counsellor again assured Hanna about confidentiality of the session and that no information would be shared with her employer. Hanna described the similarities and differences she felt in the workplace in Canada compared to her experience of working as a professional in her home country. The career counsellor decided to inquire about actions in the workplace that triggered a sense of comfort or discomfort. Hanna's ensuing narrative highlighted the sexist nature of the workplace, with a hierarchy of male managers and the male engineers receiving the best projects. Hanna felt that her talents were not being utilised and she was often excluded from important discussions. The counsellor invited Hanna to discuss her preferred future at the workplace and to outline what would be similar, different, how she would feel, and how she would be behaving differently, and how she would be treated in the workplace by other people. Taking a solution-focused approach with Hanna helped her to move from a narrative of oppression to opening possibilities for positive engagement in the work role. As a form of assessment of the cultural influences on her life, the counsellor used both direct and indirect inquiry. Directly, the career counsellor selectively posed questions and probes about aspects of Hanna's life, to encourage a fuller narrative and to explore possible cultural influences. Indirectly, the counsellor listened carefully to Hanna's narrative to weave together connecting strands to reflect aspects of her cultural identity that Hanna revealed in the stories about her life. Through both direct and indirect inquiry, Hanna and the counsellor co-constructed the cultural influences on her presenting concerns in the current context, encouraging Hanna to begin constructing a possible future where she could feel more positively engaged with her professional identity.

The career counsellor offered a challenge to Hanna about the ways in which she was polarising her experience in Canada versus life in her home country as "good" or "bad". The career counsellor invited Hanna to provide more details about aspects of her life roles that had improved and areas where she felt she was gaining mastery. In this way, Hanna was encouraged to acknowledge the strengths that she had demonstrated and to recognise the vast amount of change that she has managed for herself and her family since immigrating to Canada. The career counsellor decided to introduce a narrative thread about the nature of oppression in the workplace and some of the barriers, naming some of the examples that Hanna provided as sexist. In doing so, the career counsellor invited Hanna to make a shift from a narrative of personal failure, to surfacing some of the interpersonal and organisational influences that were adversely affecting her. The career counsellor was more than a sounding board, filling the role of a cultural teacher and offering ideas about the meaning of behaviour in the local context, inviting Hanna to discuss her own interpretations and meanings, and to collaborate on developing relevant strategies.

The career counsellor acknowledged Hanna's fear of speaking up and the importance of safety in making choices in the workplace and in telling her family story. In a parallel process, the career counsellor tried to create a safe space for Hanna to speak about her career concerns, while allowing her to test out the ideas and strategies that she might choose to implement. The career counsellor was mindful of the time that they had together for this first session, honoured Hanna's presenting agenda, and invited her to return for more discussion and ideas for family resources. The career counsellor reframed some of the issues that Hanna presented as the family's career dilemmas to acknowledge the family system and the family members' settlement experiences. At the end of this session, the career counsellor invited Hanna to talk about her experience of seeking help, what stood out for her, and what ideas she felt she might use in her life. Through asking Hanna to summarise the session, the counsellor was again encouraging Hanna to feel more empowered about the changes she was making in a new cultural context.

The career counsellor reflected about the many clients she had worked with who were facing conditions of underemployment or unemployment due to the lack of recognition of their international credentials. Beyond interventions directly with Hanna, the career counsellor followed up with a meeting at the immigration settlement agency to learn more about their programming for internationally educated professionals. The career counsellor was invited to serve on an advisory committee that was comprised of multiple community stakeholders. The career counsellor brought unique perspectives to advocate for gender considerations in shaping policy and program development.

Case study: reflective questions

1   What aspect of Hanna's identity might feel similar to or different from your own experience that might lead to making assumptions?
2   How would you approach Hanna to learn about which aspects of her cultural identity are most relevant to her presenting issues?
3   Considering the information presented in the case study, compare how your interventions might unfold, based on the following scenarios:

   a   You consider that the issues are "within" Hanna, such as language proficiency, low self-efficacy, low self-esteem, and the client does not have a career plan.
   b   You focus on the workplace dynamics and coaching Hanna to take action to improve her situation at work and to pursue professional status as an engineer.
   c   You work as an employee assistance counsellor with the organisation where Hanna works and your plan for intervention addresses organisational change.
   d   You notice similar barriers in the experiences of internationally educated professionals and decide to use your professional role and network to address barriers for immigrant women and advocate for systemic change.

Chapter summary

The CICC model was developed to address a lack of attention paid to cultural context in conceptualising people's career concerns. The CICC model offers an overarching approach for assessing key influences on how people construct their cultural identities for understanding their presenting career concerns. Career practitioners are invited to consider the compatibility of this model with incorporating other theories and concepts. Additional strengths of the CICC model include the call for active reflective practice about practitioners' personal cultural identities, the identities of the people they serve, and the tools and resources they draw upon, including which theories of career development align with their clients' worldviews. Career practitioners are also invited to reflect about cultural influences on the working alliance and how they can collaborate with clients to determine meaningful and relevant counselling goals and processes. As a social constructivist orientation to career counselling, the CICC model is intended to draw attention to the importance of negotiating shared meaning in the working alliance between counsellors and their clients.

Given that not all people and their cultural identities are treated equally in our society, career practitioners are inevitably dealing with people whose lives have been adversely affected by structural and societal inequities. People's cultural identities are linked to their social locations, and practising from a CICC perspective incorporates a social justice lens in counselling interventions and in other professional practice roles to address social inequities. Moving beyond cultural sensitivity, practitioners are encouraged to take a social justice lens to determine appropriate forms of intervention, including social justice advocacy.

Research has been conducted to investigate the ways that career practitioners conceptualise culture and social justice in their views of client concerns and interventions (Arthur, 2016; Arthur et al., 2009) and their perceived competencies (Arthur et al., 2013; Collins, Arthur, McMahon, & Bisson, 2015). Additional research across country contexts could add perspectives about how practitioners incorporate the central concepts from the model into their practice contexts and the outcomes for service delivery.

Beyond research that incorporates the perspectives of career practitioners, research is needed to shift the focus from what we do *to* clients and the processes of engaging *with* them. For example, researchers could focus on clients' views of career counselling and how their cultural identities and contexts were taken into account, or not, during the career counselling process. Research is also needed to consider how clients conceptualise social justice issues in relation to their career concerns and how clients' perspectives might inform social justice interventions. These examples illustrate some potential ways that research from the perspectives of clients might strengthen understanding about how culture and social justice can be further infused into practical applications of the CICC model.

Learning activities

Learning activity 1

This learning activity is intended for use with students in a class or for use during a professional development event with career practitioners. The larger group will be divided into two groups for the purpose of a debate. Group A will be asked to take the position that social justice is a central value to guide the roles and responsibilities of career practitioners. Group B will be asked to take the position that social justice is not a central value to guide the roles and responsibilities of career practitioners. As the groups offer their position points, the facilitator takes notes. Once the points are exhausted from each group, the facilitator reviews the main points and invites the group to add additional points, from either perspective.

Learning activity 2

Develop and design a career genogram, tracing the influences on the career development for yourself, your siblings, parents, grandparents and extended family. What were the values and beliefs in your family regarding education and employment, the nature of jobs, or the role of work in your life? Consider how those values were transmitted to you between generations through sayings, attitudes, or through forms of action. How have you embraced those values in the pursuit of your own career development? Next, consider how your values and beliefs regarding work and/or career may be similar or different than other people, noting how you have or might be able to address values conflicts that surface in your role as a career practitioner.

Learning activities: reflective questions

1   Reflect on the relationships between people's cultural identities and their experiences of social inequities.
2   Generate examples of how career practitioners can intervene at different levels, including with individual clients, on behalf of clients, with policymakers, and through addressing change in external systems such as schools, government policy makers, employers.
3   Reflect on the meaning of social justice for you and select one action that you could take to address a social inequity related to education or employment. Share with a colleague what that action would be and your plan for implementing that action.

References

Arthur, N. (2005). Building from cultural diversity to social justice competencies in international standards for career development practitioners. *International Journal for Educational and Vocational Guidance*, 5(2), 137–149.

Arthur, N. (2014). Social justice in the age of talent. *International Journal for Educational and Vocational Guidance*, 14(1), 47–60.

Arthur, N. (2015). Voices of women from Canada. In J. Bimrose, M. McMahon, & M. Watson (Eds.), *Women's career development throughout the lifespan: An international exploration* (pp. 113–126). New York: Routledge.

Arthur, N. (2016, November). *From reflection to social justice action: Examples from career practitioners in Canada*. Presentation at the annual conference of the International Association of Educational and Vocational Guidance, Madrid, Spain.

Arthur, N. (2017). Constructivist approaches to career counselling: A culture-infused approach. In M. McMahon (Ed.), *Career counselling: Constructivist approaches* (2nd ed., pp. 54–64). Abingdon, Oxon, UK: Routledge.

Arthur, N. (in press). Culture-infused career counselling: Connecting culture and socially just professional practices. In N. Arthur, R. Neault, & M. McMahon (Eds.), *Theories and models at work: Ideas for practice.* Manuscript submitted for publication. Ottawa, ON: CERIC.

Arthur, N., & Collins, S. (2011). Infusing culture in career counselling. *Journal of Employment counselling, 48,* 147–149.

Arthur, N., Collins, S., Marshall, C., & McMahon, M. (2013). Social justice competencies and career development practices. *Canadian Journal of Counselling and Psychotherapy, 47,* 136–154.

Arthur, N., Collins, S., McMahon, M., & Marshall, C. (2009). Career practitioners' views of social justice and barriers for practice. *Canadian Journal of Career Development, 8,* 22–31.

Arthur, N., & McMahon, M. (2005). A systems theory framework for multicultural career counselling. *The Career Development Quarterly, 53*(3), 208–222.

Arulmani, G. (2017). Contexts and circumstances: The cultural preparation process approach to career development. In M. McMahon (Ed.), *Career counselling: Constructivist approaches* (pp. 79–90). Abingdon, Oxon, UK: Routledge.

Bimrose, J., & McNair, S. (2011). Career support for migrants: Transformation or adaptation? *Journal of Vocational Behavior, 78,* 325–333.

Bimrose, J., Watson, M., McMahon, M., Haasler, S., Tomassini, M., & Suzanne, P. (2014). The problem with women? Challenges posed by gender for career guidance practice. *International Journal for Educational and Vocational Guidance, 14*(1), 77–88.

Blustein, D. (2013). The psychology of working: A new perspective for a new era. In D. Blustein (Ed.), *The Oxford handbook of the psychology of working* (pp. 3–18). New York: Oxford University Press.

Collins, S., & Arthur, N. (2010a). Culture-infused counselling: A fresh look at a classic framework of multicultural counselling competencies. *counselling Psychology Quarterly, 23*(2), 203–216.

Collins, S., & Arthur, N. (2010b). Culture-infused counselling: A model for developing cultural competence. *counselling Psychology Quarterly, 23*(2), 217–233.

Collins, S., & Arthur, N. (2018). Challenging conversations: Deepening personal and professional commitment to culture-infused and socially just counselling practices. In D. Pare & C. Oudette (Eds.), *Social justice and counselling: Discourse in practice* (pp. 29–42). New York: Routledge.

Collins, S., Arthur, N., McMahon, M., & Bisson, S. (2015). Assessing the multicultural and social justice competencies of career development practitioners. *Canadian Journal of Career Development, 14*(1), 4–16.

Flores, L. (2009). Empowering life choices: Career counselling in the contexts of race and class. In N. Gysbers, M. Heppner, & J. Johnson (Eds.), *Career counselling: Contexts, processes, and techniques* (pp. 49–74). Alexandria, VA: American counselling Association.

Kang, H., Callaghan, J., & Anne, M. (2015). An intersectional social capital model of career development for international marriage immigrants. *The Career Development Quarterly, 63,* 238–252.

Kennedy, T., & Chen, C. (2012). Career counselling new and professional immigrants: Theories into practice. *Australian Journal of Career Development, 21*(2), 36–45.

Patton, W., & McMahon, M. (2017). Constructivism: What does it mean for career counselling? In M. McMahon (Ed.), *Career counselling: Constructivist approaches* (pp. 3–16). Abingdon, Oxon, UK: Routledge.

Richardson, M. (2012). counselling for work and for relationship. *The Counseling Psychologist, 40*(2), 190–242.

Stead, B. G. (2004). Culture and career psychology: A social constructionist perspective. *Journal of Vocational Behavior, 64*(3), 389–406.

Watson, M. (2017). Career constructivism and culture: Deconstructing and reconstructing career counselling. In M. McMahon (Ed.), *Career counselling: Constructivist approaches* (pp. 43–53). Abingdon, Oxon, UK: Routledge.

14 The cultural preparedness framework
Equilibrium and its alteration

Gideon Arulmani

Learning objectives

The purpose of this chapter is to:

- describe cultural learning as a human faculty through which learning is consolidated and ideas about work are transmitted,
- explain the formation and alteration of cultural preparedness equilibrium as outcomes of enculturation and acculturation, and
- aid in developing greater sensitivity to the acculturative influences of contemporary, global trends and their effect on career development.

Introduction to the chapter

Every one of us is born into a cultural environment characterised by a particular arrangement of beliefs, customs, practices, and other social expressions that hold individual life in common with the group, thereby imbuing it with a unique cultural meaning. As a result, our engagement with work, occupation and career could, in turn, be imbued with the meanings attributed to them by our cultures. The cultural preparedness framework proposes that this uniquely human tendency transmutes human engagement with work into a manifestation of culture. Five propositions undergird the framework: (1) global conditions, trends, and transformations form the backdrop against which human engagement with work and career occurs; (2) career development is influenced by three key factors (patterns of social organisation along the individualism–collectivism continuum, patterns of value attribution, and the processes of role allocation); (3) cultural learning through the processes of enculturation and acculturation mediates the interaction between global trends and influences on preparedness; (4) the socialising forces of enculturation place the individual/group in a unique state of equilibrium that influences engagement with career development; and (5) this equilibrium is affected by acculturative forces which could be consonant or dissonant with the individual/group's cultural preparation status, leading to the requirement for a new equilibrium. The concept of cultural preparedness postulates that peoples' engagement with the world is a manifestation of the manner in which they have been prepared by their cultures for this engagement (Arulmani, 2014a). The chapter is organised around a case study of the author's encounter with Maldivian culture when he implemented a project on guidance and counselling in that country between 2006 and 2011.

Culture as a mediator of learning and work

Culture is reflected in human behaviour that cannot be attributed to genetic or biological inheritance but rather to social learning (e.g., Tomasello, 2000). The propensity to learn from experience, to accumulate these learnings through systems of symbolic codification (e.g., language, numerals, art), and transmit these learnings to others is a defining human characteristic. By Neolithic times, work was no longer merely linked to hunting and gathering to meet survival needs. Customs, laws, value attributions, social standards, religious beliefs, and traditions began to influence the manner in which people engaged with work roles. The impact of culture on work is palpable in the way in which attitudes began to form toward work in general as well as toward specific occupational clusters. We have described these culturally mediated ways of thinking as social cognitive environments: culturally mediated learning environments within which experiences are assimilated and interpreted (Arulmani & Nag-Arulmani, 2004). From a guidance and counselling view point, we have referred to these cognitions as career beliefs: "a conglomerate of culturally mediated attitudes, opinions, convictions and notions, which cohere together to create mindsets that underlie and influence people's orientation to the idea of a career and to their engagement with career development" (Arulmani & Nag-Arulmani, 2004, p. 107).

There could be as many variations in social cognitive environments as there are cultures. For example, almost polar opposites are seen in the evolution of social cognitions toward work between Western and non-Western cultures. The Greek word for work was *ponos*, taken from the Latin *poena*, which meant sorrow, when manual labour was meant for slaves (Tilgher, 1930/1958). Social cognitive environments in medieval England promoted the belief that it was the duty of a worker to remain in his class, passing the family occupation on from father to son (Tilgher, 1930/1958). It was after the protestant reformation that all forms of work became culturally acceptable for all persons, including the wealthy. The protestant work ethic (Weber, 1905/2002) gave "moral sanction to profit making through hard work, organization, and rational calculation" (Yankelovich & Immerwahr, 1984, p. 247). By contrast, traditional Indian orientations to work rest on the notion of *dharma*: a code of behaviour that fosters a reciprocally supportive, sustaining rather than exploitative worldview. Work within this cultural matrix is understood as a duty and a contribution (Prabhu, 1963). Various cultural groups could interpret similar experiences in different ways. For example, a certain culture (e.g., the Japanese work ethic until recently) may espouse a work ethic that places a positive moral value on loyalty between employer and employee (Banda, 2014). By contrast, the neoliberal work ethic, influenced as it is by instrumental rationality, breaks with the notion of a social contract existing between employer and employee (e.g., Sultana, 2014). Therefore, culture mediated attitudes toward work and career development could vary.

Cultural preparedness results from the accumulation over time, of the learnings and experiences of a certain group of people, so assimilated and systematised into the group's ways of engaging with the world that it can be said to exemplify that group and distinguish it from other groups. These ways of engaging rest upon a social cognitive environment typified by an interconnected system of beliefs, values, rituals, social organisation and mores, that have become deeply embedded within the conventions and routines to which a given group is habituated. The understanding that culture facilitates learning and work leads us to three important constructs in the cultural preparedness framework: cultural learning, enculturation and cultural preparedness equilibrium. With a view to illustrating these key concepts, they are introduced and applied to a case study from the Maldives.

Cultural learning

Adapted from biological anthropology, cultural learning is a construct that is fundamental to the cultural preparedness approach. Tomasello's (2000) comparisons of human and nonhuman learning show that human beings are biologically prepared for culture in ways that other primates are not. Every child is born into a particular environment typified by culturally anchored symbolic artefacts represented by traditions, rituals, tools, language, conventions and institutions such as family and religion. As Tomasello points out, "the cultural context is not just a facilitator or motivator for cognitive development but rather a unique 'ontogenetic niche' (i.e., a unique context for development) that actually structures human cognition in fundamental ways" (Tomasello, 2000, p. 37). By 9 to 12 months of age, the human child begins to show a stronger tendency toward imitative learning through a focus on the action that produces a result, rather than emulation learning that focuses on the outcomes of the action, which is also seen in nonhuman species. Subsequently, through instructed and collaborative learning, the human individual becomes not only a recipient but also a transmitter of culture. An important observation that Tomasello makes is that individuals acquire the use of cultural practices in a relatively exact form, which "serves as a kind of ratchet – keeping the practice in place in the social group, perhaps for many generations, until some creative innovation comes along" (Tomasello, 2000, p. 137). The cultural preparedness framework proposes that it is this capacity for cultural learning that transforms the human being's engagement with work into a manifestation of culture.

Case study

Extracted with permission from The Promise Foundation, 2010.[1]

The Maldives is a small South Asian developing island-nation in the Indian Ocean comprising 1192 coral islands of which 188 are inhabited (Ministry of

Planning and National Development [MPND], 2006). With populations of fewer than 1000 on some islands and a total population of about 393,500 inhabitants, this is smallest Asian country and the most geographically dispersed (MPND, 2006). [CL] While the earliest written history of the Maldives is marked around 543 BCE, folklore and mentions in other histories (e.g., Indian history), point to the possibility that the Maldives has been peopled for over 2000 years (Bell, 1940).

[CL/EC/EQ] The collectivist nature of Maldivian society is seen in its deeply traditional orientations, small, closely knit social units with clear lines of leadership, strong family values and kinship ties which are passed on across generations (Bell, 1940). The leader of an island is the Island Chief (katheebu), who plays a paternal role in community life.

[CL/EC] Given that over 90% of this nation comprises the ocean, the ways of the sea have been [EQ] absorbed into the lives of these islanders. [EC] Ancient Maldivian folktales are replete with stories about the tuna fish, and other sea creatures which create a cultural foundation even from childhood for a deep connection with the sea.

[EC] Surrounded as it by the ocean, fish is essential to the Maldivian diet. [EC] Fishing is an ancient Maldivian profession and a major economic activity. Boat-building is the other essential occupation in the Maldives. [EQ] Using material available on the islands, traditional Maldivian boat-building has evolved over many centuries. [CL/EC] The work ethic surrounding fishing and boat-building [EQ] is embedded in Maldivian culture and has been [CL] transmitted across generations. [EC/EQ] Both these professions enjoy high social status as do all occupations associated with them.

[AC] The inception of the tourism industry in 1972, marked a defining milestone in the history of work in the Maldives. Tourism replaced fishing as the largest industry in the Maldives, accounting for 28% of the Maldivian GDP and more than 60% of the Maldives' foreign exchange receipts (MPND, 2006). [EQA] The tourism industry opened up the erstwhile culturally insulated islands to the rest of the world and thereby it has also altered Maldivian ways of living.

It is against this cultural and economic background that this project was implemented. [AC] The objective of the project was to establish a national career guidance system, within a larger national vocational skills programme. At the inception of the project, I conducted a survey on a number of islands, to understand Maldivian culture and occupational orientations. I present here a paraphrased recounting of my encounter with a highly respected Maldivian fisherman whose wisdom played a significant role in my formulation of the cultural preparedness approach. I first met him as a participant in one of my focus group discussions on the island of Kulhudhuffushi, in northern Maldives, well known for its fishermen, blacksmiths, rope makers and boat builders. I first noticed him because of his [EC/EQA] restlessness as a participant in the FGD. [EC/EQA] He seemed annoyed and in deep disagreement with my description of career and occupation. [AC] After the meeting I went up to him and through my interpreter explained that I valued his opinion and that I was disappointed that he did not express his views in the meeting. At first, he seemed disdainful but gradually he began to talk. The discussion gathered momentum and continued over the next three days of my stay on the island. [EQA] His anguish at how tourism was upsetting a 2000 year old history, as well as traditional Maldivian values, was palpable. He took me around the island and explained the boat making industry to me. [CL] Gazing at the graceful contours of a 100-foot fishing boat (Mas Dhoani) that was under construction I realised that the boat was entirely hand crafted. [CL/EQ] He explained that traditional Maldivian boat building used the technique of tying hand hewn planks of coconut wood with rope twisted from coconut fibre (roanu). [EC/EQ] I saw also that Maldivian master boat-builders did not use diagrams or sophisticated instruments. [CL/EC] They did it all, relying on experience and observation. [CL/EC] I also noticed that over the ages other occupations ranging from carpentry and anchor casting to rope making and caulking had clustered around the profession of boat making, in an informal hierarchy.

My fisherman friend also allowed me to accompany his crew on a fishing trip. [EC/EQ] Here again I noticed that a variety of occupations including navigation, identification of fishing locations, fish-hook making and fish processing had evolved around the fishing profession. I saw that on the boat too, [EC/EQ] a code of occupational roles was in place. [EQ] My fisherman friend was at the prow of the boat, looking keenly at the sea and the sky above. At first it did not seem that the boat was heading toward a specific fishing spot. But I was mistaken. [CL/EC] The crew was following instructions from my fisherman friend. He was interpreting signs from the sea surface, and cloud and bird formations in the sky. At his sudden a cry, specific crew members sprayed baskets of tiny bait fish into the sea. In an instant the boat was surround by thousands of tuna, gulping the bait fish. Then the fishing began. The sea was brimming with fish swimming close to the surface. [CL/EC] Yet, the fishing method used was the pole-and-line technique. Fish were hauled into the boat, one-at-a-time. Large quantities were caught, but [EQ] still it was just one-at-a-time! After a while, the shoal moved away. The boat was heaped with silvery tuna. [CL/EC] As another team began to process the fish, I asked my friend, why they didn't use a large net to catch more fish. He gave me a long (despairing) look and said, [EC] "If we use a net, there are no fish for tomorrow." It was my last night on Kulhudhuffushi. [AC] Many of my (largely neoliberal) ideas about career and occupation had been challenged and shaken. My friend's words as we walked along the island shore that night transformed my thinking in an almost epiphanic manner. He said, [EC] "As long as there are fish in the sea, there is no need to think of what you describe as 'career'"! Early the next morning as I sailed away from that island (on a fibre glass motor boat, ironically), I asked how it was that my fisherman friend could find that huge shoal of tuna. [CL] "Ah", my young interpreter said, "He is the fish father".

Cultural learning: illustration from a case study in the Maldives

The transmission of ideas and values associated with the traditional Maldivian way of life is exemplified through the 2000-year-old traditions of fishing and boat making. Cultural learning is seen all through the case study, showing it to be the substrate upon which the consolidation and transmission of a culture's learning rests. This is particularly well illustrated in the final sentence of the case study "Ah! He is the fish father", revealing the younger person's reverential acceptance of the wisdom and experience of the much older fisherman. Other aspects of the case study that illustrate cultural learning are marked with the superscript CL.

Enculturation

Enculturation is the process of learning to become one's culture. From birth, through cultural learning, a person assimilates the values of the culture that enfolds him or her and acquires the behaviours that are suitable and obligatory. Enculturation is used within the cultural preparedness framework to describe specific and circumscribed phenomena within a particular culture.

Illustration from case study

The attribution of primacy to two occupations (fishing and boat making), the traditions surrounding these occupations, the clustering of occupations around these two occupations, the existence of a code of occupational roles and even the fisherman's initial disenchantment with the author, are all examples of enculturation. The fisherman's statements "If we use a net, there are no fish for tomorrow" and "As long as there are fish in the sea, there is no need to think of what you describe as 'career'", are a poignant revelation of enculturated work values. Other illustrations of enculturation are marked with the superscript EC.

Cultural preparedness equilibrium

Cultural preparedness equilibrium is the outcome of the workings of enculturation and cultural learning, reflecting Tomasello's (2000) ratchet effect mentioned above. Through the faculty of cultural learning the individual is enculturated to view and engage with the world in a certain way. This view is not about right or wrong, appropriate or inappropriate. It is about how an individual has been brought up to behave. The person's cultural preparedness equilibrium reflects an internal stability and the mental and emotional balance that results from the habituation of doing something in a certain way.

Illustration from case study

The case study shows that enculturation through the process of cultural learning had instilled a sense of equilibrium with regard to family relationships and work values. An equipoise and certainty has emerged with regard to navigating life's daily routines and challenges. While strong overtones of a patriarchal social organisation exist, this has been absorbed and normalised within this culture. Emerging from a deep, almost reverential connection with nature, this equilibrium has instilled restraint and self-control, as exemplified by the pole-and-line style of fishing despite the availability of mass fishing techniques. The superscript EQ indicates aspects of the case study that illustrate cultural preparedness equilibrium.

Acculturation

Acculturation could result from major external factors that affect the individual/group but over which the individual/group has little or no control. It also refers to the outcomes of the intermingling between cultures. While cultural learning and enculturation describe within-group, endogenous processes that influence cultural preparedness, human behaviour is at the same time influenced by acculturative forces of exogenous origin. Although acculturation can be reciprocal, in reality it is the minority/submissive group that is usually required to adapt to the requirements of the dominant group. The notion of career is an example. It originated in a Western, industrialised culture but has today become a reality in many other cultures around the world. The nature of work itself is changing in many of these countries, replacing the older and more holistic practice of pursuing livelihoods. An accultural approach to career development could transpose definitions of career that are not indigenous to the local context and displace already present, culturally grounded orientations.

Alteration of cultural preparedness equilibrium

The history of acculturation is perhaps as old as humankind's ability to voyage and travel and thereby meet and engage with other cultures. The cultural preparedness framework makes the point that acculturative forces could be consonant or dissonant with the individual/group's cultural preparation status. Consonance would mean that acculturation supports, enhances, or further stabilises the existing cultural preparedness equilibrium. Dissonance would mean that the forces of acculturation disturb the existing cultural preparedness equilibrium.

Illustration from case study

The most obvious acculturative influence in this case study is the arrival of tourism: an example of a macro, global trend. However it must also be noted that the fisherman and the author were acculturative influences upon each other: an example of the intermingling of cultures. Over the months following the author's encounter with him, the neoliberal ideas in the author's mind were gradually supplanted by the idea of cultural preparedness. The fisherman on his part became less cynical and bitter. In fact he began to consider giving contemporary twists to traditional occupations. Specific aspects of the case study that illustrate acculturation and the alteration of equilibrium are marked with the superscripts AC and EQA respectively.

Applying cultural preparedness for research and practice: examples from the development of a career guidance system for the Maldives

The experience of culturally embedding a career guidance programme into the Maldivian context and other such cultures caused the author to almost entirely move away from his universalistic approach and instead focus on the evolution of culturally mediated systems of career development. Five salient conceptual guidelines based on the cultural preparedness framework that guided this process are outlined briefly in the following sections. A more detailed description of the Maldivian career guidance system that emerged from this exercise is available in Arulmani and Abdulla (2007).

Recognising cultural leadership

Firstly, the author recognised that if a truly resonant system of guidance were to be developed, his own role could only be secondary to the already present leadership structure within this cultural system. Therefore, the elders and leaders of these island communities were acknowledged as the culturally sanctioned mediators of cultural learning. Their experiences, ideas and views informed the development process and were embedded into the career guidance system that finally emerged. These individuals participated in the vetting of the activities, tools and methods and in the training of guidance counsellors.

Expanding the definition of "client"

The programme redefined for whom the career guidance programme was actually meant. Keeping in view the collectivist enculturation of this culture, the family (particularly parents) were drawn into the guidance and counselling process. Exercises were developed to bring the individual and family together and thereby facilitate family-based decision making.

Integrating livelihood with career

In many cultures, livelihood is the daily reality while career is notional. For example, traditional ways of working (such as those described in the case study) were acknowledged as valid occupations and included in the career dictionary developed for the country as a part of this project. The prevailing system of work-based learning was valorised and integrated into the overall system. Although the existing cultural preparedness equilibrium was recognised and strengthened in this way, it is acknowledged that the programme did have an acculturative influence. For example, career development exercises were developed to view traditional occupations from a contemporary viewpoint (e.g., the value of receiving formal training related to a traditional occupation). The programme also introduced contemporary occupations and careers that required formal education.

Research in brief

Illustrative research examples undergirding the cultural preparedness framework

The Maldivian project was informed at all stages by research on local social cognitions and cultural practices. A qualitative study and an outcome analysis are given in the following sections as examples of research that have informed the cultural preparedness framework.

Identifying career beliefs

The cultural preparedness framework points out that social cognitions in the form of career beliefs, resulting from enculturation and cultural learning, have a defining impact on the career development process. For intervention planning therefore, identification of career beliefs characterising Maldivian culture was a first step. Data were collected through interviews and focus group discussions. The sample comprised 523 individuals including students, parents, teachers, and island leaders representing all project locations. Thematic analyses were conducted to identify patterns in career beliefs and frequency analyses showed how widespread these beliefs were. Commonly occurring belief themes within each project location were identified and presented to key stakeholders. Their feedback pertaining to the pervasiveness of these social cognitions helped to validate the findings. Following a deductive approach, the career beliefs framework developed by Arulmani and Nag-Arulmani (2004), was used to further validate the analysis. Briefly, thematic analyses pointed to four main career belief themes, which are listed and illustrated in Table 14.1 (Arulmani, 2006).

Findings such as this point to the processes of cultural learning and enculturation – constructs that are fundamental to the cultural preparedness framework. Our research shows that such career beliefs vary across cultures (e.g., Vietnam: Arulmani, 2014b; Sri Lanka: Arulmani, 2016) and thereby enculturating varied orientations to work, livelihood, and culture. It is vital that activities for career guidance are designed around such culturally mediated thought processes.

Outcomes of a culturally sensitive intervention versus a career guidance-only intervention

Continuing to keep the cultural preparedness framework in view, a social marketing campaign was designed for the Maldives that integrated culturally mediated social cognitions into the career guidance project. A quasi experimental study following a pretest–posttest design was conducted on a sample of

Table 14.1 Career belief themes, examples of common statements reflecting these beliefs and the frequency of their occurence ($N = 523$) (Translated from the original Dhivehi into English; source: Arulmani, 2006).

Career Belief Theme	Examples of Common Statements	Frequency of Occurrence
Gender	The girl's first priority is to stay at home and take care of the family.	86%
	Girls will get spoiled if they take up a career.	90%
Importance of education	Exams are too difficult to pass. So, it is better to try for a job without trying to pass exams.	70%
	People study and even get a university degree. But they still do not have a job. Therefore studying is no use.	65%
Control and self-direction	I live on a small island. There are not many jobs here. We cannot say what the future holds. So I cannot really plan for a successful career.	61%
	I am not a good student. I get low marks. Therefore I cannot get a good job.	56%
Persistence toward career development goals	I was selected for a 12-months course in carpentry. But I found the course very hard. So I dropped out after one week.	82%
	I have been paid my wages today. I will go back to work when my money finishes.	49%

291 grade 10 students (waiting control group, 77 students) to compare changes in career beliefs (Arulmani & Abdulla, 2007). Students were randomly assigned to a career guidance–only intervention (CG) or a social marketing plus career guidance intervention (SMCG). Following the intervention, the CG group showed significant reductions of negativity in career beliefs (t (104) = 14.91, $p <$ .001). The SMCG group also showed significant reductions in negativity in careers beliefs (t (108) = 51.47, $p <$ .001). Changes in the control group were not significant. Important for this discussion is the finding that the extent of decrease in negative career beliefs following the interventions was greater in the group that received the culturally mediated programme (the SMCG group) when compared to the CG-only group (t (212) = –30.68, $p <$ .001).

Similar trends have also been found in other Asian countries (e.g., Vietnam: Arulmani, 2014b; Sri Lanka: Arulmani, 2016). Such converging qualitative and quantitative evidence give support to the argument that an intervention that is grounded in the cultural preparedness of a community has better outcomes.

Contemporary global trends as acculturative influences

It is said that today we are at the threshold of the Fourth Industrial Revolution (4IR) (Schwab, 2017). Technological advances are leading not merely to automation but to the autonomisation of work tools and processes (e.g., driverless cars) leading in turn to a reduced dependence on human effort. These are acculturative influences that lie in the interface between financial capitalism and an amoral technological evolution on the one hand, and the forced abdication of human, cognitive and cultural engagement with work on the other hand. Trends such as these carry the strong potential for dominant cultures to push economically weaker cultures to align with their dictates. This in turn could lead to the homogenisation of cultures. The applicability of an intervention is likely to be affected when "universal" principles are applied without adapting them to the "particular" characteristics of a specific setting (Arulmani, 2014a). The effectiveness of an intervention could be higher when the ideas and concepts that lie behind an intervention cohere with the history, values, and beliefs of a particular community (Arulmani, 2011). Committing to the notion of cultural preparedness requires researchers and practitioners to recognise, acknowledge, and work with prevailing cultural practices rather than replace them.

Strengths and limitations

Viewed along the universalist–particularist continuum, the cultural preparedness framework leans more toward the particularist position and rests on the argument that a culture must be understood on its own terms. At the same time, it must be kept in mind that if applied without due consideration, such an approach could suffer the limitation of promoting ethnocentrism: viewing other groups exclusively through the lens of one's own culture. As a result, the benefits that could accrue from a universal common ground could be lost. Although the universalist position is committed to understanding nomothetic trends and commonalities, it could miss the trees for the forest and runs the risk of becoming hegemonic. On the other hand, the particularist position, as a result of its idiographic commitment to specify, examine details, and celebrate uniqueness could miss the forest for the trees and thus risks becoming exclusivist. Being acutely aware of these potential limitations, the cultural preparedness framework aims at the middle ground. Although it recognises overarching, universal principles, it cautions against the smothering of preexisting, culture-specific uniqueness. It encourages the examination of universals in the light of a specific culture, preferably by the people of that culture. It asks for space within which universals could be adapted to resonate with the cultural preparedness equilibrium of a specific culture. It also asks that provisions be made when necessary, for the rejection of what is considered to be a universal principle in favour of a principle particular to a culture.

Future directions

Embedded within the cultural preparedness framework is the notion of cultural equivalence. The knowledge, ideas and systems emanating from non-Western epistemologies merit more than indulgent descriptions as "alternative" or "indigenous" approaches. A general recommendation for future directions is that these repositories of wisdom are acknowledged as in fact being "mainstream" thought for a given culture and hence warranting acceptance as valid frameworks for generating hypotheses, formulating designs for research, and intervention and for making interpretations (Arulmani, 2011).

The political events of the present times (e.g., Brexit), point to a future that could be characterised by diminishing interdependence, an erosion of ties between nation-states, the closing of borders and a return to nationalism, possibly leading to a deglobalising trend (Schwab, 2017). To be noted here is that deglobalisation would occur in contexts that are already pluralistic in their cultural composition. The drawing back of an economy from erstwhile economic ties with other countries does not account for the cultural pools and islands that would remain within its own borders. The cultural preparedness framework could have future applications in such situations.

Conclusion

Encounters with leaders of the Maldivian community such as the fisherman described in the case study, planted the first seeds of the idea of cultural preparedness in the author's mind. The author could see that orientations to work in the Maldivian context rested on a deeply enculturated, livelihoods perspective where work is not just a means of earning money, but went deeper and was embedded into the community's ways of living. The notion of career was relatively alien to this culture and learning an occupation was embedded in the processes of enculturation and cultural learning. Over the last few centuries, the ramp in the flow of knowledge and influence has largely been tilted from Western industrialised cultures to other parts of the world. This has caused widespread alteration in the cultural preparedness equilibrium of recipient cultures, often leading to the devalorisation of indigenous ways of thinking and behaving. Understanding the relativity of cultural preparedness equilibrium across cultures could contribute to the formulation of interventions that facilitate the emergence of a viable, new equilibrium

---

Learning activities

Learning activity 1

"I am a lotus eyed, slim-waisted, long-limbed beauty with lovely slender fingers. Who am I?"

Your response could reflect your cultural learning and enculturation. To my zoologist friend who coined this sentence, the answer is, *Hyla squirella.* (Look it up!) Reflect on how our upbringing causes us to view the world in a certain way and on the fact that different cultures enculturate us differently.

Learning activity 2

Imagine a girl in bikini, wearing outsize sunglasses. Also imagine another girl in an all-encompassing burqa that leaves only her face visible. The girl with the sunglasses looks at the burqa clad one and thinks "Everything covered but her eyes. What a cruel male-dominated world". The burqa-clad girl looks at the bikini-clad, sunglasses-wearing one and thinks, "Nothing covered but her eyes. What a cruel male-dominated world".

Learning activities: reflective questions

1 Is either of these girls right or wrong?
2 In what ways would the girls' respective cultural preparedness equilibrium be disturbed by acculturative forces, if they had to cross over to work and develop a career in each other's cultural locations?
3 Most work environments formally or informally prescribe dress codes. If you were an employer of multicultural work force, how would the cultural preparedness framework influence your decisions about dress codes in your office?
4 What could be a new cultural preparedness equilibrium that could emerge in their lives?

Note

1 This case study is based on the author's experience during a project on guidance and counselling (2006–2011) in the Republic of Maldives. All figures and statistics are from 2006 when this study was conducted. Abbreviations: CL = cultural learning; EC = enculturation; EQ = cultural preparedness equilibrium; AC = acculturation; EQA = alteration of equilibrium.

References

Arulmani, G. (2006). *Employment skills training project (Asian Development Bank 2028-MLD): Career guidance and social marketing component.* Male, Maldives: Asian Development Bank.

Arulmani, G. (2011). Receive in order to give: Eastern cultural values and their relevance to contemporary career counselling contexts. *Occasional Paper: Faculty of Education, Canterbury Christ Church University*, 16–22.

Arulmani, G. (2014a). The cultural preparation process model and career development. In G. Arulmani, A. J. Bakshi, F. T. L. Leong, & A. G. Watts (Eds.), *Handbook of career development: International perspectives* (pp. 81–104). New York: Springer International.

Arulmani, G. (2014b). *Preparing a guide on career guidance for rural areas and piloting it in Vietnam: Final report.* Hanoi, Vietnam: International Labour Organisation.

Arulmani, G. (2016). Pilot assessment to identify training needs of career guidance officers in north Sri Lanka: Final report to Deutsche Gesellschaft Fur International Zusammenarbeit (GIZ), Sri Lanka Colombo, Sri Lanka.

Arulmani, G., & Abdulla, A. (2007). Capturing the ripples: Addressing the sustainability of the impact of social marketing. *Social Marketing Quarterly, 13*(4), 84–107.

Arulmani, G., & Nag-Arulmani, S. (2004). *Career counselling: A handbook.* New Delhi, India: Tate McGraw-Hill.

Banda, K. (2014). Transition from school to work of university students in the Japanese context. *Indian Journal of Career and Livelihood Planning, 3*(1), 26–31.

Bell, H. C. P. (1940). *The Maldive islands: Monograph on the history, archaeology and epigraphy.* Male, Maldives: Ceylon Government Press.

Ministry of Planning and National Development. (2006). *Republic of Maldives: Seventh national development plan, 2006–2010 (Working draft).* Male, Maldives: Author.

Prabhu, P. H. (1963). *Hindu social organizations: A study of socio-psychological and ideological foundations.* Bombay, India: Popular Prakashan.

Schwab, K. (2017). *The fourth industrial revolution.* New York: Crown.

Sultana, R. G. (2014). Career guidance for social justice in neoliberal times. In G. Arulmani, A. J. Bakshi, F. T. L. Leong, & A. G. Watts (Eds.), *Handbook of career development: International perspectives* (pp. 317–334). New York: Springer.

The Promise Foundation. (2010). *Interventions for youth development and potential realisation: An overview.* Bangaluru, India: Author.

Tilgher, A. (1930/1958). *Homo faber: Work through the ages (trans. D. C. Fisher.).* New York: Harcourt Brace (Original work published in 1930).

Tomasello, M. (2000). Culture and cognitive development. *Current Directions in Psychological Science, 9*(2), 37–40.

Weber, M. (1905/2002). *The Protestant ethic and the spirit of capitalism* (trans. P. Baehr and G. C. Wells). New York: Penguin Books (Original work published 1905).

Yankelovich, D., & Immerwahr, J. (1984). Putting the work ethic to work. *Society, 21*(2), 58–77.

15 Career development
Insights from organisation theory

Hugh Gunz and Wolfgang Mayrhofer

Learning objectives

The purpose of this chapter is to:

- identify the contributions of coevolutionary theory for informing the field of career development,
- reflect on the significance of coevolutionary relationships to the field of career development, and
- understand the dynamics of coevolutionary relationships.

Introduction to the chapter

As careers are lived in and between organisations, the nature of the organisations in question has a powerful influence on individual careers. Organisations vary considerably in their characteristics and contextual embeddedness, all of which affect the kind of career that their members might have, within and between them. Organisation theorists attempt to explain what organisations are and why they behave as they do (Clegg, Hardy, Lawrence, & Nord, 2006; Tsoukas & Knudsen, 2005). Our chapter addresses this question: How might theories of organisations inform the field of career development? We focus on coevolutionary theory (Lewin, Long, & Carroll, 1999), which helps us understand the dynamics of careers. It addresses a key, but widely overlooked point concerning careers: they are affected by, and affect, those of others.

Overview of organisation theory

Origins of the theory

As soon as one asks the question, *How might organisation theory inform the field of career development?*, it becomes evident that it would require something of the order of a book to begin to answer it. This is because there is no single unitary organisation theory on which the chapter could draw. Rather, organisation theory (OT) is a broad field of enquiry covering many different approaches to understanding organisations, suggesting many unique frameworks for examining career development that yield a plethora of differing suggestions for both research and practice. We briefly outline the scope of the field before selecting one particular, and in our view promising, approach that has emerged from OT. As we have argued elsewhere (Gunz & Mayrhofer, 2018), coevolutionary theory has the potential to suggest sometimes counter-intuitive outcomes in hitherto well-understood areas of career scholarship.

First, we explain why organisations and organisation theory might matter at all to careers. Career itself is a term that is used in many different senses (Young & Collin, 2000). Here, we draw on the idea that the study of career involves the simultaneous application of three perspectives to do with space, being, and time, such that when we examine careers we are interested in the condition of a career actor, in other words, the individual who has the career (Gunz & Mayrhofer, 2018), where they are in a given geographical and social space, and how this changes over time. We label these perspectives respectively spatial, ontic (meaning "of or relating to entities and the facts about them"; OED, 2017), and temporal (Gunz & Mayrhofer, 2018), so that a career is a pattern of a career actor's positions and condition within a bounded social and geographic space over their life to date.

To the extent that careers are lived within and between organisations, organisations define a major part of the geographical and social space within which this happens, and this is why OT is such a fruitful source of ideas about career. Concepts emerged from OT, such as (a) bounded rationality (Simon, 1947/ 1957); (b) the difference between mechanistic and organic organisations (Burns & Stalker, 1961); (c) distinctions between charisma, power, and compliance (Etzioni, 1961); (d) questioning pure rationality (Cyert & March, 1963) or using the metaphor of a garbage can (March & Olsen, 1976) in viewing organisational decision-making; (e) the effect of production technology (Woodward, 1965), environment (Lawrence & Lorsch, 1967), uncertainty reduction (Thompson, 1967), or transaction costs (Williamson, 1975) on organisational structures and processes; and (f) viewing organisations as open systems (Katz & Kahn, 1966) or systems of power relations dependent on the external environment (Pfeffer & Salancik, 1978). The theme underpinning these views is one of organisations and the individuals working in them being nothing like the machine-like entities of classical management theory. Critical and unforeseen life events, power, conflicts and contradictions, uncertainties, decisions, and the like all play an important role alongside formal structures and processes. Organisations are seen as social universes in themselves, embedded in a broader economic, legal, and social environment.

More recently, interest has also gone beyond single organisations to populations of organisations. One stream draws on population ecology (Hannan & Freeman, 1977), examining the viability of organisations within ecological niches, and the other on neo-institutional theory (DiMaggio & Powell, 1983), based on the idea that organisations are institutions whose behaviour is governed by their need for legitimacy within their social, political, and economic context. It is this last stream of research and writing that brought the notion of coevolution to the study of organisation (Lewin, Long, & Carroll, 1999), on which we focus here.

Lewin et al. introduced coevolution to organisation theory as a way of understanding how "firm strategic and organisation adaptations coevolve with changes in the environment (competitive dynamics, technological, and institutional) and organisation population and forms, and ... new organisational forms can mutate and emerge from the existing population of organisations" (Lewin et al., 1999, p. 535). Coevolution is a term that is used quite widely, and not always with any real precision of meaning (Hodgson, 2013). We adopt the definition of Heylighen and Campbell (1995), who explain that

> the environment [of an evolving entity] changes in part because it also often consists of evolving systems that try to optimize their fitness. This inter-dependency, where the change in fitness of one system changes the fitness function for another system, and vice-versa, is called co-evolution.
>
> (p. 184)

Key theoretical principles

"Fitness" is a key concept in evolutionary biology. In the previous quote, the authors use it to mean "a complex function of the system and its environment, an index of the likelihood that the system would persist and replicate. Those systems will be selected that have the highest fitness" (Heylighen & Campbell, 1995, p. 184). Fitness is an index of the evolutionary success of the entity in question. In career terms, we can think of fitness as an indication of career success, so the careers of two career actors can be thought of as coevolving if the career success of one has an impact on the other, and vice versa. For example, a successful mentor (Ragins & Kram, 2007) provides career support to their protégé, thereby increasing the chances that the protégé will experience greater career success than otherwise. This in itself does not represent coevolution, because it says nothing about the effect that the protégé's success (or lack of it) may have on the career of the mentor. For this we need to move to what has been called relational mentoring (Fullick-Jagiela, Verbos, & Wiese, 2015; Ragins, 2012), which involves mutual learning by both protégé and mentor. To the extent that this mutual learning is seen as a career advance by *each* party, their careers are coevolving; here we are viewing career success mainly from a subjective perspective (Hughes, 1937). The mutual learning may, over time, translate into objective success (e.g., promotion and/or enhanced status in the firm) for each party. To sum up, coevolution happens when the mentor's career is affected by what happens to the protégé's career, and the protégé's career is affected by what happens to the mentor's career.

Evolutionary biologists use the concept of fitness landscapes (Kauffman, 1993) to visualise both evolution and coevolution; more recently, they have been applied to organisations (Van de Ven, Ganco, & Hinings, 2013). In a fitness landscape, the genotype of an organism is depicted on the horizontal dimensions of the landscape and its fitness on the vertical dimension. Similar organisms are close to each other horizontally, while dissimilar ones are distant, and fitter organisms are higher on the landscape than less fit organisms. Evolution is conceived of as a process of climbing fitness "mountains". Some landscapes have a single peak – there is one way of evolving – while others may be very rugged, with many independent peaks of differing heights separated by valleys. These rugged landscapes describe a situation in which there are many independent evolutionary routes, some leading to higher levels of fitness (higher peaks) than others.

When we say that an organism is coevolving with another, we mean that its fitness landscape is changed by what happens to the other organism. Positive coevolution means that its landscape – or parts of it – are pushed up as a result of what happens to the other organism, and vice versa. Returning to our mentoring example, coevolution happens if the mentor's fitness landscape is affected by what happens to the protégé, and vice versa. For example, as a result of the mentor's coaching, the protégé experiences greater success in pitching ideas for new projects, and starts rising through the organisation as a result. The protégé involves the mentor in the projects which leads to the mentor's career benefitting from the projects' success. The mentor's fitness landscape has been "pushed up" by the protégé's success.

We need to add two more observations from the coevolution literature to our account of this facet of organisation theory, concerning coevolutionary theory's predictions about the dynamics of coevolving systems.

First, there is a built-in tendency for coevolving systems to change over time, and not for the better. Heylighen and Campbell (1995) describe a five-way classification of such systems, ranging from synergetic, in which each benefits from the other, to what they call super-competitive, in which "free riders" eventually lead to "the erosion and eventual collapse of the cooperative system" (Heylighen & Campbell, 1995, p. 190; the other three intermediate states are labelled independent, partially competitive, and competitive). Because of problems such as that of the free-rider, coevolving systems have a built-in tendency to turn to super-competition: "The problem is that everybody profits from cooperation, but that noncooperators benefit more, since they reap the additional resources produced by synergy, while investing nothing in return" (Heylighen & Campbell, 1995, p. 190). To return to our mentoring example, synergetic coevolution involves mentor and protégé mutually benefitting in career terms from the relationship. But if the relationship degrades into a competitive one, or leads to clique formation, both to the detriment of the organisation as a whole, we have something more closely resembling super-competition.

Second, the ruggedness of a fitness landscape has important implications for the organisms evolving on it. If the landscape has a single, Mt. Fuji-style peak, there is only one best evolutionary outcome. But if the landscape is rugged, with many sub-peaks, the chances are much greater that the organism will get trapped on a sub-peak. Once that has happened, there is no way for it to evolve to a higher level of fitness. Baum (1999) draws on the simulations of Kauffman

(1993) to show that there are a variety of strategies, for example to do with the uniformity with which reward practices are applied, that can be adopted to alter the chances of getting stuck on sub-peaks. For example, if an organisation wants to reduce the chances of mentoring relationships developing into cliques, it should create a rugged landscape with lower peaks by avoiding uniform rewards for mentorship behaviour across the organisation; if on the other hand it wants to allow people to develop as much as they can, it should choose uniform rewards, generating a single peak for everyone to climb (see Gunz & Mayrhofer, 2018, pp. 177–180, for a more detailed explanation).

Cultural validity of the theory

The assumptions underlying coevolutionary theory are essentially universalistic. They ignore time related and contextual specifics of the cultural and institutional sort and are "space-time-invariant".

However, cultural circumstances might affect coevolutionary influences on careers. In a highly collectivist culture, for example, the unit of analysis may shift from the individual career actor to the career actor as a member of an extended family. The coevolutionary pressures experienced by the actor will be of a different quality. Compared to an individualistic culture with a common assumption that "work comes first", the individual may not be as free to accept promotions, geographical transfers, working relationships with members of another sex, or the like without consulting with, and being strongly influenced by, their extended family.

Similarly, there is a tacit assumption of equality between the organisms that populate the fitness landscape. However, depending, for example, on the view on men's and women's role in a specific culture, it makes a big difference if we look at a male/male, female/male, or female/female configuration in the coevolving unit of analysis. Similarly, the coevolving careers of supervisor – employee have a different dynamic in a context that tolerates/requires a high power differential between different hierarchical levels (e.g., that deteriorating tendencies will occur later and at slower speed).

These examples do not invalidate the basic assumptions of coevolutionary theory. Yet, they suggest that its application may require the recognition that career actors are the subject of complex and varying influences, and that a full analysis requires a proper recognition of this complexity.

Research in brief

Mentoring has been widely studied (Ragins & Kram, 2007), but the application of coevolutionary theory to it is new. Similarly, there has been little work on relational mentoring. Ghosh, Reio, and Hayes (2012) examined a group of managerial and non-managerial employees of three US-based corporations. They find that perceptions of "reciprocal support" (Ghosh et al., 2012, p. 42) between mentor and protégé, an indication of relational mentoring, are linked to increased affective organisational commitment and organisation-based self-esteem. These affect the protégés' intentions to display helping organisational citizenship behaviour (OCB). Tentatively, organisational commitment is linked to career satisfaction, a component of subjective career success (Romzek, 1989), while self-esteem is a component of core self-evaluations (Judge, Locke, & Durham, 1997) that relates to career success, as does OCB (Heslin & Latzke, in press). This implies that relational mentoring, at least in the perceptions of some protégés, is connected with the protégé's success. However, the impact of this mentoring on the careers of the mentors requires additional research.

Research in brief: reflective questions

Looking at people with whom you had a mutually beneficial professional relationship resulting in a positive influence on your career development:

1   Did the relationship have any effect on how you viewed the organisation you were working with at that time?
2   What effect did the mutually beneficial professional relationship have on you personally, in particularly with regard to your position within the organisation and what you could achieve?
3   What consequences did this relationship have for your career satisfaction as well as changes in income and advancement?

Case study

Restructuring and rising through the ranks

The restructuring of Siemens in the aftermath of a bribery scandal unfolding in the early 2000s provides the canvas for illustrating these principles. Siemens, founded in 1847 with headquarters in Berlin and Munich, Germany, is a global player in electrical engineering and electronics employing about 351,000 employees worldwide with an overall revenue of €79.644 billion (figures as of September 30, 2016; Anonymous, 2017a). In 2007, Peter Löscher was brought in as the first external CEO in the history since its foundation in 1847 to handle the emerging crisis as a consequence of the widespread bribery. He was ousted in 2013 after poor financial results and Joe Kaeser (originally Josef Käser, changing his name after a stint in the San Jose, California, operation of Siemens) was appointed as new CEO, with a renewal of his contract in 2017 for another term until 2021.

Kaeser (born 1957) has spent his whole professional life at Siemens. After studying business administration in Germany he joined the company in 1980, moved to the semi-conductor branch of Siemens in 1987, soon focused on finance, became Siemens's Chief Strategy Officer in 2004 and replaced Heinz-Joachim Neubürger (a key figure in the bribery scandal who killed himself in 2015) as Chief Financial Officer in 2006. When taking over as CEO, Kaeser initiated Vision 2020, a change program with massive changes such as cutting one layer of leadership and reducing the number of business units. Lately, he planned to divide Siemens into two major parts: Siemens Industry and Siemens Medical Technology. A small group of trusted people very loyal to the new CEO, often based on a joint history in Siemens, played a key role in this restructuring.

A prominent member of this inner circle was Janina Kugel. Born in 1970 and educated as an economist in Germany and Italy, she started out as a management consultant at Accenture, one of the largest globally operating consulting firms. In 2001, she joined Siemens Communications and became Vice President Business Transformation & Knowledge Management. There she met, among others, Joe Kaeser, who attracted his attention as someone with the potential for a larger role in the company (Löhr, 2014). In 2005, she changed to Corporate Development and then switched to HRM, becoming Chief Diversity Officer in 2014. In 2015, Kaeser paved the way for her becoming a member of the managing board as Chief Human Resources Officer.

Kaeser and Kugel often presented Siemens together to the outside world, and Kugel was sometimes called "the queen of the K + K monarchy at Siemens" (Ziesemer, 2017). Well-equipped in terms of technical competence, appearance, and personal communication skills, she was an ambassador for Vision 2020 and represented the new style that Kaeser wanted to see at Siemens: charming, open and easy going. In November 2017, however, Kugel came under considerable fire. When Siemens announced massive layoffs worldwide (about 7,000 jobs), the works council accused her of lack of communication that constituted a slap in the face of all employees and of the organisational culture (Anonymous, 2017b). Some signs of tension were also visible between the CEO and his Chief HRM officer when, symbolically, she was reminded of her difficult task by Kaeser during the balance sheet press conference (Meck, 2017).

Discussion of theoretical building blocks

In the following, we use the Siemens case to illustrate the significance of the four major theoretical building blocks: coevolution, fitness, fitness landscapes, and tendency of coevolutionary systems to deteriorate over time.

Coevolution

Two or more entities can be said to be coevolving when the change in fitness of one affects the other(s), and vice versa. To implement a drastic restructuring program, initially skeptically commented on in the business press (Bilanz, 2014), CEO Kaeser needed, among others, allies who credibly represented the new era both within Siemens and in the outside world. Kugel came in handy in this respect: young compared to many of her colleagues in positions of similar responsibility, female in an organisational culture deemed to male-dominant compared to the *zeitgeist*, and, judging by her previous achievements, obviously capable of getting a job done, not to mention with a high degree of loyalty. She increased the options for Kaeser and the likelihood of successfully implementing the planned steps. For Kugel, the rise of Kaeser clearly influenced her own personal and professional prospects. As CEO, Kaeser was able to strongly influence the composition of the managing board at Siemens. Despite the supervisory board's formal appointment rights, the CEO's voice was heard in practice. In the case of Kugel's rise to Chief HRM Officer joining the managing board, Kaeser clearly used his influence. Taken together, the individual developments of both Kaeser and Kugel influenced the other. Their own professional advancement increased the options for the other person and, in this case, for professional success as indicated by hierarchical advancement.

Fitness

Fitness is an index of the evolutionary success of the entity in question. In the case example of Kaeser and Kugel coevolving through the ranks of Siemens, this dyad clearly was successful both as a dyad and as participating individuals. Individually, Kaeser and Kugel continuously rose in the Siemens hierarchy. It took them 33 and 14 years, respectively, to move from their entry level positions at Siemens to the highest level, the managing board, with Kaeser becoming its chairman. Also as a dyad, they were very successful in their coevolution. Strongly depending on each other due to their positions at Siemens, this dyad was also seen as working hand in hand, mutually enabling each other – though, to be sure, to a different degree due to the power differential between the two – to be successful both as individuals and as a dyad.

Fitness landscapes

Fitness landscapes depict the terrain, the context within which organisms, or, in our case, career actors in firms, make their moves. In our example, the fitness landscape is not a simple one, for example of the Mt. Fuji-type with one major peak and various more or less direct ways to the top. True, the managing board of Siemens AG is formally the highest decision making authority. However, depending on the overall situation in terms of economic and societal development, the importance of the various country organisations, divisions, and functional areas can vary considerably. This makes for a very rugged fitness landscape constantly in motion. Kaeser's cut of hierarchical layers and of the number of business units led to massive changes in the landscape. In turn, this allowed various organisms – here: career actors – to pursue different routes through this landscape. Kugel, Siemens' Chief HRM Officer, clearly profited from the changing landscape. However, in all likelihood Kugel was stuck on her current sub-peak. Given the organisational history of Siemens and the status of

HRM officers in general, it is highly unlikely that she will be able to move up to CEO in Siemens, regardless of however much the landscape may be pushed up beneath her by Kaeser's success.

Tendency for coevolving systems to deteriorate over time

Coevolution theory posits that different types of coevolving systems have a common tendency towards deterioration over time, i.e., a move towards the destructive pole of super-competition. In the Siemens example of the coevolving system of the CEO and his CHRMO, until 2017 this system was potentially synergetic. Some deterioration became evident in 2017. The announcement of cutting roughly 7,000 jobs despite substantial profits put the coevolving system in a new situation with a changed fitness landscape. For Kaeser, it was a critical situation since there was a lot of publicity linked to the announcement and another litmus test for his leadership abilities as CEO. For this he needed Kugel, his CHRMO. At the same time, if there was a considerable negative fallout of these activities, he had to be careful not to be too much in the centre of it and to have a scapegoat that took much of the blame and ultimately also the fall. For Kugel, this was a critical moment, too. While the situation brought her a lot of spotlight, it was dominated by harsh criticism from different kinds of employee representatives and an overall negative press (Anonymous, 2017b). If she was able to weather the storm, it would improve her standing within the coevolving system. However, the symbolic signals sent by the CEO at the balance sheet press conference (Meck, 2017) do not seem to bode well for future cooperation.

Intervention notes

Possible interventions in this case relate to both the organisational and the individual level. At the organisational level, the substantial restructuring that Joe Kaeser drove over an extended period of time modified the career-related fitness landscape. This had consequences for the way in which careers are made in the company. Helping the organisation to identify this newly evolving landscape and the related consequences is an important accompanying measure to integrate these changes into organisational and individual career development considerations.

An appropriate intervention can consist of a half-day workshop with participants from different parts of the company and representing different groups of employees, with the aim of producing a joint view of the newly emerging career-related fitness landscape. Guiding questions for exchanging their views could be:

1   Peaks and valleys

    a   Can we observe new peaks and valleys due to the ongoing changes?
    b   What has happened to the traditional ones?

2   Routes through the landscape

    a   How do the landscape changes affect well-established career routes?

    b   What potential new routes are emerging?

3   Career actors

    a   Who belongs to the current set of career actors populating the fitness landscape?

    b   Who is (no longer) an important career actor?

4   Power relations and rules

    a   What effects does the new landscape have for the existing power relations?

    b   Are new explicit and/or implicit rules governing the landscape emerging?

At the dyad level of CEO Joe Kaeser and CHRMO Janina Kugel, a potential intervention has to address at least three issues. First, it seems helpful to check and possibly raise the level of awareness about the kind of relationship – a coevolving dyad in a dynamic fitness landscape – that they form. Although this might be obvious from the outside, the views of the participating persons might be quite different.

Second, being on a joint path and mutually depending on each other has a number of strengths such as harvesting secondary gains, if the other part of the dyad is successful, e.g. by reaching important strategic goals such as restructuring Siemens or downsizing an existing operation without high social cost and negative publicity. At the same time, there are a number of pitfalls threatening the relationship. Examples include being tied to the other person in times of failure and having to cope with the fluid social recognition the two people in this dyad receive within the company and in the wider public. In addition, how people perceive the coevolving dyad in terms of its genesis, the assumed mutual benefits, and its future potential is critical to the effects it has on the company and for the dyad members.

Third, like every other relationship, a coevolving dyad has a limited life span. In this particular environment, i.e. a company in a changing environment in the process of restructuring and an average term of office of the CEO since the mid-1960s of 7.5 years (www.siemens.com/global/en/home/company/about/history/people/chairmen-of-the-managing-board-of-siemens-ag.html), it seems safe to predict that this will not be a bond over decades. Consequently, contemplating how to handle a relationship at the tail-end of its life cycle and, ultimately, deliberately manage its end should that be necessary seems to be not far-fetched.

All this points towards the need to deliberately acknowledge this kind of relationship and actively manage it. The social form of such an intervention could be high-level coaching, presumably with the CHRMO who should be more open to this kind of support due to her area of responsibility. In turn, insights and behaviour changes acquired by Janina Kugle will influence the coevolving dyadic relationship.

Chapter summary and conclusion

OT in general, and coevolutionary theory in particular, provides a unique perspective on careers because of the attention they draw to the importance of context. As we note earlier, examining careers involves the application of three perspectives – spatial, ontic, and temporal – and OT potentially provides many important insights into the spatial to the extent that the social space in question is organisational. Coevolutionary theory is a particularly useful perspective on careers because of the focus it brings to the way that careers interconnect.

Coevolutionary theory is new to OT and the study of careers which reflects a general feature of the careers literature: it has been slow to draw on theoretical frameworks outside its own field (Gunz & Mayrhofer, 2018). It has been noted that

> institutions are but the forms in which the collective behaviour and collective action of people go on. In the course of a career the person finds his place within these forms, carries on his active life with reference to other people, and interprets the meaning of the one life he has to live.
>
> (Hughes, 1937, p. 413)

Schein (1980) noted that careers "[fall] at the intersection between the individual and society" (p. 357).

A great deal has been learned about the nature of institutions and organisations since the time of Hughes and the early writings by Schein, but we are only beginning to apply some of this understanding to the study of careers. OT is a very rich and complex area of scholarship, and it will take some time for careers scholars to exploit this richness. We have suggested elsewhere (Gunz & Mayrhofer, 2018) an approach, the social chronology framework, which has the potential to provide a structured approach to exploring how the field of career studies can contribute to OT. We believe that there is great potential for career studies to develop in new and interesting directions as a result of these explorations.

Career development is rightly seen as an individually focused activity in the sense that its focus is on the development of individuals' careers. But it is equally important to remember that careers are not lived in isolation: our careers touch those of many others as we proceed through life, and theirs touch ours. If we are to understand fully how these mutual influences may play out we need to think beyond our own individual career paths and towards the complex social space that these paths lead through. However, because of the complexity and dynamic nature of this social space, this is not easy to do. Coevolutionary theory in particular, and OT in general, suggest intriguing new approaches to making sense of this complex world.

Learning activities

Set some time aside for the following exercises in advance to ensure you are undistplaced, in a reasonably good mood, in an environment that stimulates your creativity, and with little if any time pressure beyond the time budget you allocate to yourself. Have something ready to note down your thoughts and insights (e.g., a piece of paper, your tablet or smartphone, a notebook).

Learning activity 1: ideal profile of my coevolution partner

Coevolutionary partnerships can have strong positive effects on one's career development, for example with regard to personal growth or hierarchical advancement. However, especially because of the dynamics of such relationships, there are potential dangers, such as slowing down your own development because of actions of your coevolution partner regarded as negative by important decision makers, or emotional upheaval due to conflict in the partnership. Therefore, it is wise to choose such a partner carefully. This exercise helps you explore this issue by following these steps:

1   Set up two columns and mark them with '+ +' and '– –'. In the '+ +' column, list those people who have had a profoundly positive influence on your life; in the '– –' column, put down the names of people who left negative traces in your life.
2   Choose the people whose influence was most profound from both the positive and negative lists of influencers. Reducing the list to something like 3–5 of the 'big hitters' per column will help you focus.
3   Looking at the set of most profound influencers, list in some detail:

    a   What was their personality like, what were their most notable characteristics?
    b   What kinds of behaviour were most remarkable?
    c   What effects did their personality characteristics and their behaviour have on you? How long-lasting was it?

4   Against this backdrop:

    a   Make a list of 3–5 attributes related to personality and behaviour that you would like to see and not see in a potential coevolution partner.
    b   Looking around in your current professional social context: who would be the top two people you would choose as partner in such a relationship? Why? What would be your expectations?

Learning activity 2: mapping your personal fitness landscape

In terms of careers, fitness landscapes describe the terrain, the context within which you make or plan for your moves. Using the image of landscape with attributes such as beautiful vs. ugly, interesting vs. boring, uplifting vs. depressing, calming vs. eerie etc., please list in some detail:

1   Describe your current career landscape. Put specific emphases on

   a   Peaks that

      i   you can identify
      ii are specifically attractive for you

   b   Valleys and precipices that

      i   you can identify
      ii seem especially dangerous

   c   Established routes that people before you have taken

      i   What do they look like?
      ii   How fast do people move along these routes?
      iii What do these established routes require in terms of knowledge, skills, abilities, other things (KSAOs)?
      iv   What happened to the people who took these routes?
      v   Would you be able and willing to follow these routes? If yes, why; if no, why not?

   d   Are there alternative routes that have rarely, if ever, been taken?

      i   What do they look like?
      ii   What do these alternative routes require in terms of knowledge, skills, abilities, other things (KSAOs)?
      iii Would you be able and willing to go these routes? If yes, why; if no, why not?
      iv   What are potential benefits and drawbacks of these alternative routes?

2   Introduce the time dimension into the picture and look to the future:

   a   (How) Will the picture change in the future?
   b   If yes,

      i   in which direction?
      ii What does that mean for you and your development?

Learning activities: reflective questions

1   Of the individuals who have affected your career, positively or negatively, are you aware of the effect the relationship had on their careers?

> 2   If you have been able to identify any individuals with whose careers you have had a coevolving relationship (or you know of someone else in this situation), have you noticed any changes over time in the nature of the relationship?
>
> 3   If these relationships developed within a single organisation, were there any policies, for example to do with the way that people are/were rewarded, that had an effect on the relationships? What was/were the effect(s)?

References

Anonymous. (2017a). Retrieved from www.siemens.com/global/en/home.html

Anonymous. (2017b). Arbeitnehmer attackieren Siemens-Führung. Retrieved from www.handelsblatt.com/unternehmen/industrie/jobabbau-arbeitnehmer-attackieren-siem ens-fuehrung/20556900.html

Baum, J. A. C. (1999). Whole-part coevolutionary competition in organizations. In J. A. C. Baum & B. McKelvey (Eds.), *Variations in organization science: In honor of Donald T. Campbell* (pp. 113–135). London: SAGE.

Bilanz. (2014). Retrieved from http://docplayer.org/19958257-Luxus-die-kaeser-show-vw-porsche-alles-mueller-laden-der-kreuz.html

Burns, T., & Stalker, G. M. (1961). *The management of innovation*. London: Tavistock.

Clegg, S. R., Hardy, C., Lawrence, T., & Nord, W. R. (Eds.). (2006). *The SAGE handbook of organization studies*. London: SAGE.

Cyert, R. M., & March, J. G. (1963). *A behavioral theory of the firm*. Englewood Cliffs, NJ: Prentice Hall.

DiMaggio, P. J., & Powell, W. W. (1983). The iron cage revisited: Institutional isomorphism and collective rationality in organizational fields. *American Sociological Review*, 48(2), 147–160.

Etzioni, A. (1961). *A comparative analysis of complex organizations*. New York: The Free Press.

Fullick-Jagiela, J. M., Verbos, A. K., & Wiese, C. W. (2015). Relational mentoring episodes as a catalyst for empowering protégés. *Human Resource Development Review*, 14(4), 486–508.

Ghosh, R., Reio, T. G., & Haynes, R. K. (2012). Mentoring and organizational citizenship behavior: Estimating the mediating effects of organization-based self-esteem and affective commitment. *Human Resource Development Quarterly*, 23(1), 41–63.

Gunz, H., & Mayrhofer, W. (2018). *Rethinking career studies: Facilitating conversation across boundaries with the social chronology framework*. Cambridge, UK: Cambridge University Press.

Hannan, M. T., & Freeman, J. (1977). The population ecology of organizations. *American Journal of Sociology*, 82(5), 929–964.

Heslin, P. A., & Latzke, M. (in press). Individual difference antecedents of career outcomes. In H. Gunz, M. Lazarova & W. Mayrhofer (Eds.), *The Routledge companion to career studies*. Abingdon, Oxon, UK: Routledge.

Heylighen, F., & Campbell, D. T. (1995). Selection of organization at the social level: Obstacles and facilitators of metasystem transitions. *World Futures*, 45(1–4), 181–212.

Hodgson, G. M. (2013). Understanding organizational evolution: Toward a research agenda using generalized darwinism. [Review]. *Organization Studies*, 34(7), 973–992.

Hughes, E. C. (1937). Institutional office and the person. *American Journal of Sociology*, *43*, 404–413.

Judge, T. A., Locke, E. A., & Durham, C. C. (1997). The dispositional causes of job satisfaction: A core evaluations approach. *Research in Organizational Behavior*, *19*, 151–188.

Katz, D., & Kahn, R. (1966). *The social psychology of organizations*. New York: John Wiley.

Kauffman, S. A. (1993). *The origins of order: Self-organization and selection in evolution*. New York: Oxford University Press.

Lawrence, P. R., & Lorsch, J. W. (1967). *Organization and environment: Managing differentiation and integration*. Boston, MA: Harvard University Press.

Lewin, A. Y., Long, C. P., & Carroll, T. N. (1999). The coevolution of new organizational forms. *Organization Science*, *10*(5), 535–550.

Löhr, J. (2014). Die stille Reserve der Wirtschaft ist weiblich. Retrieved from www.faz.net/aktuell/wirtschaft/managerinnen-der-zweiten-reihe-die-stille-reserve-der-wirtschaft-ist-weiblich-12798320/janina-kugel-12798530.html

March, J. G., & Olsen, J. P. (1976). *Ambiguity and choice in organizations*. Bergen, Norway: Universitetsforlaget.

Meck, G. (2017). Der neue Star bei Siemens. Retrieved from www.faz.net/aktuell/wirtschaft/unternehmen/siemens-personalchefin-janina-kugel-im-haertetest-15288181.html

OED. (2017). *Oxford English Dictionary*. Retrieved from www.oed.com

Pfeffer, J., & Salancik, G. R. (1978). *The external control of organizations – a resource dependence perspective*. New York: Harper & Row.

Ragins, B. R. (2012). Relational mentoring: A positive approach to mentoring at work. In K. Cameron & G. Spreitzer (Eds.), *The handbook of positive organizational scholarship* (pp. 519–536). New York: Oxford University Press.

Ragins, B. R., & Kram, K. E. (Eds.). (2007). *The handbook of mentoring at work: Theory, research, and practice*. Thousand Oaks, CA: SAGE.

Romzek, B. S. (1989). Personal consequences of employee commitment. *Academy of Management Journal*, *32*(3), 649–661.

Schein, E. H. (1980). Career theory and research: Some issues for the future. In C. B. Derr (Ed.), *Work, family, and the career: New frontiers in theory and research* (pp. 357–365). New York: Praeger.

Simon, H. A. (1947/1957). *Administrative behavior: A study of decision-making processes in administrative organization* (2nd ed.). New York: Free Press.

Thompson, J. D. (1967). *Organizations in action*. New York: McGraw-Hill.

Tsoukas, H., & Knudsen, C. (Eds.). (2005). *The Oxford handbook of organization theory*. Oxford, UK: Oxford University Press.

Van de Ven, A. H., Ganco, M., & Hinings, C. R. (2013). Returning to the frontier of contingency theory of organizational and institutional designs. *Academy of Management Annals*, *7*(1), 393–440.

Williamson, O. E. (1975). *Markets and hierarchies: Analysis and antitrust implications*. New York: Free Press.

Woodward, J. (1965). *Industrial organization: Theory and practice*. London: Oxford University Press.

Young, R. A., & Collin, A. (2000). Introduction: Framing the future of career. In A. Collin & R. A. Young (Eds.), *The future of career* (pp. 1–17). Cambridge, UK: Cambridge University Press.

Ziesemer, B. (2017). So herrscht die Königin der K+K-Monarchie. Retrieved from www.welt.de/wirtschaft/bilanz/article167112162/So-herrscht-die-Koenigin-der-K-K-Monarchie.html

16 Counselling/psychotherapy
A vocational perspective for psychotherapy

Mary Sue Richardson

Learning objectives

The purpose of this chapter is to:

- introduce counselling/psychotherapy as a psychotherapy theory that incorporates a vocational perspective,
- describe the four components of counselling/psychotherapy, and
- illustrate the four components and related theoretical principles of counselling/psychotherapy in a case study.

Introduction to the chapter

This chapter is a product of many years of professional experience in psychotherapy and vocational psychology through an amalgam of practices: teaching vocational development and counselling theory courses in an academic setting, and practising psychotherapy in an independent setting. In those years, I have witnessed and participated in significant historical shifts in the counselling professions with major implications for the practice of psychotherapy and career counselling. The story I tell about changes in the counselling professions is rooted in the U.S. experience, though I believe it is relevant to other national contexts as well. After setting this context, I present a model for psychotherapy that incorporates a vocational perspective. Following is a case study illustrating central features of this model.

The professional context

The widening split between psychotherapy and career counselling

Briefly, career theory and practice had its roots in the early 20th century in the work of Frank Parsons (1909), who recognized the need to help people make decisions about the kind of work they were going to do for a living. This marked the beginning of the counselling profession and the practice of vocational guidance. In the mid-20th century, one of vocational psychology's most significant theorists, Donald Super (1963), brought counselling into the profession of psychology by formulating a theory of career fashioned on the procrustean bed of psychological developmental theory. Thus was born counselling psychology, largely legitimized by its contribution to the developmental zeitgeist of the times in the profession of psychology (Richardson, 1993). In fairly short order, however, change in health care having to do with the licensure of psychotherapy initiated a trend towards the marginalization of career theory and practice in the professions of counselling psychology and counselling, or at least mental health counselling, that continues to this day.

The change in health care I refer to has to do with the recognition of the important role of psychotherapy in meeting mental health needs, the legitimization of these services through professional licensure, and the inclusion of psychotherapy in health insurance reimbursement. Applied psychologists of all persuasions, including counselling psychologists, flocked to the rapidly expanding and mostly well-compensated practice of psychotherapy. The same process occurred a few decades later in the counselling profession with the advent of licensure for mental health counsellors (Cummings, 1990). Psychotherapy is a major player in the world of health care; career counselling is not a player in this world at all. Career counselling continues to be rooted in an educational model that is not reimbursable and does not contribute to developing the psychotherapeutic expertise needed for licensure. The split between psychotherapy and career counselling that has always existed is not only alive and well: It is even more deeply fractured by professional developments associated with licensure.

Counselling/psychotherapy

Beyond integration: a vocational perspective for psychotherapy

One response to the split between psychotherapy and career counselling has been to champion efforts to integrate these practices (McIlveen, 2015). Rather than integration, my goal is to propose a theoretical model for psychotherapy, counselling/psychotherapy, that enables a vocational perspective on psychotherapy practice, and to illustrate this model with a case study. Counselling/psychotherapy locates vocational concerns within the realm of psychotherapy, acknowledges that clients who are struggling with mental health issues are, in many cases, also struggling with finding their way in the contemporary worlds of work, and takes the position that the challenges of working in today's world may, in fact, be responsible for not only exacerbating, but also for causing mental health problems.

Counselling for work and relationship: a first step toward counselling/psychotherapy

Counselling/psychotherapy builds on the practice-driven theoretical approach of counselling for work and relationship (CWR) (Richardson, 2012, 2017;

Richardson & Schaeffer, 2013). CWR posits a shift from helping people develop their careers to helping people co-construct their lives through work and relationships. It is a theory grounded, first of all, in contextualism.

CWR does not consider a career to be a part of a self that develops, as in career development, but rather, considers work as two contexts of development through which people develop. The context of market work has to do with the work a person does for pay. The context of unpaid care work refers to the work of caring for others in personal and family lives, such as raising children and caring for aging parents. A person's experience in the contexts of work may take different routes, described as work paths. Work paths are the joint products of persons interacting with the opportunities and constraints in the work contexts in which they participate. Shifting from the language of career to discourse about market work and unpaid work contexts and work paths is a major and consequential shift in thinking. It challenges the ideology of career (i.e., that career is a separate, psychologized, and privileged part of self) and decenters the locus of change from self to the interaction between self and context.

CWR construes people as developing throughout their lives in multiple, interdependent contexts, with three major contexts for most adults, consisting of (a) market work (work done for pay), (b) unpaid care work (the work of caring for others in personal lives), and (c) relationships. Focusing for the moment on two of the three major life contexts having to do with work, CWR acknowledges that the work that is needed for any society to function is twofold. It includes economic production. People have to produce goods and services for the economy to function and for them to support themselves. The work of society also includes social reproduction. People have to care for themselves, their children, families and friends, their communities, and the natural world in order to reproduce the social world that, in turn, drives economic production. In short, all work is not paid: Work is not synonymous with market work.

CWR, second of all, is grounded in narrative theory. Narrative is a burgeoning approach for studying human development and the human experience across disciplines (Gergen, Josselson, & Freeman, 2015). It is one of the major exemplars of the new subjective paradigm of human science that takes the study of human subjectivity as its primary data (Zittoun et al., 2013). Narrative is also the body of theory that considers the dimension of time central to the human experience. In this chapter, the words, narrative and story, are used interchangeably.

It is my contention that implicit in career development theory and practice is a fundamental concern with time, specifically with the future. When a person is engaged in a process of figuring out what to do in the world of market work, how to get started or how to get back on a market work path, that person is engaged in dealing with their future, with the struggle to co-construct a future in market work. It is a short step from this concern with the future, with what a person is going to do in regard to market work to concerns most people have about their futures in all other contexts of life: "What am I going to do to earn a living?" shares future space with "Whom am I going to marry?", "Will I have children", "What am I going to do about my elderly parents?", "How can I improve my relationships with my adult children?" CWR takes concerns about the future that underlie career concerns and extrapolates and extends them to encompass concerns about the future across the life contexts that structure experience for most people for most of their lives.

The theorist most noted for placing narrative in time, inclusive of past, present, and future is Ricouer (1980, 1984). According to Ricouer (1984), the actions that shape future directions emerge from the telling and retelling of the story of the past in the present. Limiting the focus for the moment on the actions that lead to future directions in lives, Ricouer posits that actions are the building blocks of lives. More specifically, what is important are agentic actions, actions that people, on some level, can identify as actions they want to take. It is not the specific direction of an action that is important: it is that the action itself has the quality of intentionality or directionality.

In CWR, the focus of practice is to facilitate agentic action per se, with the notion that agentic action in whatever life context it may arise, may lead, in some way, at some point in time, to progress in co-constructing the multiple paths of lives through contexts of work and relationship. It is also this focus on agentic action that provides the opportunity to explore and challenge the ways in which societal forces and internalized identities shape and constrain the agentic actions that emerge in lives.

Contextualism and psychotherapy

The shift to contextualism basic to CWR is mirrored in the shift to contextualism in theories of psychotherapy. Contemporary theories of psychotherapy posit the significance of relationships for the genesis of psychological distress and for healing or recovering from this distress. While this is most explicitly acknowledged in what is loosely referred to as relational psychodynamic theories (Coleman & Hirsch, 2011), the significance of relationships is also important in contemporary cognitive behavioral theories. Relational-cultural theory is particularly helpful for elucidating both healing and damaging aspects of interpersonal relationships in cultural contexts (Comstock et al., 2008). Across the board, theory and research in psychotherapy attests to the fact that the quality of the relationship between therapist and patient is the major factor predicting positive outcomes (Wampold & Imel, 2015). In other words, the relationship between therapist and client is a significant interpersonal context in which healing can occur.

What the model of counselling/psychotherapy does is to expand this acknowledgement of the significance of the relationship context for mental health to encompass the two contexts of work. Much has been written about what it is about relationships with significant others that cause psychological problems and how these problems can be rectified with healing relationships. The significance of the contexts of work for mental health is a new frontier (Wachtel, 2017). Space does not permit exploration of this new frontier in this chapter. However, Smith's (2015) work on poverty and mental health points to important directions for future theory and research. Within vocational psychology, Blustein's (2006) model of the needs satisfied by market work, power/survival/self esteem, social connectedness, and self-directedness, have clear implications for mental health. Let's just take self-esteem for example. Having a job, being able to support oneself, feeling like a productive member of society is essential for self-esteem in today's world. The reams of research on the negative effects of unemployment on mental health suffice to make this point.

Narrative and psychotherapy

The centrality of time and narrative fundamental to CWR is addressed by Hansen (2006) in relation to psychotherapy theory. He proposes that all psychotherapy theories posit a story about how people get into psychological trouble and a story about how to resolve this trouble in psychotherapy. Further, all psychotherapy practices have to deal with the stories that people carry with them into psychotherapy about what has happened to them in their lives and how it has affected them. The process of psychotherapy, regardless of theoretical orientation is, on some level, about helping people tell and revise the stories they tell about themselves in ways that enable them to develop more functional, adaptive, and meaningful lives. It is a collaborative conversation between the therapist and the patient shaped by the stories about the past that people carry with them into therapy and the story or stories shaping their therapists' theoretical orientation or orientations. Psychotherapy is, thus, a conversation in which patients' narratives are therapeutically revised. What is therapeutic is the process of the revision of patients' stories.

The significance of action is also prevalent in psychotherapy across the board. While research by Williams and Levitt (2007) supports the notion that the restitution of agentic action is a goal across psychotherapeutic modalities, Hill's (2016) model of the psychotherapy process across therapeutic modalities posits taking action as the third and final stage of psychotherapy.

Pulling together CWR and psychotherapy: counselling/psychotherapy

Returning to Ricouer's (1984) thesis that the actions of the future emerge from the telling and retelling of the stories of the past, counselling/psychotherapy is a practice encompassing psychotherapy, the therapeutic telling and revising of the stories of the past, and counselling for work and relationship, facilitating agentic actions that lead to the co-construction of lives going forward through work and relationships.

Counselling/psychotherapy is situated in present time in which there is synergistic movement between telling and revising past narratives and co-constructing life paths. Counselling/psychotherapy is a practice that does not split concerns with the inner lives of clients from their outer lives. Similar to Wachtel's (2009) psychotherapy model that pays attention both to behavioral contingencies in the therapeutic relationship and behavioral contingencies that shape people's lives outside the therapy encounter, counselling/psychotherapy focuses attention on both inner and outside worlds as they shape and construct experience. Instead of espousing one or more specific models of therapeutic change in psychotherapy or one or more specific theories of career or vocational development, counselling/ psychotherapy is a kind of metatheory that enables practitioners to draw from the wealth of therapeutic modalities in psychotherapy and the richness of approaches to career or vocational development in the vocational literature. In other words, counselling/psychotherapy is pantheoretical with respect to theories of psychotherapy and theories of vocational or career development. Narrative theory according to Ricouer (1984) provides the glue that pulls together both past and future in the present in the same practice.

Cultural validity of the theory

The cultural validity of the proposed model of counselling/psychotherapy is two-fold: It is responsive to the global forces restructuring work contexts across the world, and it is based on narrative as a mode of thinking ubiquitous across cultures.

Market work across the world has radically altered in recent decades. The notion of a career developmental model in which people finish school, choose an occupation, and embark on a lifelong progression in a line of work no longer matches the realities of the occupational structure and the kinds of employment opportunities afforded by our economic system (Borgen & Neault, 2014; Savickas et al., 2009). Career as an orderly developmental process has been replaced by radical discontinuities in work paths, the erosion of stable and reliable relationships between employers and employees, the loss of stable jobs, and the loss of jobs themselves to the increasing uberization of the economy (uberization refers to the economic trend in which agents exchange an under-utilized capacity of existing assets or human resources, typically through a website or software platform, while incurring only low transaction costs. The term is derived from the company name "Uber" (Standing, 2015). The precariousness of employment is further accentuated by the demise of institutions that protect workers, such as unions, and the failure of laws protecting workers to keep up with the changes in how people are employed (Reich, 2015). All of these factors coalesce to present mental health challenges for many (Bude, 2018).

At the same time as market work across the world has been transformed (Folbre, 2012; Trask, 2014), so too has care work. Although it may have been normative in the 20th century for many women to forego market work in favor of domesticity that is no longer economically feasible for most women. Women and men are working at jobs and dealing with a range of family and care responsibilities. Policy accommodation of market work structures to the care responsibilities of families vary across countries and employers. Depending upon the country of residence and socioeconomic status, families have adapted with a range of strategies including the outsourcing of care work to lower paid care workers who do care work for a living, that is, paid care work. Across the board, it is a challenge for families to handle the increasingly unpredictable demands of market work and the ongoing demands of their own familial and personal unpaid care work.

The ubiquity of narrative as a mode of thinking across cultures (Bruner, 1990) has been instrumental in the growth of narrative theory, research, and narrative-based practices worldwide (Savickas et al., 2009). Although psychotherapy as a professional practice may be more highly valued in western cultures, the use of narrative as a metatheory for psychotherapy practice in the model of counselling/psychotherapy may actually help to destigmatize psychotherapeutic practice in parts of the world where mental health issues and treatment for such issues are more taboo. Talking about telling and retelling the story of one's past in the present, while fostering the future directionality of lives, which is what counselling/psychotherapy is essentially about, may be more culturally palatable from an international perspective than discourse about psychotherapy per se.

Research in brief

Research was designed to study the processes by which conversations that focus on telling the stories of the past and on future aspirations foster agentic action (Richardson et al., 2009). Students were asked to write a reflexive journal after each of three group discussions focusing on their past work and relationship paths, their future work and relationship aspirations, and the ways in which their social identities might have affected or be affecting these developmental paths. In these reflexive journals, students responded to a single question having to do with how the conversations in the groups affected their thoughts and feelings about themselves and about their lives.

A qualitative analysis of these journals identified three processes in student texts: **intentional process,** which included attitudes, feelings, and intentions about the future; **identity process**, which included attitudes, thoughts, and feelings about the self; and **emotional process**, which had to do with students' feelings about participating in the group discussions. Themes of active engagement, uncertainty or conflict, and fear or resignation were identified in the intentional process data. Themes of self-awareness, self-revision, and deeper sense of self were identified in the identity process data. Across both sets of processes, students shifted their intentional states in response to the group conversations as well as recommitted to the intentional states they had prior to the conversations.

Although both positive and negative feeling states appeared in the emotional process data, positive feelings having to do with emotional support predominated. Most students found that the group discussions helped them become clearer about themselves, about the directionality of their lives, and more able to cope with the uncertainty of the future.

According to Bruner (1990), actions are framed and emerge from sets of intentions such as those identified in the reflexive journals. Thus, one can surmise that the intentional and identity processes identified in these students' journals enabled them to develop more deeply considered sets of intentional states likely to frame their future agentic actions, which, in turn, might enhance their ability to take agentic action when opportunity arises.

Interpretation of these results suggests that group conversations about past narratives and future directions with the encouragement of the reflexive processing of that experience may be a powerful counselling intervention for helping people co-construct their lives going forward. With respect to individual counselling situations, these results suggest that the active encouragement of intentional and identity process in the counselling dyad may be instrumental in enabling agentic action to emerge in clients' lives.

Research in brief: reflective questions

1   How does this research relate to the major theoretical dimensions of the counselling/psychotherapy model of practice?
2   Can you identify in your own experience a time when a conversation with another person made a significant impact on how you thought or felt about your future directions in your life? Please describe this experience and explain why you think it had the impact that it did.
3   What do you see as the connection between intentional and identity process and the emergence of directionality in lives?

Case study

Matthew (pseudonym) was a white, single, heterosexual man in his mid-30s, of medium build and fairly attractive, who began therapy with me for serious depression. A second presenting problem was that he was marginally employed and very worried about his economic future. It also quickly became apparent that Matthew had a serious drinking problem.

Matthew grew up in a small town, the only son of an alcoholic and abusive father who worked as a highly skilled mechanic and a mother who was creative and musical but frequently sick and had a serious psychological condition requiring frequent hospitalizations. The family was essentially middle class. Matthew had a difficult childhood that he described as "hardscrabble". He turned out to be musically talented and he had the good fortune of having teachers who supported his talent. He became an excellent musician. His musical talent and skills were significant factors enabling him to cope with his problematic home environment. He managed to graduate from high school and go to college where he majored in education because it was "easy". He continued to pursue his musical gifts in college, but did not have the self-confidence or wherewithal to pursue a degree in music. After college, Michael joined the army and then moved to a large metropolitan area where he had vague hopes of doing something in music.

By his mid-30s, when he began psychotherapy, Matthew had given up ever being able to make a living as a musician. He had occasional gigs that provided supplementary income, but did not have the self-confidence to pursue the auditions that might have led to more and better market work in music. He was also facing the reality that making a living in an artistic field was a daunting challenge. He knew he was not up to this challenge. Instead, he had cobbled together a set of part-time jobs that included doing cleaning work as a porter in a small building and freelance jobs painting people's apartments. Matthew was also socially isolated. He was miserable due to his depression, loneliness, and unsatisfying, unrewarding, and, what he considered, demeaning market work.

In the first phase of psychotherapy, guided by a relational psychodynamic theoretical orientation, we focused on exploring Matthew's problematic relationships with his parents and how these relationships were echoed in the emotionally abusive relationship he had with his boss in the cleaning job, in the frequent exploitative relationships with clients he experienced doing freelance painting jobs, and in his transference reactions with me. As he became more aware of what was going on in his relationships that was contributing to his ongoing depression, Matthew began to take significant agentic actions to improve his life. This initiated the second phase of therapy.

During the second phase of therapy, Matthew quit his cleaning job and began to more carefully vet prospective employers for his freelance painting work to weed out those whom he suspected might be exploitative. Although he was not developing any more satisfying and lucrative market work paths, he was taking steps to get away from an oppressive boss and away from exploitative employers. He constantly complained that he did not know what he was going to do to make a more decent living and be able to retire some day. Although he could have developed his freelance painting work into something more substantial, he hated being an entrepreneur, always hustling for the next job. He just wanted some kind of stable job. He talked about going back to get an M.A. in education that would enable him to teach, and although he did look into some degree programs, he made no progress in pursuing this path. Getting an M.A. degree seemed too daunting on too many levels. This lack of progress and ongoing complaints about not being able to find a better market work path extended through the second phase of the therapy.

Early in the second phase of therapy, as Matthew began to feel less depressed, he joined Alcoholics Anonymous (AA), quit drinking, and became a very active member of AA. He attended meetings regularly and gradually took on a leadership role in the organization. Matthew's participation in AA not only helped him quit drinking: It also provided him with a set of relationships, friends, and colleagues through engagement in the unpaid care work of AA. Joining AA was an agentic action with significant positive ramifications for the relationship and unpaid care work paths of his life, and eventually for his market work path.

Early in this second phase of therapy, Matthew talked about his childhood dream of being able to ski. This was a strong and compelling dream that Matthew pursued, taking skiing lessons, going on ski trips, and joining a local ski club. Matthew was a good athlete and he loved skiing. Through the ski club, he met a young woman who interested him. In a fairly short time, the relationship blossomed and they began to live together. In this case, Matthew's agentic actions to pursue a childhood dream led to a significant and rewarding relationship path.

The third phase of therapy was initiated at an AA meeting Matthew attended where one of his friends, also a musician, spoke about his problem finding someone to take over his position, teaching music, so that he could take a one year sabbatical to pursue some exciting professional opportunities. His principal had given him permission to appoint a replacement outside of the regular academic channels. After the meeting, Matthew approached his friend and said that he was interested in the position. This was the beginning of the end of psychotherapy for Matthew. He managed to get the necessary certifications and permissions to enable him to teach, had a difficult but rewarding first year teaching, and eventually was able to leverage his year of teaching into a full-time job teaching music in elementary school. Matthew left therapy with a stable and satisfying intimate personal relationship and a good job. His depression abated and disappeared over time as he co-constructed his life going forward in the last two phases of his therapy.

This case study illustrates how the therapy with Matthew started with a predominant focus on the past and a reconstruction of narrative and gradually shifted to an increasing focus on the co-construction of new directions in Matthew's life. A major theoretical principle of counselling/psychotherapy is that the reconstruction of the past and the co-construction of future directionality are closely linked, frequently occur simultaneously, and are synergistic.

With respect to the reconstruction of the story of Matthew's life, another major theoretical principle is that all theories of psychotherapy are essentially a story about how problems develop and how to resolve problems. In this case, the specific theoretical orientation or the story that guided the reconstruction of Matthew's life story was relational psychodynamic theory. For example, Matthew's dysfunctional early relationship with his father shaped his later dysfunctional relationships with bosses and clients. Exploration of these dysfunctional relationships in the past, in the present, and in the context of an empathic relationship with the therapist, enabled growth and development to occur and new and improved relationships to develop. As a result of these new and improved relationships, Matthew's depression was resolved.

Another basic principle of counselling/psychotherapy is to encourage agentic action across life domains. This principle is based on a holistic and contextual understanding of persons participating in interdependent and interpenetrating life contexts: What is most important is agentic action regardless of context.

Hence, in the story of Matthew's therapy, his capacity for agentic action first emerged in the contexts of sports and Alcoholics Anonymous. These actions eventually led to satisfying market work and relationship paths.

In addition to the principle to facilitate agentic actions across life domains, theories from the vocational literature helped to inform the understanding of how to help Matthew resolve his problems with market work. According to planned happenstance theory (Mitchell, Levin, & Krumboltz, 1999), taking action and becoming engaged with the world enables a person to create opportunities in the contexts of their lives. Certainly, this is what happened with Matthew. Taking action and becoming engaged with Alcoholics Anonymous led to a situation in which Matthew had the opportunity to get a temporary teaching position without first getting an M.A. degree. It was the beginning of a more stable and satisfying market work path.

The influence of a second theoretical model from the vocational literature can also be seen in this case study. It is not at all surprising from the perspective of relational vocational theory (Schultheiss, 2007) that a satisfying intimate relationship was most likely a positive factor affecting Matthew's ability to step forward, pursue the opportunity of a temporary teaching position, and make it through the rigors of becoming a teacher.

What is important to note is that counselling/psychotherapy is not a model that integrates career counselling with psychotherapy. Rather, it is a theory of psychotherapy based on narrative theory that acknowledges the synergistic relationship between past and future time dimensions in lives. It is in the attention to the future where theories from the vocational realm are most likely to inform the practice of counselling/psychotherapy.

Case study: reflective questions

1   According to the model of counselling/psychotherapy, what is the rationale for not referring Matthew to a career counsellor to deal with his market work problems while dealing with his depression in psychotherapy?
2   What is the difference between counselling/psychotherapy informed by a vocational theory such as planned happenstance and career counselling based on the theory of planned happenstance?
3   What do you think might be the connection between Matthew's ability to pursue and develop competence as a skier and his overall progress in resolving problems and developing a better and more meaningful life?

Summary and conclusions

The model of counselling/psychotherapy described in this chapter attempts to bridge the gap between psychotherapy, located in health care practice, and career counselling, located in educational practice, in order to enrich the practice of psychotherapy with a vocational perspective. While located primarily in psychotherapy practice, counselling/psychotherapy is a model that extends the scope of psychotherapy into the future and into the social and economic contexts in which lives are embedded.

One of the strengths of this model, which is its breadth and potential relevance to a broad range of practitioners, is the mirror image of one of its major limitations. As a metamodel that is pantheoretical with respect to psychotherapy theory and vocational theory, it is abstract and difficult to operationalize. Research on the relationship between processes of narrative reconstruction and the co-construction of life paths, and on the role of agentic action in both processes is needed to further develop this model. It is encouraging that agentic action is a focus of theoretical and research attention across disciplinary fields in psychology (Young, 2018). Further research on intentional and identity processes in different contexts, under different conditions, and with different populations will help to elucidate how narrative-based conversations foster forward movement in lives. Most importantly, research is needed to investigate the effectiveness of this model for a range of different kinds of clients in different life contexts.

To conclude, I would like to offer some reflections on the implications of the discourse of counselling/psychotherapy, language that challenges prevailing ideologies of power and hierarchy. First and foremost, the discourse of counselling/psychotherapy challenges the psychologizing of career that splits off the individual embedded in the social and economic circumstances of life from personal and emotional realms of experience. Second, it challenges the split between inner and outer worlds reified in the split practices of psychotherapy and career counselling, practices that can be critiqued as mystifying the emotional implications of living lives structured by hierarchies of power and oppression due to social and economic inequality. Third, by locating the practice of counselling/psychotherapy in the domain of psychotherapy, the discourse of counselling/psychotherapy acknowledges the power of the disciplinary cleavages between health and educational practices. Fourth, it enables the richness of the historical legacy and contemporary developments in vocational psychology to inform the practice of psychotherapy.

Last, but not least, the discourse of market work and unpaid care work advances the cause of promoting the value of care as equal to and synergistic with market values. This discourse may contribute to the degenderization of care work and to the overall improvement of conditions for optimal human development. On a more pragmatic level, the advancement of care in personal lives as work may afford some modicum of stability in a precarious world. One may be out of a job, but, in the presence of care work, one is not out of work, thereby extending a sense of being a socially valued citizen beyond the boundaries of market work.

Learning activities

Learning activity 1

Please partner with a fellow student or colleague for two narrative-based conversations, approximately 30–45 minutes long over the course of 2 weeks. In the first conversation, share the stories of your lives to date, being sure to include the stories of your work and relationship paths. Be sure to include unpaid care work if that has been part of your life to date. In the second conversation, focus on where you see yourself headed in your life – in the short term? In the long term? After each of these conversations, take some time to write down a journal entry (one to two pages of typed text) any thoughts and feelings about yourself and about your life that were stimulated by that conversation.

Please note: this experiential activity calls upon you to self-disclose to another person. Both members of these conversational dyads need to make active efforts to be careful and considerate of one another, to listen respectfully and empathically, to be respectful of the confidentiality of the dyad, and to be sure that both members of the dyad share time equitably.

The following questions use the language of life paths – that is, the course of your development with respect to the major life contexts in which you participate. For most people, this is likely to include work and relationship contexts. For you, there may be other significant life contexts – such as health, sports, church or religious contexts.

1   After you have written both journal entries, review what you have written to see if you can identify any impact the conversation had on your sense of yourself or on the thoughts and feelings about the future.
2   Can you discern in your journals any ways in which your social identities (gender, race, socioeconomic status, sexual orientation, etc.) have shaped or constrained your life paths to date?
3   Is there any way that your social identities are shaping or constraining your life paths going forward?

Learning activity 2

Please interview three people you know who have different kinds of market work experiences. It could be that they are working in very different industries, or they have varying degrees of stability in their work, or they are at very different points in their life. Ask them if and how their work affects their feelings about themselves, their sense of well-being, their worries or concerns. Attempt to engage your interviewees in a discussion about the impact of their market work on them rather than just asking them a set of questions. You do not need to tape these interviews, but you should be sure to take good notes about the interview shortly afterwards.

Learning activities: reflective questions

1   Did you find any commonality among your interviews regarding the impact of their market work on their sense of self, well-being, worries or concerns?

2   Did you find any evidence of anxiety in your interviewees caused by the precariousness of market work?

3   What, if anything, did you learn about the impact of market work on people's sense of self, well-being, worries or concerns?

References

Blustein, D. L. (2006). *The psychology of working*. Mahwah, NJ: Lawrence Erlbaum.

Borgen, W., & Neault, R. (2014). Orienting educators to contemporary ideas for career counseling: An illustrative example. In G. Arulmani, A. J. Bakshi, F. T. L. Leong, & A. G. Watts (Eds.), *Handbook of career development: International perspectives* (pp. 709–726). New York: Springer.

Bruner, J. S. (1990). *Acts of meaning*. Cambridge, MA: Harvard University Press.

Bude, H. (2018). *Society of fear*. Cambridge, UK: Polity Press.

Coleman, R.C., & Hirsch, I. (2011). Relational psychoanalytic psychotherapy. In S. G. Messer & A. S. Gurman (Eds.), *Essential psychotherapies: Theories and practice* (3rd ed., pp. 72–106). New York: The Guilford Press.

Comstock, D. L., Hammer, T. R., Stresstzsch, J., Cannon, K., Parsons, J., & Salazar II, G. (2008). Relational-cultural theory: A framework for bridging relational, multicultural, and social justice competencies. *Journal of Counseling & Development, 86,* 279–287.

Cummings, N. A. (1990). The credentialing of professional psychologists and its implications for other mental health disciplines. *Journal of Counseling and Development, 68,* 485–490.

Folbre, N. (Ed.). (2012). *For love and money: Care provision in the United States*. New York: Russell Sage Foundation.

Gergen, K. J., Josselson, R., & Freeman, M. (2015). The promises of qualitative inquiry. *American Psychologist, 70*(1), 1–9.

Hansen, J. T. (2006). Counseling theories within a postmodernist epistemology: New roles for theories in counseling practice. *Journal of Counseling and Development, 84,* 291–297.

Hill, C. E. (2016). *Helping skills: Facilitating exploration, insight, and action* (4th ed.). Washington, DC: American Psychological Association.

McIlveen, P. (2015). Psychotherapy, counseling, and career counseling. In P. J. Hartung, M. Savickas, & W. B. Walsh (Eds.), *APA handbook of career interventions, Volume 1: Foundations* (pp. 403–417). Washington, DC: American Psychological Association.

Mitchell, K. E., Levin, A. S., & Krumboltz, J. D. (1999). Planned happenstance: Constructing unexpected career opportunities. *Journal of Counseling and Development, 77,* 115–124.

Parsons, F. (1909). *Choosing a vocation*. Boston, MA: Houghton Mifflin.

Reich, R. (2015). *Saving capitalism: For the many, not the few*. New York: Knopf.

Richardson, M. S. (1993). Work in people's lives: A location for counseling psychologists. *Journal of Counseling Psychology, 40*, 425–433.

Richardson, M. S. (2012). Counseling for work and relationship. *The Counseling Psychologist, 40*(2), 190–242.

Richardson, M. S. (2017). Counseling for work and relationship: A practice-driven theoretical approach. In J. P. Sampson, E. Bullock-Yowell, V. C. Dozier, & D. S. Osborne (Eds.), *Integrating theory, research, and practice in vocational psychology*. Tallahassee: Florida State University Library.

Richardson, M. S., Meade, P., Rosbruch, N., Vescio, C., Price, L., & Cordera, A. (2009). Intentional and identity processes: A social constructionist investigation using student journals. *Journal of Vocational Behavior, 74*, 63–74.

Richardson, M. S., & Schaeffer, C. (2013). Expanding the discourse: A dual model of working for women (and men's) lives. In W. Patton (Ed.), *Women's working lives: Moving the boundaries of our discourse* (pp. 23–50). Rotterdam, The Netherlands: Sense.

Ricoeur, P. (1984). *Time and narrative*. Chicago, IL: University of Chicago Press.

Savickas, M. L., Nota, L., Rossier, J., Dauwalder, J-P, Duarte, M. E., Guichard, J., Van Vianen, A. E. M. (2009). Life designing: A paradigm for career construction in the 21st century. *Journal of Vocational Behavior, 75*, 239–250.

Schultheiss, D. E. P. (2007). The emergence of a relational cultural paradigm for vocational psychology. *International Journal of Educational and Vocational Guidance, 7*, 191–201.

Smith, L. (2015). Reforming the minimum wage: Toward a position for psychology. *American Psychologist, 70*, 557–565.

Standing, G. (2011). *The precariot: The new dangerous class*. New York: Bloomsbury.

Super, D. E. (1963). *Career development: Self-concept theory*. New York: College Entrance Examination Board.

Trask, B. S. (2014). *Women, work, and globalization: Challenges and opportunities*. New York: Routledge.

Wachtel, P. L. (2009). Knowing oneself from the inside out, knowing oneself from the outside in: The "inner" and "outer" worlds and their link through action. *Psychoanalytic Psychology, 26*, 158–170.

Wachtel, P. L. (2017). *The poverty of affluence* (2nd ed.). New York: Free Press.

Wampold, B. E., & Imel, Z. E. (2015). *The great psychotherapy debate: The evidence of what makes psychotherapy work*. New York: Routledge.

Williams, D. C., & Levitt, H. M. (2007). Principles for facilitating agency in psychotherapy. *Psychotherapy Research, 17*, 66–82.

Young, R. A. (Chair) (2018, June). *Human action and the future of applied psychology*. Symposium conducted at the meeting of the International Congress of Applied Psychology, Montreal, Canada.

Zittoun, T., Valsiner, J., Vedeler, D., SalgadoJ., Goncalves, M. M., & Ferring, D. (2013). *Human development in the life course: Melodies of living*. Cambridge, UK: Cambridge University Press.

Part III

Implications for theory and practice

Moving the field forward

Part III contains one chapter that synthesises the key themes raised in the chapters included in Parts I and II and poses questions for future career theory development, research, and practice.

17 Contemporary career development theories

Expanding international perspectives

Nancy Arthur and Mary McMahon

Learning objectives

The purpose of this chapter is to:

- Synthesize themes related to the aims of the book,
- Highlight global trends in the changing world of work, and
- Consider future directions for career theory.

Introduction to the chapter

The world of work is changing at a rapid pace in ways that make people's career planning and decision-making more complex. Change is an ever-present force in social evolution, but the pace and scope of change in recent decades compounds people's need to be prepared, skilled, and adaptable. Participation in the labour force will typically entail several shifts within and between employment settings throughout the life course, often precipitating disruption and adjustment in relation to their other life roles and responsibilities. In tandem, our understandings about the changing world of work need to be reflected in the theories and practices that underpin educational and career guidance for people of all ages.

In 1993, Savickas noted that changes in the world of work were outpacing changes in approaches to career counselling. The risk of this identified gap is that clients may not fully benefit from career-related services or they may view career-related services as outdated and unnecessary (Savickas, 1993). We are living in an era when people require career-related services that are responsive to increasing complexities of life in the 21st century. Neither interventions nor the theories that inform interventions can remain static. We agree with the position that theory informs practice and practice informs theory; both domains are essential for responding to people's needs for education and work as markers of social participation. It is timely to consider the ways in which contemporary career development theories can anchor practices in an evolving landscape of global change.

As noted in the preface, this edited collection was conceptualized with four general aims. In this closing chapter, we revisit those aims and reflect on the contemporary status of theories of career development. To recap, the first aim was to develop a career theory book that would emphasize the contemporary theories in the field of career development. Second, we were eager to expand the disciplinary contributions and to include multiple voices that inform contemporary career theories. Third, we wanted to give more primacy to the cultural applications of theory across diverse populations within and between countries. Fourth, we wanted to create a career theory resource with strong linkage between theory and practice. With these priorities in mind, we brought together authors for chapters that represent current thinking, innovation, and new theoretical developments. This chapter aims to revisit the purposes of the book and reflect on the contemporary career development theories included in it. We outline some common themes in the theories, particularly in light of selected global trends and the changing world of work.

The contemporary status of theories of career development

Our first aim was a career theory book that emphasizes contemporary career development theories. As noted earlier in the preface, we believe that it is important for readers to appreciate the historical origins of career development theories. We also encourage readers to notice the many theoretical threads that have informed and will continue to shape the tapestry of theories in the field. However, we have noticed that, in practice, the texts, resource materials, and the curriculum in many courses continue to emphasize early foundational theories and do not devote enough time to the newer and leading edge developments in career theory. There are inevitably choices to be made about which content is emphasized in coursework or professional development workshops. It is often not practical or possible to cover all theories in depth. Choices have to be made about which theories to foreground and which theories will be given less emphasis. To that end, the material in this text provides readers with an array of theoretical perspectives that we believe will give readers essential foundations in contemporary career theory.

A spectrum of theoretical advances

We encourage readers to consider the stage of theoretical development represented in the book. Some of the theories presented in this book are well established, while other theories are newer and at earlier stages of development. Some foundational theories have been updated through ongoing research and revision, and application across a variety of country contexts. There is also variation in the epistemological stances embedded in theories.

There has been major growth in the field from the positivist traditions to the burgeoning growth in constructivist perspectives and theories that lend themselves to narrative approaches in their application (Patton & McMahon, 2017).

Thus, some theories illustrate the complementarity of positivist matching approaches and the more holistic perspectives associated with constructivism. There have also been advances in the field in terms of broadening the focus to incorporate systems influences, within, between, and beyond the individual to incorporate relevant local, national, and global influences on people's career development. This more holistic perspective has been made possible not only through the influence of constructivism and social constructionism but also through the introduction into career development of theories from other disciplines (e.g., systems theory, chaos theory, action theory, social learning theory). There is increasing recognition that external forces are often the drivers of opportunities and barriers; the best of plans may be interrupted or derailed through chance, luck, and people's willingness to embrace risk and unforeseen opportunities.

More than a name: conceptualization of work, livelihoods, and career

The meaning and definition of the term *career* itself has been contested (Collin & Young, 2000). The continued ambiguity, stemming from the lack of conceptual clarity, has led to different understandings and thinking (Patton & McMahon, 2006) that is evident in the evolvement of career theory. Critique has been levied about the relevancy of the term career for representing the realities of people's lives in many countries around the world (Blustein, 2013). This critique resonates for the current discussion of theory and some underlying assumptions that (a) people have freedom of choice and agency in selecting and securing work, (b) all people are able to secure meaningful work, (c) people value work as a primarily life role, and (d) work is central to their identities. These assumptions sharply contrast people's experience with mundane and tedious tasks of work secured as basic income or as a means of survival. The terms *livelihood* and *livelihood planning* have been suggested as alternatives to *career* and *career guidance* (Arulmani, 2011; Organization for Economic Co-operation and Development [OECD], 2015; Sultana, 2014a). There are concerns that contemporary career theories and guidance interventions that emphasize personal agency in the construction and design of meaningful careers may not sufficiently address contextual and environmental conditions (Sultana 2017).

Further, longstanding concerns about the ways that opportunities afforded to people and their experiences in the workplace, shaped by notions of gender, race, and social class, have not disappeared. As detailed in Chapter 13, social processes position some individuals and groups in our society with privilege and/or disadvantage for accessing education and paid employment. There is growing recognition that a single category of identity does not capture the fluid and intersecting nature of people's identities that may be additionally constrained through social and structural barriers (Arthur, 2017). Further, the emphasis on paid work has often overshadowed the nature of care work, in which the caring for other people is essential for the functioning of society, yet much of it is devalued as 'women's work' and unpaid (Klugman & Melnikova, 2016; Richardson, 2017).

Different conceptualizations of work in various parts of the world lead to some key question: How do we apply theory? To whom do we apply theory? How does theory translate to other cultures and country contexts? Such critical thinking and discussion is an important part of introspection and examination of the assumptions embedded in theory and practice, which often mirror broader economic and political discourses (McIlveen & Patton, 2006; Sultana, 2014b). As noted in this discussion and in Part II of the book, contemporary career theories have moved the field forward by going some way to addressing concerns that have persisted in the field for several decades. Concerns and challenges remain however, for future advances in theory.

Revisiting the personal-career interface

In addition to the questions posed in the previous section, we pose another one: Is career personal? This question is posed in light of the longstanding and arbitrary separation of work and vocational matters from other life domains. We remind readers of the seminal work of Donald Super (1990), who was the first theorist to specifically acknowledge the career and personal life interface in his life-span lifespace theory. Contributors to the articles in the special issue of *The Career Development Quarterly* (Subich, 1993) offered varying positions about the personal-career interface and the implications for counselling interventions. Regardless of the lack of unity in perspectives, it seems that career matters and the related field of career counselling have been relegated to a secondary role as 'less serious' and the 'poor cousin' to other modes of helping, such as general counselling and psychotherapy. However, the integration of career-related issues in people's lives, and vice versa, cannot be neatly assigned to one profession over another. We acknowledge differences in the aims and scope of practice in various professions and their sub-specialities. Yet, efforts to overcome the legacy of arbitrary separation of personal and career issues continue to be fuelled by misinformation at best, and the hierarchy of professional status, at least. Vocational issues inevitably surface in the lives of clients who seek services from a range of helping professions. Consequently, theoretical knowledge needs to be widely distributed to enhance the preparation of practitioners for addressing people's career-related concerns as the main presenting issue, or as inextricably woven into people's life concerns.

Inspiring multiple voices in theoretical development

Our second aim for the book focused on the expansion of disciplinary contributions and the inclusion of multiple voices that inform contemporary career theories. We wanted to consider which disciplines are represented in the theories of career development that are commonly featured in texts. For example, we have noticed the disciplinary silos that have existed since the 1950s in relation to career development practice. These silos originate when students learn about career theory in programs steeped in disciplinary foundations such as education, psychology, or business and management, and students rarely have opportunities for interdisciplinary learning. This silo effect continues through the organization of separate professional development associations and events, leading to the lack of interdisciplinary collaboration for new directions in career theory and practice. Further, we have noticed a great divide between career development practices that occur in public institutions such as schools or community-based agencies and the practices that occur in organizations. There seems to be an arbitrary line between supporting people to prepare for work and supporting people who are working within organizations. We felt strongly about the importance of including a chapter on organizational career theory. In doing so, we encourage readers to consider the range of career development activities that occur within organizations and the contributions of organizational career theory for supporting workers and supporting the management of organizations.

Psychological career theory

In psychological career theory, the focus on the individual persists, with the goals of helping people to gain understanding of who they are, and the personal factors that can be mobilized for strengthening personal agency and for making vocational choices. The emphasis on intrapersonal and intrapsychic factors continues to hold a primary position in the field for explaining vocational behaviour. This has led to a burgeoning career assessment industry evident in the widespread use of quantitative assessment that underpins career guidance in many countries. However, the more recent emphasis on meaning and story in contemporary theories and practice has seen a growing number of qualitative career assessment instruments rapidly transforming the connections between the philosophical underpinnings of theory with practice (see McMahon & Watson, 2015). Additionally, we are witnessing innovation in the 'mixed methods' of modern and post-modernist career theories (Sampson, 2009) and the integrative approaches to career interventions (Rottinghaus, & Eshelman, 2015), including the use of both qualitative and quantitative tools. The current move toward integration is reminiscent of the pioneering work of Parsons (1909), who integrated both worldviews in his work.

Psychological career theory with its primary focus on individuals may be too narrow to fully account for the complex and ever present systemic influences of the contexts in which individuals live. A more complete understanding of career development may be garnered through greater recognition of contributions from other disciplines and from multidisciplinary understandings. Throughout the chapters in this edited collection, theorists have acknowledged that people do not live in isolation and their experiences are strongly influenced by the environments around them. There is growing attention paid to the social and organizational contexts in which people's career development emerges and the opportunities afforded to people or barriers posed.

What happened to sociological theory?

Sociological theorists have historically been concerned with social norms, social relations, and organizational structures that influence the nature of work, people's identities in their working lives, and structural forces related to occupational attainment and mobility. Sociological perspectives also drew attention to the influences of gender, race, and social class and the social inequities arising from discrimination and other forms of oppression. We see evidence that these concepts are being integrated into contemporary theories. Yet, sociological theories seem to have lost their position in making contributions to career theory and are rarely included in the texts or curriculum of courses on theories of career development. Perhaps this is a sign that more recent work is needed to update theories and to propose sociological perspectives in more contemporary forms. Further, we encourage greater collaboration between theorists from different disciplines to inspire creative theoretical integration for application across the contexts of families, schools, communities, and organizations.

Cultural validity of theory

Our third aim for the book was to give more primacy to the cultural applications of theory across diverse populations within countries and to expand learning from theorists who attend to cultural contexts between countries. Contemporary career theory needs to be comprehensive and relevant for diverse populations throughout the world (Brown, 2002), accounting for the cultural dimensions of their social roles and values (Hartung, 2002). For example, psychological theory originates from Western cultural and historical perspectives (Gergen Gulerce, Lock, & Misra, 1996) that may "aid or limit our understanding of the world" and human functioning (Kim, Park, & Park, 2000, p. 72). It is critical to learn from other countries and cultures in order to enrich the field. For example, shifting and emerging economies and labour market trends in the global economy are motivating an increased interest in Eastern perspectives (Chatzichristou & Arulmani, 2014).

We have noticed however, that discussions of culture in other texts are often relegated to a minor role, in passing, with only a few sentences, one or two paragraphs, or simply ignored. Consequently, we set out to intentionally foreground the cultural considerations of each theory featured in this book. Theories are developed in particular eras and contain particular cultural assumptions. There is no such thing as a neutral theory, as each career theory is imbued with assumptions that are representative of the beliefs and values of theorists who hold particular worldviews (Arthur, 2017). Given the greater diversity among the populations of many countries, theorists need to be concerned with the representations of culture in their perspectives.

Approaches to conceptualizing culture in theory

There has been debate about whether theorists should pursue validation of their career theories across populations or aim for theories that are population-specific (Leong & Brown, 1995; Leong & Hardin, 2003). Consequently, we invited each of the chapter authors to offer commentary about the cultural validity of their theories. Some chapter authors preferred to use terminology such as cultural sensitivity or applications, as opposed to validity, given the historical association of the latter term with quantitative research.

Authors referenced particular populations and the attention to diversity paid in research on their theory. Several of the authors have tested their theory through research with a variety of populations, within and across countries. For example, chapter authors highlighted individuals and groups, who have been marginalized and/or racialized, also highlighting gender, age, and social class, while there was little mention of ability/disability, religion, or sexual orientation. These examples are important to counteract a prevailing narrative that all people have equal opportunity in the current world of work (Arthur, 2014). People who lack economic resources in the first place are often disadvantaged in terms of gaining equitable access to education and/or employment, resulting in a cycle of economic disparities. Advocates of constructionism have emphasized the focus on clients telling their stories and using narrative methods to centralize the lives of clients. In moving forward, we encourage theorists to move beyond the identity politics associated with positioning people according to a single identity or group membership. The intersections of people's identities are not static; across contexts, people are often afforded additional privilege or constraints in the lives (Allan, Tebbe, Bouchard, & Duffy, 2018; Arthur, 2017)

Cultural applications and internationalization

Chapter authors connected their discussions about the cultural applications of theory to a broader theme of internationalization of the field. Chapter authors commented on the importance of considering how their work may or may not be transferable to other countries. Again, some theorists are further along in the testing of central concepts of their theories and have provided documentation about the relevancy of their theories between selected countries. This point was a note of caution posed by the same authors who acknowledge the need for further research pertaining to the transferability of career theory across countries.

One of the main points that we wish to raise is opening up the field to include new perspectives and contributions to theories from a variety of countries. We are advocating for more inclusivity of established and emerging perspectives. Popular theories are often perpetuated by ethnocentrism, expressed through the selection of articles for publication in journals or who is repeatedly featured as the main speakers at conferences. It is important to introduce new people and their perspectives, and to recognize the contributions of theorists from many countries. In a global and contemporary society, we can aim for better balance between exporting theories from western countries and learning from the diversity of perspectives offered from a wider range of countries. A related point is the position of English as the dominant language of the most influential career development journals, which renders some authors who are less proficient in English as potentially voiceless (Hou & Zhang, 2007). Achieving "a multi-directional flow of philosophy, theory, practice and research across cultures and cultures" (McMahon & Yuen, 2010, p. 110) remains a challenge. Internationalization of the field of career development will only advance when we are able to open space for new, culturally and linguistically diverse perspectives to be supported.

These suggestions surface a turning point in the field in which the relevancy of career theories is called into question: for whom are theories written, by whom, and how well do theories apply to the lives of people in different countries around the world? In Section I of the book, these questions are taken up in substantive ways by the authors in the first three chapters, through consideration of the historical legacy and domination of the field by Western theories. These questions are examined directly and indirectly in the discussion and self-critique offered by theorists in each of the chapters. With increasing opportunities for the export of theory and related tools for practice, there are commercial interests at stake. The risks for exploitation and colonization cannot be overlooked at a time when many countries are seeking resources to shape their national frameworks and to prepare career and guidance personnel.

Linking theory and practice

The fourth aim in developing this edited collection of theory was to strengthen the linkage between theory and practice. Although we respect the generation of theoretical knowledge for knowledge sake, the creation of this edited collection was motivated, in part, by our commitment to increasing the accessibility of theory. To reiterate an earlier point, knowledge of contemporary career theory is important not only for professionals who identify as career practitioners, but also for other helping professionals and personnel working in management and industry settings.

Staying current with theory: an ethical standard for practice

In reviewing the codes of ethics and standards of practice for many national and international associations, we have noted what is stated about the role of theory. In essence, practitioners need to be grounded in career theory in order to have a foundation for case conceptualization and intervention planning. Moreover, practitioners need to be discerning about their use of theory. For example, in the South African context, Watson and Stead (2006) asked "What should our theory base be? Are our theories sufficiently sensitized to local cultural, socioeconomic, and social conditions? What should our role be and who are the clients? What values should be promoted?" (p. 8). We emphasize the importance for practitioners to be grounded in theoretical knowledge that is contemporary and leading-edge, to make discerning decisions about the applications of theory, and to evaluate the relevance of theory in their practice setting and with their clients, as advocated by Watson in Chapter 2. It is a professional and ethical responsibility for practitioners to keep abreast of developments in the field, including the theory that underpins the tools and techniques that they apply in practice. Therefore, practitioners are urged to engage critically and reflectively with career theory in order that they apply it in ways that best serve their clients.

If we look across to other professions, it is highly unlikely that consumers would be satisfied working with professionals who neglected to update their knowledge and solely relied on theory that was developed several decades ago. The same situation should apply to the provision of career services. Whether or not consumers are informed of such matters in order to question the qualifications of practitioners is one matter; following the professional ethics and standards of practice in the field is clearly a matter of concern for practitioners. To that end, we encourage readers to update their knowledge about career theory to consider newer perspectives and updates to foundational theories that continue to lead the field. The challenge for theorists and practitioners is to stay current and update their perspectives and approaches to practice within a global context.

Learning from case studies

One of the strengths of Part II of the book pertains to the original case studies presented by the authors in each of the chapters. Authors were invited to create case studies that they felt would help readers to see how key concepts could resonate with ideas for practice. As a result, there are thirteen chapters with case studies that feature diverse client identities, presenting issues, and approaches to case conceptualization and intervention. Chapter authors crafted the details of fictitious client scenarios, resulting in an array of individual clients, individuals and their families, individuals and managers in organizations, and entire communities. The case studies illustrate the rich nuances of peoples' lives and the many ways that theory can be used to ground approaches to practice. The practical utility of the theories in this book is underscored, as evident in the original contributions made by authors to linking theory and practice.

Moving theory forward in the global context

One of the underlying goals of developing an edited collection with contemporary theories was to expand the discussion about global perspectives. In doing so, we recognize that any writing in the field is akin to a snapshot that represents the field at a particular time. We have emphasized the importance of theory responding to current forces that shape people's career development. It is also important that theorists consider ways to be more proactive in moving the field forward. To that end, we have identified ten overarching trends that reflect the United Nations' (2015) Sustainable Development Goals, www.un.org/susta inabledevelopment/sustainable-development-goals/, and highlight the changing nature of work and work settings in a global context. We offer these trends as pivotal points for informing future directions and innovations in career theory. Selected references offer readers additional sources for information about these trends.

1 The global economy is interconnected to the economic stability of individual nations and communities, opening up new opportunities, while governments are also pressuring for educational systems and curriculum in schools to produce workers to fulfill labour market needs for economic utility (Irving, 2011, 2018).

2 Workplaces are changing with the unprecedented use of technology, artificial intelligence, and automation. Many work functions historically performed by people have been replaced by robotics and new jobs have been created around the integration of technology in the workplace, requiring employees to develop new skills (Hooley, 2018; The Economist Intelligence Unit, 2018).

3 The 'green economy' is resulting in job creation and losses. 'Green' jobs, products and services are becoming economic priorities for governments (Georgeson, Maslin, & Poessinouw, 2017; Nations Environment Program [UNEP], 2011), also offering new directions for practitioners to promote "green guidance" (Plant, 2014).

4 The depletion of resource and craft-based industries has resulted in limited job opportunities and options for people to maintain their lifestyles in smaller communities, prompting many people to leave those industries and pursue work in urban centres (Chatzichristou & Arulmani, 2014; Kalyanram, Gopalan, & Kartik, 2014).

5 An unprecedented number of people are mobile between countries, seeking new opportunities for education and employment. On the spectrum of voluntary and forced mobility and migration, securing employment is critical for economic and social integration in a new country (Arthur, 2012; Newman, Bimrose, Nielsen, & Zacher, 2018).

6 There is growing concern for youth in many countries with high rates of youth unemployment. Youth not engaged in employment or education (NEETS) face major barriers to enter the labour market (International Labour Organization [ILO], 2017). During economic downturns, educated youth are experiencing delayed entry to the workforce or the beginning of long-term unemployment (Bell & Benes, 2012).

7 Many countries have focused on the participation of women in the workforce as a way to strengthen their labour force and improve economic productivity. Girls' participation in education and household labour, workplace conditions, and wage parity with men continue to be cited as barriers (Afiouni & Karam, 2018; Bimrose, McMahon, & Watson, 2015)

8 A disturbing trend globally is an unprecedented number of workers in vulnerable and precarious forms of employment, most evident in developing countries (ILO, 2018). The call for decent work has been connected to human rights (Blustein, Kenny, Di Fabio, & Guichard, 2018; Pouyaud & Guichard, 2018).

9 The connections between employment, unemployment, and people's mental health are well established (e.g., Paul & Moser, 2009; Wanberg, 2012). Beyond the personal effects, there are economic effects due to lost productivity in the workplace (Fryer & Stambe, 2012).

10 Polarization is increasing between the 'rich and the poor', and the 'haves and the have nots' in many countries. Worldwide efforts at poverty reduction also show widening gaps in the number of people who are not making a living wage and live in poverty, coined as working poverty (ILO, 2018).

These trends, although not an exhaustive list, are useful in contextualizing our consideration of career theory and its future directions. In citing these examples, it is important to guard against stereotyping groups of people as homogeneous; not all individuals within and between countries will experience access to, and mobility in educational and employment systems in the same ways. It is important to acknowledge that the world of work is not neutral. Individuals from nondominant groups often experience racialization, sexism, ageism, social class discrimination, and other intersecting forms of oppression that perpetuate social inequities (Arthur, 2017).

Despite these cautions, the selected trends are connected to a number of persistent and emerging social issues that are relevant for framing discussions about people's career development in contemporary time. Clearly, there are challenges in responding to the multitude of complex forces that are influencing the world of work. The challenge for theorists is be responsive to trends while being proactive in ways that lead and create new understandings.

Charting future directions

In view of the themes identified in the previous sections of this chapter, there are multiple directions for the future of career theories. To that end, we offer several challenges and recommendations for theorists and researchers.

1 Theorists and researchers are challenged to consider a philosophical question in positioning their work, "For whom will this theory be relevant, under what conditions, and in which contexts?" It is of paramount importance to address the diversity of populations within and between countries, who have differential access to education and employment.

2 Theorists are urged to specifically address the cultural contexts of their work and generate evidence that their theories can be transferred and applied across and between countries.

3 The historical roots of contemporary theory are grounded in the work of pioneers who demonstrated strong social justice values. Theorists are invited to consider how their theories can be applied to the large number of people in the world who experience social inequities, unstable and precarious workplace conditions, and structural barriers to becoming established in the workforce.

4 Many theorists are paying increasing attention to the micro-, meso-, and macro-forces and influences on people's educational and occupational opportunities. Theory-based interventions are needed at all three levels and theorists are encouraged to offer advice and support to practitioners and policy-makers in this regard.

5 There is strong demand from practitioners for theorists to illustrate the application of their theories in practice; practitioners want to know how to apply theories and want practical tools and approaches that are informed by theory. In turn, practitioners offer unique viewpoints and experiences to inform the theoretical development and reform.

6 The agendas of professional conferences and workshops can be strengthened through showcasing contemporary theories and their applications to practice. Tools and techniques are linked to theoretical advancements.

7 Incorporating the expertise of the public and service users could be used to inform theory and its application in practice. Flipping top-down to ground-up approaches may increase the theory-practice connections.

8 Work and career issues inevitably surface in the lives of clients who seek services from a range of professions. Theoretical knowledge needs to be widely distributed to enhance the preparation of practitioners for addressing work and career concerns directly or as part of a more holistic view of their lives.

9 Although authors from several countries have informed contemporary career theories, we encourage a more inclusive approach to recognizing and supporting new theoretical work from authors in different countries.

10 Theorists and researchers are urged to engage in collaboration with other disciplines in order to facilitate comprehensive understanding of career issues. The time is ripe to address the myriad of complexities in the changing world of work through interdisciplinary collaboration.

Concluding comments

This chapter began with a recap of the four central aims that shaped the content of this edited collection. As noted in the opening chapter of the book, the field of career development has historical roots in social justice through the pioneering action of leaders in several countries who were concerned about the welfare of people who were disenfranchised in society. More than a century later, many of the theorists in this book have addressed the importance of career guidance for helping people to make sense of their lives and to help them pursuing options for work. Chapter authors have commented on the increasing influences of global issues for the lives of individuals, families, and communities. On thing that particularly stands out is the recognition of structural and societal influences that afford access or barriers for people's entry into the labour market and their occupational mobility. Readers are encouraged to consider what the chapter authors state directly and indirectly in tying their theoretical perspectives and applications to social inequities and social justice.

The unique and contrasting perspectives offered by chapter authors represent theoretical innovations in career theory for the 21st century. A noticeable feature of this book that warrants mention in this concluding chapter is that theorizing in career development is active and ongoing. Moreover, many of the perspectives offered in the chapters of this book have built on pioneering theories that have come before them. Although the chapters of this book present diverse perspectives, across the chapters there many similarities, which suggest that scholars and practitioners new to the field may be more easily able to comprehend core concepts of contemporary career theory.

In closing, we recognize that the publication of this book is occurring at a particular point in time. We encourage continued debate and discussion about the changing world of work in relation to the continued call for theoretical updates and new theoretical innovations. Theory has a growing role to play in explaining people's vocational behaviour and in guiding interventions that are relevant for people in their life contexts. We encourage readers to discuss and debate the ways that career development theory helps us to make sense of who we are and of the world around us.

Learning activities

Learning activity 1

Refer to the ten global trends identified in this final chapter. Individually, reflect on these trends and how they have influenced your own career development. You may also choose to informally interview relatives or other members of your local community to consider how those trends have shifted over time and are likely to persist as influences on people's career development in the future. Share your examples in discussion with a partner or in a small group context. Generate a summary of the points raised from the examples for further discussion about the implications for contemporary career development practices.

Learning activity 2

This exercise is designed for use in a group setting with students or for professionals who are already working in a variety of practice settings. Members of the group are assigned to read a different chapter of the book, depending on the size of the group. An alternative format for this learning exercise can be used, with all members of the group reading the same chapter. Group members are invited to take a social justice lens in reviewing the chapters. After reading the assigned chapter(s), group members are invited to explore and share their reviews of the theory. Questions that may be used in this learning activity include the following:

1   How do authors of the selected chapter(s) directly or indirectly discuss matters pertaining to social inequities and social injustices?
2   In which ways do the theories inform practices for addressing social inequities and social injustices?
3   How has your understanding about the connections between career theory and social justice been informed through reading the selected chapter(s)?

Learning activities: reflective questions

1   What roles and responsibilities do career practitioners have in supporting clients to understand the influences of global forces on their career development?
2   What considerations need to be made regarding the cultural applications of theory for diverse populations within a country or between countries?
3   What insights have you gained through reading this chapter about practitioners' use of theory to inform their practices?

References

Afiouni, F., & Karam, C. (2018). Debunking myths surrounding women's careers in the Arab Region: A critical reflexive approach. In R. Sultana (Ed.), *Career guidance and livelihood planning across the Mediterranean* (pp. 55–70). Rotterdam, The Netherlands: Sense.

Allan, B., Tebbe, E., & Bouchard, L., & Duffy, R. (2018). Access to decent and meaningful work in a sexual minority population. *Journal of Career Assessment.* doi:10.1177%2F1069072718758064

Arthur, N. (2012). Career development and international transitions. In M. McMahon & M. Watson (Eds.), *Career development: Global issues and challenges* (pp. 93–110). Hauppauge, NY: Nova Science.

Arthur, N. (2014). Social justice in the age of talent. *International Journal of Educational and Vocational Guidance, 14*(1), 47–60.

Arthur, N. (2017). Constructivist approaches to career counseling: A culture-infused approach. In M. McMahon (Ed.), *Career counseling: Constructivist approaches* (2nd ed., pp. 54–64). New York: Routledge.

Arulmani, G. (2011). Striking the right note: The cultural preparedness approach to developing resonant career guidance programmes. *International Journal for Educational and Vocational Guidance, 11*, 79–93.

Bell, D., & Benes, K. (2012). *Transitioning graduates to work: Improving the labour market success of poorly integrated new entrants (PINEs) in Canada.* Ottawa, ON: Canadian Career Development Foundation.

Bimrose, J., McMahon, M., & Watson, M. (Eds.). (2015). *Women's career development throughout the lifespan: An international exploration* (pp. 113–126). New York: Routledge.

Blustein, D. L. (Ed.). (2013). *The Oxford handbook of the psychology of working.* New York: Oxford University Press.

Blustein, D. L., Kenny, M. E., Di Fabio, A., & Guichard, J. (2018). Expanding the impact of the psychology of working: Engaging psychology in the struggle for decent work and human rights. *Journal of Career Assessment.* doi:10.1177%2F1069072718774002

Brown, D. (2002). Introduction to theories of career choice and development. In D. Brown & Associates (Eds.), *Career choice and development* (4th ed., pp. 3–23). San Francisco, CA: Jossey-Bass.

Chatzichristou, S., & Arulmani, G. (2014). Labor market and career development in the 21st Century. In G. Arulmani, A. Bakshi, F. Leong, & A. Watts (Eds.). *Handbook of career development: International perspectives* (pp. 241–254). New York: Springer.

Collin, A., & Young, R. (Eds.). (2000). *The future of career.* Cambridge, UK: Cambridge University Press.

Fryer, D., & Stambe, R. (2012). Unemployment and mental health. *International Encyclopedia of the Social & Behavioral Sciences* (2nd ed.), 733–737.

Georgeson, L., Maslin, M., & Poessinouw, M. (2017). The global green economy: A review of concepts, definitions, measurement methodologies and their interactions. *Geo: Geography and Environment, 4*(1), 1–23.

Gergen, K. J., Gulerce, A., Lock, A., & Misra, G. (1996). Psychological science in context. *American Psychologist, 51,* 496–503.

Hartung, P. (2002). Cultural context in career theory and practice: Role salience and values. *The Career Development Quarterly, 51*(1), 12–25.

Hooley, T. (2018). A war against the robots? Career guidance, automation and neoliberalism. In T. Hooley, R. Sultana, & R. Thomsen (Eds.), *Career guidance for social justice: Contesting neoliberalism* (pp. 93–108). New York: Routledge.

Hou, Z., & Zhang, N. (2007). Counselling psychology in China. *Applied Psychology: An International Review, 56,* 33–50.

International Labour Organization (ILO). (2017). *Global employment trends for youth 2017.* Geneva, Switzerland: Author. Retrieved from www.ilo.org/global/publications/books/global-employment-trends/WCMS_598669/lang–en/index.htm

International Labour Organization (ILO). (2018). *World employment and social outlook: Trends 2018.* Geneva, Switzerland: Author. Retrieved from www.ilo.org/global/research/global-reports/weso/2018/WCMS_615594/lang–en/index.htm

Irving, B. (2011). Career education as a site of oppression and domination: An engaging myth or a critical reality? *Australian Journal of Career Development, 20*(3), 24–30.

Irving, B. (2018). The pervasive influence of neoliberalism on policy discourses in career/education: Delimiting the boundaries of social justice in New Zealand. In T. Hooley, R. Sultana, & R. Thomsen (Eds.), *Career guidance for social justice: Contesting neoliberalism* (pp. 93–108). New York: Routledge.

Kalyanram, K., Gopalan, R., & Kartik, K. (2014). Tensions in livelihoods: A rural perspective. In G. Arulmani, A. Bakshi, F. Leong, & A. Watts (Eds.). *Handbook of career development: International perspectives* (pp. 377–397). New York: Springer.

Kim, U., Park, T., & Park, D. (2000). The challenge of cross-cultural psychology: The role of indigenous psychologies. *Journal of Cross-Cultural Psychology, 31,* 63–75.

Klugman, J., & Melnikova, T. (2016). *Unpaid work and care: A policy brief.* UN Secretary-General's High-Level Panel on Women's Economic Empowerment. Retrieved from www.empowerwomen.org/-/media/files/un%20women/empowerwomen/resources/hlp%20briefs/unpaid%20work%20%20carepolicy%20brief.pdf?la=en

Leong, F. T. L., & Brown, M. T. (1995). Theoretical issues in cross-cultural career development: Cultural validity and cultural specificity. In W. B. Walsh & S. H. Osipow (Eds.), *Contemporary topics in vocational psychology. Handbook of vocational psychology: Theory, research, and practice* (pp. 143–180). Hillsdale, NJ: US: Lawrence Erlbaum.

Leong, F. T. L., & Hardin, E. (2003). Career psychology of Asian Americans: Cultural validity and cultural specificity. In G. Nagayama & S. Okazaki (Eds.), *Asian American psychology: The science of lives in context* (pp. 131–152). Washington, DC: American Psychological Association.

McIlveen, P., & Patton, W. (2006). A critical reflection on career development. *International Journal for Educational and Vocational Guidance, 6*(1), 15–27.

McMahon, M., & Watson, M. (2015). *Career Assessment: Qualitative approaches.* Rotterdam, The Netherlands: Sense.

McMahon, M., & Yuen, M. (2010). Internationalisation and career counselling. *Asian Journal of Counselling, 16*(2), 91–112.

Newman, A., Bimrose, J., Neilsen, I., & Zacher, H. (2018). Vocational behavior of refugees: How do refugees seek employment, overcome work-related challenges, and navigate their careers? *Journal of Vocational Behavior, 105,* 1–5.

Organisation for Economic Co-operation and Development (OECD). (2015). *Securing livelihoods for all: Foresight for action.* Development Centre Studies. Paris, France: Author.

Parsons, F. (1909). *Choosing a vocation.* Boston, MA: Houghton-Mifflin.

Patton, W., & McMahon, M. (2006). *Career development and systems theory: Connecting theory and practice.* Rotterdam, The Netherlands: Sense.

Patton, W., & McMahon, M. (2017). The systems theory framework of career development. In J. P. Sampson Jr., E. Bullock-Yowell, V. C. Dozier, D. S. Osborn, & J. G. Lenz (Eds.), *Integrating theory, research and practice in vocational psychology: Current status and future directions* (pp. 50–61). Tallahassee: Florida State University.

Paul, K. I., & Moser, K. (2009). Unemployment impairs mental health: Meta-analyses. *Journal of Vocational Behavior, 74,* 264–282.

Plant, P. (2014). Green guidance. In G. Arulmani, A. Bakshi, F. Leong, & A. Watts (Eds.), *Handbook of career development: International perspectives* (pp. 309–316). New York: Springer.

Pouyaud, J., & Guichard, J. (2018). A twenty-first century challenge: How to lead an active life whilst contributing to sustainable and equitable development. In T. Hooley, R. Sultana, & R. Thomsen (Eds.), *Career guidance for social justice: Contesting neoliberalism* (31–46). New York: Routledge.

Richardson, M. S. (2017). Counseling for work and relationship: A practice driven theoretical approach. In J. P. Sampson Jr., E. Bullock-Yowell, V. C. Dozier, D. S. Osborn, & J. G. Lenz (Eds.), *Integrating theory, research and practice in vocational psychology: Current status and future directions* (pp. 40–49). Tallahassee: Florida State University.

Rottinghaus, P. J., & Eshelman, A. J. (2015). Integrative approaches to career intervention. In P. J. Hartung, M. L. Savickas, & W. B. Walsh (Eds.), *APA handbook of career intervention: Volume 2: Applications* (pp. 25–39). Washington, DC: American Psychological Association.

Sampson, J. P. (2009). Modern and post-modern career theories: The unnecessary divorce. *The Career Development Quarterly, 58,* 91–96.

Savickas, M. (1993). Career counseling in the postmodern era. *Journal of Cognitive Psychotherapy: An International Quarterly, 7,* 205–215.

Subich, L. (1993). How personal is career counselling? *The Career Development Quarterly*, 42(2), 129–131.

Sultana, R. G. (2014a). Career guidance for social justice in neoliberal times. In G. Arulmani, A.J. Bakshi, F.T.L. Leong, & A.G. Watts (Eds.), *Handbook of career development: International perspectives*. New York: Springer.

Sultana, R. G. (2014b) Pessimism of the intellect, optimism of the will? Troubling the relationship between career guidance and social justice. *International Journal for Educational and Vocational Guidance*, 14, 5–19.

Sultana, R. G. (2017). Anchoring career guidance in the Mediterranean? In search of southern perspectives. In R. Sultana (Ed.), *Career guidance and livelihood planning across the Mediterranean* (pp. 3–18). Rotterdam, The Netherlands: Sense.

Super, D. E. (1990). A life-span, life-space approach to career development. In D. Brown and L. Brooks (Eds.), *Career choice and development* (2nd ed., pp. 197–261). San Francisco, CA: Jossey-Bass.

The Economist Intelligence Unit. (2018). *The automation readiness index: Who is ready for the coming wave of automation?* London: Author. Retrieved from http://automationreadiness.eiu.com/whitepaper

United Nations. (2015). *Sustainable development goals: 17 goals to transform our world.* Retrieved from www.un.org/sustainabledevelopment/sustainable-development-goals/

United Nations Environment Program (UNEP). (2011). *Towards a green economy: Pathways to sustainable development and poverty eradication – a synthesis for policy makers.* Retrieved from www.unep.org/greeneconomy

Wanberg, C. R. (2012). The individual experience of unemployment. *Annual Review of Psychology*, 63, 369–396.

Watson, M. B., & Stead, G. (2006). An overview of career theory. In G. B. Stead & M. B. Watson (Eds.), *Career psychology in the South Africa context* (2nd ed., pp. 13–34). Pretoria, South Africa: Van Schaik.

Index

Locators in *italics* refer to figures and those in **bold** to tables.